Dictionary of
Existential Psychotherapy
and Counselling

Dictionary of
Existential Psychotherapy
and Counselling

Emmy van Deurzen and Raymond Kenward

Los Angeles | London | New Delhi
Singapore | Washington DC

First published 2005
Reprinted 2009, 2011 (twice)

SAGE Publications Ltd
1 Oliver's Yard
55 City Road
London EC1Y 1SP

SAGE Publications Inc.
2455 Teller Road
Thousand Oaks, California 91320

SAGE Publications India Pvt Ltd
B1/I 1 Mohan Cooperative Industrial Area
Mathura Road, New Delhi 110 044
India

SAGE Publications Asia-Pacific Pte Ltd
33 Pekin Street #02-01
Far East Square
Singapore 048763

British Library Cataloguing in Publication data

A catalogue record for this book is available from the
British Library

ISBN: 978-0-7619-7094-1 (hbk)
ISBN: 978-0-7619-7095-8 (pbk)

Library of Congress Control Number: 2004099431

Typeset by C&M Digitals P Ltd., Chennai, India
Printed and bound in Great Britain by the MPG Books Group

MIX
Paper from
responsible sources
FSC
www.fsc.org   FSC® C018575

To our mothers, Anna and Sylvia, for introducing us to our first existential concepts and experiences

Contents

Introduction

This book is meant as a simple, robust and reliable reference work for both the lay person and the experienced professional. It assumes no previous knowledge of the subject, yet has sufficient depth to be of use to the trained therapist. It is arranged in straightforward alphabetical order, and has a generous number of cross-references, each indicated in **bold**, so that readers may quickly find what interests them, and then, if they wish, go on to discover related ideas. We have included many quotations from the great existential thinkers, as an aid to understanding, and to whet the appetite of the browser to consult the original texts.

The ideas in this work are generally philosophical rather than directly psychological, so that the reader coming to existential psychotherapy for the first time may wonder how philosophy could be relevant to the process of psychotherapy. For such a reader, the entries on **philosophy** and on **existential psychotherapy** might prove a helpful starting-point.

The entries in this book are generally of three kinds:

1 *Theorists*, e.g. **Arendt, Binswanger, Camus**. We have included a number of non-existential writers considered to have contributed to existential thinking or where their ideas have provoked a reaction amongst existential thinkers, e.g. **Descartes**.
2 *Existential Terminology*, e.g. **essence, falling, generosity**. We have tried to avoid mere jargon, and to include concepts that are interesting in their own right, and for which the reader might imagine some psychotherapeutic relevance.
3 *Related Subjects*, e.g. **humanistic psychology, identity, judgement**. These are subjects not exclusively existential but in which existential writers have had something special to say.

All reference books are guilty of sins of omission. Certainly this book might be twice the size it is, and we have had to make difficult decisions on what to include and what to leave out. But of course we accept full responsibility for its inadequacies, and content ourselves with the knowledge that we have striven to make this book, with all its limitations, errors and inevitable bias, one that will provide the reader with a ready reference to the wide range of fascinating and passionate ideas that form the background to the practice of existential psychotherapy and counselling. However, we extend an open invitation to the enthusiastic reader who wants to help make the second edition of this dictionary yet more accurate and complete. Please send your suggestions to either of the authors through Sage Publications, or directly by email to:

Raymond Kenward
raymond.kenward@nhs.net

Emmy van Deurzen
emmy@dilemmas.org

absurd, the

The notion that life is absurd is an idea closely linked with existential philosophy. The absurd is a term used in a variety of ways. For atheist writers, such as **Sartre**, it is the belief that there is no idea behind the **world**, and no rational underpinning to the universe, so that humankind is simply **thrown** into a world without **meaning**. For religious writers, such as **Kierkegaard**, it is the belief that a rational understanding of God is beyond human capability. Kierkegaard argued that Christianity is absurd, so any search for rational proof of God is a hindrance to faith; instead, what is required is a **leap of faith**. But **Heidegger** argues that human being itself has meaning, and only outside of human being is there absurdity:

> [A]ll beings whose mode of being is unlike Da-sein must be understood as *unmeaningful*, as essentially bare of meaning as such ... *And only what is unmeaningful can be absurd.* (Heidegger, 1927b: 152)

In *The Myth of Sisyphus* (1942a), **Camus** argues that the absurd is a useful starting point from which to begin appreciating the world in an aesthetic and experiential way.

See also **art and existential thought; Being;** *Da-sein;* **knowing and knowledge; meaning and meaninglessness**

abyss

See **anxiety; Nietzsche**

Achenbach, Gerd

See **philosophical counselling and consultancy**

action

See **bad faith; Beauvoir, de; change; choice; existence precedes essence; freedom and free will; Merleau-Ponty;** *praxis;* **Sartre; will to live**

actualisation

Actualisation (*Verwirklichung*) of things that are ready-to-hand (see **world**) is to bring about their potential, according to **Heidegger**. They remain able to repeat that potential. With human beings, actualisation refers to the possibility of making something that is possible become real and actual. Such actuality needs to be created at each time and can never be taken for granted. In **death** the possibility of actualisation ceases:

> Death, as possibility, gives Dasein nothing to be 'actualized', nothing which Dasein, as actual, could itself *be*. (Heidegger, 1927a: 262)

Whilst *Dasein* may achieve actuality, *Dasein* has always the **possibility** of actualisation.

actualising tendency
See **client-centred psychotherapy**

Adorno, Theodor
See **Frankfurt School, the**

adumbrations
See **profiles**

adversity
See **coefficient of adversity**

aesthetic life
See **Kierkegaard**

aletheia/a-letheia
See **thinking; truth**

alienation
The concept of alienation, or – literally – *estrangement*, is one of the most fundamental concepts of existential thinking, and for many theorists, the most important. And in turn it is one of the most significant areas of **existential psychotherapy**. There are four kinds of alienation: from oneself, from others, from the **world**, and from **God**.

The general reader may possess a familiarity with this term as used by Marx, or perhaps by **Hegel**, its originator. For Hegel and Marx, it applies to a person unable to realise their potential, and who is thus diminished and frustrated. For Marx, the working class are through their wage-slavery estranged from their own work. For Hegel, humans generally, in creating their own **world**, are estranged from nature.

Alienation occurs through the fact or perception of opposed dualities, for instance, mind–body, freedom–causality. **Buber** tells us that humankind thinks dichotomously. If this is so, it may suggest how humankind so easily excludes and alienates. More specifically, Buber argues that in objectifying other beings, we are rarely aware of their full being, and thus we are alienated from them. Many existential theorists hold that we protect ourselves from full awareness of our alienation by absorbing ourselves in the social mass. Thus, **Kierkegaard's** notion of the **crowd**, Nietzsche's of the **herd**, and **Heidegger's** of the **They**.

As existential writers have made alienation a fundamental concern, so many of them see it as involving an emotional and spiritual loss. For instance, Kierkegaard, a profoundly religious writer, sees humankind as spiritually alienated from God. We do not see the meaningfulness that there is, we lack faith, lack the personal relationship to God. For Heidegger, human beings have become alienated from **Being**. We are therefore homeless. And (following Hegel) he argues we have alienated ourselves further with our **technological attitude**. Hegel had a further idea, that of disalienation, which is to progress towards the Absolute, and is rather like self-actualisation (see **client-centred psychotherapy**). For the more pessimistic **Sartre**, we are essentially alienated, because life is **absurd**, with the **meaninglessness** of **being-for-itself**.

The psychotherapeutic notions of **congruence** and incongruence refer to psychological integration and alienation, respectively. These are purely intrapsychic concepts, with no existential reference. All psychological **defences** result in estrangement, at least from the **self** (usually in that the person loses direct awareness of their emotions), and often also from others.

alterity
See **Levinas**

ambiguity
A word used in a technical sense by **Heidegger**, as an aspect of everyday, inauthentic **Being**, which is a consequence of our being fallen with other people, and living in a *They-self* manner. It is the counterpart of **curiosity** and **idle talk** and leads to our living in a meaningless and confusing **world** in which things can be anything we want:

> When in everyday being with one another, we encounter things that are accessible to everybody and about which everybody can say everything, we can soon no longer decide what is disclosed in genuine understanding and what is not. This ambiguity extends not only to the world, but likewise to being-with-one-another as such, even to the being of Da-sein toward itself. (Heidegger, 1927b: 173)

Merleau-Ponty uses the term in a more positive sense, to indicate the two-sided, ambiguous nature of human existence, where things are both one thing and the other. He refers to this as the *chiasm*: 'The chiasm, reversibility, is the idea that every perception is doubled with a counter-perception' (Merleau-Ponty, 1964: 264). This is more than a reference to subjectivity and individual difference. We are situated in the world, and our knowledge can never be comprehensive and complete, for it is situational and open to change. Human perception is not fully subjective nor fully objective, but always both. If a psychotherapist accepts this notion, then a consequence is that his or her client's words and expressions must be understood as untranslatable and irreducible. Such a philosophy or psychology of ambiguity seeks to protect and respect the complexity of human experience, accepting that much of a person's thinking seems either correct or incorrect, though much of it is neither. Our lived world is always open to **interpretation**.

Simone de **Beauvoir** spoke of an *ethics of ambiguity,* where people had to create **meaning** according to their own lights and the challenge put to them by their **freedom** to be one thing or another.

> To attain his truth, man must not attempt to dispel the ambiguity of his being but, on the contrary, accept the task of realizing it. (de Beauvoir, 1948: 13)

See also **subject and object**

amor fati

Nietzsche's concept of the love of fate, finding joy in it. This is the contrary of hating one's mortal lot, railing against the physical world. All of life is necessary, including strife, enmity and anguish. We should not wish for heaven on earth, and it is human idealism that creates the falsehood of heaven and thus makes life hell. (Compare this with **Sartre's** idea of **bad faith.**)

See also **eternal return; yes-saying**

angst
See **anxiety**

anguish
See **anxiety**

anonymous mode of relating
See **Binswanger**

answerable
See **responsibility**

anticipation

We suffer **anxiety** at the prospect of our own **death;** but according to Heidegger, whilst death is a constant **possibility** for the human being (**Da-sein**), an authentic stance towards our personal death liberates us from such anxiety. This *Vorlaufen,* or running ahead, is a **resoluteness** towards finitude, an acceptance of our own mortality, a realisation that our days are limited, and that upon our own death there will be no more possibilities in our life:

> The more clearly this possibility is understood, the more purely does understanding penetrate to it *as the possibility of the impossibility of existence in general.* (Heidegger, 1927b: 262)

Death is not impersonal, it is not something **They** have, but is one's own:

> Death does not just 'belong' in an undifferentiated way to one's own Da-sein, but it *lays claim* on it as something *individual* ... Da-sein can *authentically* be *itself* only when it makes that possible of its own accord. (Ibid.: 263)

Heidegger speaks of anticipatory resoluteness as the way in which we can realise our ownmost potentiality for being ourselves. This means to be deliberately capable of overseeing and running ahead of our own possibilities towards the ultimate possibility of our death. In this process we come authentically into our own and into the **situation**.

See also **authenticity; being-towards-death; time and temporality**

antivalue
See **slime**

Anti-Climacus
Pseudonym used by **Kierkegaard** for *The Sickness Unto Death* (1849).

anti-psychiatry
A term devised by **David Cooper** in 1967, in his book *Psychiatry and Anti-Psychiatry*. As a Marxist psychiatrist, he claimed that psychiatry often amounts to social control enacted by clinicians who suffer from political and personal ignorance, and that it suppresses difference and originality:

> The bourgeois psychiatrist succeeds when his victim (patient) is reduced to nothing more than the wretched, forsaken condition into which the psychiatrist himself has fallen. (Cooper, 1974: 55–6)

Cooper's anti-psychiatrist would, instead of employing objectifying diagnoses and depersonalising biomedical intervention, offer the *witnessing* of the patient's subjective experience. It would discourage infantilising and paternalistic practitioner–patient relationships, replacing them with relationships where reciprocity was possible, for example, in communes.

Anti-psychiatry is associated with a reluctance to rely on medication, and is remembered for novel alternatives to in-patient care, for instance Cooper's Villa 21, and **Laing's** Kingsley Hall. These projects were and remain controversial and were abandoned in favour of more moderate therapeutic community establishments. Cooper also wrote that the anti-psychiatrist should risk the investigation of his own madness and despair, knowing that otherwise his qualifications for treating madness were invalid. Most of all, the anti-psychiatrist would allow patients to open up their experiences, not close them down. It is in these respects, perhaps, that anti-psychiatry is of most interest to existential thinkers.

Other writers associated with anti-psychiatry are Thomas **Szasz** (although he denies that his contractual psychiatry was related to it in any way), R.D. Laing (who also wished to be dissociated from the movement) and **Foucault**. The term anti-psychiatry is now little used.

anxiety

When existentialists discuss anxiety, they do not, with one exception, mean worry, they mean *angst*, or *existential anxiety*. It is not the fretful state of mind that the English word *anxiety* usually refers to, but rather an apprehension of something beyond everyday concerns.

First used in a philosophical way by **Kierkegaard**, angst is a troubled awareness of **freedom**, the potential either to sin or to take a **leap of faith** and enter into a relationship with God. In *The Concept of Anxiety* (sometimes translated as *The Concept of Dread*), angst is described as a state preceding a leap from one stage of life to another. It is, says Kierkegaard, 'a sympathetic antipathy and an antipathetic sympathy' (Kierkegaard, 1844b: 42); and thus he writes:

> Anxiety may be compared with dizziness. He whose eye happens to look down into the yawning abyss becomes dizzy. But what is the reason for this? It is just as much in his own eye as in the abyss, for suppose he had not looked down. Hence anxiety is the dizziness of freedom ... (Ibid.: 61)

Kierkegaard gives as an example a small boy attracted to adventure yet at the same time repelled by the threat to his physical safety. A sinful person may suffer angst, loving his or her state of sin, in dread of the freedom he or she chooses not to embrace, not daring to take the leap of faith into uncertainty.

Angst is not overcome by a once-and-for-all leap of faith, for one must continually make such leaps. It is, for Kierkegaard, an important aspect of the human condition, needing to be mastered:

> However I will say that this is an adventure that every human being must go through. To learn to be anxious in order that he may not perish either by never having been in anxiety or by succumbing in anxiety. Whoever has learned to be anxious in the right way has learned the ultimate. (Ibid.: 155)

Angst is thus a foreboding, a sense of the loss of innocence, a dizziness before freedom, and the tension between body and soul.

Heidegger stresses the hidden nature of existential anxiety: *'Angst* "does not know" what it is about which it is anxious' (Heidegger, 1927a: 186). He uses the term to mean anxiety at one's responsibility for living life authentically. For him, anxiety is linked to our awareness of the inevitability of death and the impossibility of our possibilities. Anxiety is therefore an essential precondition for a person to become authentically aware of his or her individuality:

> *Angst* reveals in Da-sein its *being toward* its ownmost potentiality of being, that is, *being free for* the freedom of choosing and grasping itself. *Angst* brings Da-sein *before its being free for* ... (*propensio in*), the authenticity of its being as possibility which it always already is. (Ibid.: 188)

According to Heidegger, such a moment of anxiety is an epiphany, a dramatic demonstration of *Da-sein*'s predicament. It can happen when we lose the false view of the world provided by the **They**. It is a clarity that *Da-sein* finds when facing the world, and is linked to our awareness of the inevitability of **death**, and so it is most effectively responded to by a resolute anticipation of death. **Sartre** uses the term in a similar way to Heidegger, meaning anguish. He sees anxiety as a necessary experience to become free in relation to our **nothingness**.

Theorists differ in their ideas of the origin of angst. However, except for **Yalom** (see below), it is always a metaphysical source. For instance, **Jaspers** describes anxiety as the metaphysical fear of **choice**. **Tillich** distinguishes between existential anxiety and what he calls *neurotic* anxiety. The latter is mere worrying, and is a smokescreen, a distraction, a psychological evasion, so that the worrier can shift his or her attention away from their angst.

The common existential assertion is that anxiety has no direct focus, and that a direct origin of anxiety results in fear, not anxiety. But the existential psychoanalyst Irvin Yalom departs from this perspective, accounting death as a direct and primary source of anxiety.

Angst is seen by existential thinkers as a natural reaction to the vastness of choice and isolation, a predictable response to the loneliness of individual life and the choices the individual must make. Adam and Eve would have felt angst on their expulsion from the safety of the Garden of Eden. But existential authors value such anxiety, because it marks the start of our openness to the human condition. It is the necessary counterpart of being truly alive. We either accept the uncertainty of life, or we hide our heads under the bedclothes.

See also **attunement; authenticity and inauthenticity; bad faith;** *Befindlichkeit;* **Bugental; care; falling; finite and infinite, finitude and infinitude; fleeing; individuation; nausea; possibility; resoluteness; uncanniness**

Apollonian mentality
See **Dionysian and Apollonian mentalities**

apophantic speech
That which shows itself by itself. Derived from **Aristotle's** *apophansis* – propositional speech – and used by **Husserl** and **Heidegger** in their **phenomenology** to refer to concepts that speak for themselves. Heidegger explains that as the essential meaning of *logos* is speech, so the primary function of speech is to show, to make manifest, and this is in distinction from speech used to make **judgement** or **interpretation**. Apophantic discourse involves no predication, merely the illumination of what is there. Apophantic speech, providing it genuinely uncovers what is, must obviously reveal the **truth**.

appearance
See **phenomenon**

appropriation
See *Ereignis*

Archimedean point
See **Husserl**

Arendt

Hannah Arendt (1906–75). German historian and political philosopher, student of **Heidegger** and **Jaspers**, phenomenologist and author of *Origins of Totalitarianism* (1951), *The Human Condition* (1958) and *Eichmann in Jerusalem: a Report on the Banality of Evil* (1963). She stresses the importance and the potential greatness of human action, particularly political action, but also the need to reflect upon action, and that without such reflection, human beings can drift into evil-doing.

Arendt is best known for her descriptions of the public space and how this is manipulated. She distinguishes three fundamental forms of *vita activa* (human life activity) in labour, work and action. Labour is the toil necessary in order to survive; work is human productivity and creativity, and what constitutes a world; action or *praxis* is the endeavour that makes us profoundly human and which is usually undertaken in a co-operative or political fashion.

Aristotle

(384–322 BC). Greek philosopher and pupil of Plato, whose influence is felt throughout Western philosophy.

References to Aristotelian ideas can be found under: **apophantic speech; dialectic; Dilthey;** *eudaimonia;* **intentionality; metaphysics; ontological/ ontology;** *praxis;* **space; tragedy; truth**

art and existential thought

For a number of reasons, there is a close association between existential thought and the arts, especially literature. Existential thinkers typically believe that everyday language, scientific and even philosophical language overlook the nature of human being, of **existence**. They often admire or express themselves in poetry, or illustrate their ideas through dramatic narratives. Hence the enthusiasm of **Heidegger** for the poetry of **Hölderlin** and Rilke, and thus the plays of **Marcel, Sartre** and **Camus**. For whilst existential philosophers are analytically rigorous, they commonly object to simple representations of reality. Instead, they emphasise complexity, the multiplicity of views, and the impossibility of certainty. So **Kierkegaard**, in *Either/Or* (1843a), presents various perspectives, endorsing none of them. And **Nietzsche**, in his poetic writing, constantly deploys teasing, ironic aphorisms.

Existential thinkers have given serious attention to the nature of art. Sartre, for instance, in *What Is Literature?* (1948), explores the social role of the writer, and writes approvingly of the writer as a political activist. Sartre's long and thorough analysis of Jean Genet (Sartre, 1952) and of Flaubert (Sartre, 1971) illustrate this very well. For Kierkegaard, on the other hand, art is essentially inadequate, reflecting an initial and selfish developmental stage of the person, one that needs to be overcome. For Heidegger, art is in some respects superior to philosophy, for it discloses the **world**, reveals the essences of things. Unlike **science** and **philosophy**, art does not study from a distance, but instead shows subjective experience quite directly.

This is typically the existential view of art, that artistic expression represents lived experience, that it is a first-order endeavour whilst philosophical discussion is a second-order enterprise, alienated from the lived world. Furthermore, a work of art can usefully represent any number of concrete situations, and show in a holistic way the complexity of perception and life. **Merleau-Ponty,** for example, writes at length on painting, explaining how it is more than observation of the world, but is necessarily engaged with it, how the painter employs his **body** (most especially, his eyes) to paint, and the beholder must similarly use his or her body. Seen in this way, art is the undisguised product of *embodiment*, and because of this it enables a *pre-reflective encounter*. Merleau-Ponty discusses and shows admiration for a number of artists, but above all, for Cézanne. There are of course many artists who directly associated themselves with existentialism and whose paintings illustrate existential themes, amongst them Picasso, Dali and Magritte.

There is a great deal of art in which existential themes are present, but which are not rooted in a thorough-going existential philosophy. There are also many works by artists whose attitudes do not constitute a philosophy but whose thinking is sympathetic to existential thought. So, for instance, the novels of **Dostoevsky**, Turgenev and **Tolstoy**. Franz Kafka's stories abound with existential themes, including **anxiety** and **guilt**, **meaning** and **paradox**, **freedom** and **choice**, and **alienation**. The Theatre of the Absurd – of Beckett, Genet, Ionesco and Pinter – similarly portrays a world in which rationality is useless. Theirs is a world without order, in which – but this is quite unlike the existential attitude – commitment seems pointless. Other writers, like Ibsen and Brecht, depict a world in which everything must be questioned in order to achieve some existential distance.

Music does not easily lend itself to comprehensive philosophies, but Wagner should be mentioned for his historic association with Nietzsche and the broad existential themes in his work. Richard Strauss, in his tone poem, *Also Sprach Zarathustra* (1896), attempts to portray the development of human-kind. And the Danish composer, Vagn Holmboe, in his 1963–4 *Requiem to Nietzsche*, uses music and poetry to show the philosopher's psychological development. Mahler's work also resonates with existential themes.

Most of all, existential art portrays alienation, uncertainty and the arbitrariness of the world in which the individual finds himself. The term *existential* is sometimes misused and applied to any work of art preoccupied with death or rebellion, or which encourages a cynical appraisal of the world. But popular art can examine existence, and much post-war cinema, for instance Cocteau, Wenders, Fassbinder, Fellini and Bergman, may be considered to have offered existential analyses of life.

See also **Beauvoir, de; body; essence; pre-reflexive consciousness**

articulation

Heidegger's concept of *Artikulation*. The way in which the significance of **Being** is understood, which may at times be in misunderstanding: 'The They itself, for the sake of which Da-sein is every day, articulates the referential context of significance' (Heidegger, 1927b: 129). Articulating can be *artikulieren* or *gliedern* in German, and articulation refers to both the former (joining that which is divided) and the latter (connecting parts of the same thing). Articulation is about the connections that exist in the world which enable *Da-sein* to make sense of the **world**.

See also **They, the**

assertion

Heidegger's concept of a mode of positing something, the most familiar form of discourse. We frequently start out by making assertions about the world which are unchecked against reality. We sometimes try to understand matters by examining our own or other people's statements about the world, but this, according to Heidegger, is an inferior way of understanding. Assertions are at best the result of understanding, they are not the basis of it. And whilst we can make assertions about things, we can make no assertions about **Being**. We need existential experience to understand reality, not rational categories. To discover the **truth**, we must question experience itself and not expect logical analysis to uncover it.

See also **apophantic speech; phenomenological method**

assumptions

See **doubt; dreams; existential psychotherapy; Husserl; Nietzsche; phenomenological method; science and scientific method; Zollikon Seminars**

attunement

This Heideggerian notion refers to our moods and our relatedness to the **world**. Attunement, or *Stimmung*, is the way in which we are tuned into the world, and is an aspect of what Heidegger calls **Befindlichkeit**, or state of mind: how human beings are always in a particular disposition in relation to the world. However, attunement is not a psychological term, but a philosophical one, and **Heidegger** argues that moods disclose how we stand, that they are our apprehension of the world, or more exactly, of ourselves in the world. For Heidegger, our moods permit a view of our **being-in-the-world**, they let us notice particular aspects of the world: 'Mood makes manifest "how one is and is coming along"' (Heidegger, 1927b: 134). For we resonate in sympathy, we are *attuned*. Thus an anxious person is aware of the unsettledness of **Being**.

Heidegger writes of moods as he writes of being-in-the-world, that our selves and the world cannot be separated, but are always in **relationship**: 'Mood assails. It comes neither from "without" nor from "within", but rises from being-in-the-world itself as a mode of that being' (ibid.: 136).

> We may, however, ignore our moods, and what they tell us: For the most part Da-sein evades the being that is disclosed in moods ... In the evasion itself there *is* something disclosed ... Attunement always has its understanding, even if only by suppressing it. (Ibid.: 135–43)

Worse still, some moods can block our awareness. For example: 'In bad moods, *Da-sein* becomes blind to itself, the surrounding world of heedfulness is veiled, the circumspection of taking care is led astray' (ibid.: 136). We can only get away from a mood by going into another mood, for we are always in some mood or other.

When we master a mood, we do so by way of a counter-mood; we are never free of moods. Ontologically, we thus obtain as the *first* essential characteristic of states-of-mind that *they disclose Dasein in its thrownness, and – proximally and for the most part – in the manner of an evasive turning-away.* (Ibid.: 136)

According to Heidegger, we can only stand in relation to the world, we cannot see a whole and objective reality. It is thus that the ambition of science to be objective is doomed to failure, and that ambition is inauthentic, because it avoids the nature of our being, that we cannot be separated from the world.

For the phenomenological therapist, our moods – both what is present and what is not – are our psychologically unprocessed awareness of ourselves in the world, a proto-understanding that is also a working demonstration of our aspirations, hopes and fears. They are an aspect of the process of our being in the world, and ripe for philosophical and psychological analysis.

See also **anxiety; authenticity; Boss; delusion; emotions; entanglement; liberation**

Augenblick
See **Moment, the**

authenticity and inauthenticity
Eigentlichkeit and *Uneigentlichkeit*, literally meaning something like actual and not actual, owned and unowned ways of existing. **Heidegger** emphasises the importance of the tension between authenticity and inauthenticity in every human existence. For him, to be authentic is to comprehend and accept the parameters of human living, including the fact that one has one's own life to lead and that **death** is an inevitable part of the human condition. To be authentic requires us to admit to ourselves that our possibilities are our own, and that we therefore have to win our self for ourselves. We may instead prefer **fleeing** from ourselves, and it is easy to lose oneself in inauthenticity, for instance to fall into following the behaviour and thoughts of the **They**, or to absorb oneself in one's role and to neglect one's self, to have less **care** of oneself. Heidegger writes also of **indifference**; being neither authentic nor inauthentic. And he tells us that inauthenticity can never be eradicated:

[B]ecause *Da-sein* is always essentially its possibility, it *can* 'choose' itself in its being, it can win itself, it can lose itself, or it can never and only 'apparently' win itself. It can only have lost itself and it can only have not yet gained itself because it is essentially possible as authentic, that is, it belongs to itself. (Heidegger, 1927b: 42–3)

Moreover, 'Inauthenticity belongs to the essential nature of factical *Dasein*. Authenticity is only a modification but not a total obliteration of inauthenticity' (Heidegger, 1927c: 171). Thus inauthenticity is the more primary, pervasive condition.

In the worlds of finance, art and society, to be inauthentic frequently carries moral as well as practical approval. For Heidegger, inauthenticity carries only practical approval, and he often stresses the advantages of authentic living even though the two ways of being are equally important:

> [T]he inauthenticity of Dasein does not signify a 'lesser' being or a 'lower' degree of being. Rather, inauthenticity can determine Da-sein even in its fullest concretion, when it is busy, excited, interested, and capable of pleasure. (Heidegger, 1927b: 43)

These are particularly important ideas for existential psychotherapists, permitting an examination and discussion of the client's or patient's degree and kind of inauthenticity, how much they are themselves, and to what extent they have detached themselves and lost themselves.

Heidegger's idea of authenticity is not the same as the Rogerian or client-centred idea of **congruence** (even though some writers use the term 'authenticity' as a synonym). **Rogers's** idea refers particularly to the therapist being psychologically integrated enough to recognise and accept the existence of his or her own thoughts and feelings. This idea may be considered to derive from Heidegger's more general and philosophical concepts.

See also **awaiting; bad faith; Bugental; close off; cover up; forgetting; immediacy; interhuman, the; I–Thou; levelling down; Moment, the**

autonomy
See **Beauvoir, de; becoming; choice;** *Erbe*; **fate; leaping in; ontonomy; responsibility; sexuality**

availability
Disponibilité, literally *disposability*. **Marcel** is one of a number of existential writers to speak of the **I–Thou** relationship. Accordingly, he claims that to **love** another, whether a person or God, one must be truly available, and that this means transcending mere desire and the alienating sense of **self** and others. Availability consists of an openness towards the **Other**, no matter what the circumstances or the demands this places upon us. Love is a mutual availability for what the future holds in store.

averageness
(*Durchschnittlichkeit*). One of a number of expressions **Heidegger** uses to describe the human tendency to merge into the **crowd** and become anonymous. Averageness is created through being-with-one-another, the inextricability of our involvement with others, and the consequent difficulty of discovering our individuality. The appeal of the mass is such that what is not average is suppressed, and individuality is diluted. According to Heidegger, we would rather remain average, not much better and not much worse than others, than to stand out (or *ec-sist*).

See also **being-with; individual, the; They, the**

awaiting

An authentic and resolute **anticipation** of the future is one in which one is aware of one's **potentiality-for-being-oneself** and of one's **being-towards-death**. According to **Heidegger**, we usually forget this, and engage in awaiting (*gewärtigen*), considering only the everyday, superficial concerns of life as **They** indicate we should. This is a passive attitude as opposed to the active and actualising attitude of **anticipation**.

See also **authenticity and inauthenticity; time and temporality**

awareness

See **alienation; anxiety; attunement; bad faith; body; boredom; Brentano; client-centred psychotherapy; choice; congruence; consciousness and unconsciousness; *Daseinsanalysis*; defences, psychological; Husserl; leaping ahead; Moment, the; pre-reflexive consciousness; relationship; Tillich**

back to the things themselves
See **Husserl**

bad faith
(*Mauvaise foi*). Being in bad faith is to opt for self-deception. Bad faith, as described by Jean-Paul **Sartre**, is an active evasion of duty. It is the denial or refusal to recognise one's **freedom** or one's **nothingness**. To be in bad faith is to live as though one were utterly helpless or entirely free, unwilling to transcend the limiting factors of life, or to see them as an obstacle to action. In bad faith a person may pretend to be something rather than nothing, or on the contrary may deny their responsibilities for their actions or choices. For example, in bad faith, we may construe ourselves as we perceive that others construe us. For Sartre, this is to give predominance to the **Other** in the coupling of **self** and Other, and identifying too closely with our **being-for-others**. (Rogerian therapists might like to compare this with their ideas of *congruence* and *external locus of evaluation*.) Or we might see ourselves as we used to be, and lose our freedom for action through being bound in the past, an untruthful anachronism that denies both the **facticity** of the present, and our potential for **transcendence**.

> [T]here are two authentic attitudes: that by which I recognise the Other as the subject through whom I get my object-ness – this is shame; and that by which I apprehend myself as the free object by which the Other gets his being-other – this is arrogance or the affirmation of my freedom confronting the Other-as-object. But pride – or vanity – is a feeling without equilibrium, and it is in bad faith. (Sartre, 1943a: 290)

There is a seeming paradox in the idea of bad faith of the sort found by some commentators, including Sartre, in psychoanalytical accounts of unconscious censorship. How is it we are able to deliberately withhold **knowledge** from ourselves, when to suppress an idea requires first some awareness of it? Here is not the place to explore this idea fully, but in defence of it to point out that this process is paradoxical only if one takes an entirely cognitive model of the mind.

Sartre gives many examples of bad faith, both in his philosophical texts and in his fiction. For instance, he writes:

> Take the example of a woman who has consented to go out with a particular man for the first time. She knows very well the intentions which the man who is speaking to her cherishes regarding her ... she does not wish to read in the phrases which he addresses to her

anything other than their explicit meaning. If he says to her, 'I find you so attractive!' she disarms this phrase of its sexual background ... The man who is speaking to her appears to her sincere and respectful as the table is round or square, as the wall coloring is blue or gray ... But then suppose he takes her hand ... the young woman leaves her hand there, but she does not notice that she is leaving it ... she is at this moment all intellect ... the divorce of the body from the soul is accomplished; the hand rests inert between the warm hands of her companion – neither consenting nor resisting – a thing. (Sartre, 1943a: 55–6)

And in another example, Mathieu, the protagonist of the novel *The Age of Reason*, observes a barman, then considers the words of a friend, a committed and impatient communist:

A little while ago he had been smoking a cigarette, as vague and poetic as a flowering creeper: now he had awakened, he was rather too much the barman, manipulating his shaker, opening it, and tipping yellow froth into glasses with a slightly superfluous precision: he was impersonating a barman. Mathieu thought of Brunet: 'Perhaps it's inevitable; perhaps one has to choose between being nothing at all, or impersonating what one is. That would be terrible,' he said to himself: 'it would mean that we were duped by nature.' (Sartre, 1945a: 173)

Antoine Roquentin, the central character from *Nausea*, takes false comfort and reassurance from the fixed and definite: 'how I love to read my name' (Sartre, 1938: 90): Roquentin is refusing to accept the insubstantiality of the self, that it is not as fixed as the letters of a name.

Sartre's manner, in writing of bad faith, is, as the term implies, one of disapproval, and many of his examples of bad faith are of cowardice. The existential psychotherapist will be less willing to take such a view, instead seeing such self-deception merely as a frailty of humankind, but a frailty that is undermining and harmful. For the therapist who uses Sartrean ideas in their practice, the concept of bad faith may be a powerful conceptual tool for clinical assessment.

See also **engagement; good faith; look, the; subject and object; They, the**

Barth, Karl
See **theology**

Barthes, Roland
Roland Barthes (1915–81). French *structuralist*, that is, an analyst of the unconscious structures of language, in which works of art and other cultural commodities are treated as signs capable of analysis. His works include *Mythologies* (1957) and *Criticism and Truth* (1966).

The point of Barthes's analyses of cultural items is to reveal the bourgeois myths they covertly convey. Advertisements, cars, television and newspapers are full of such meaning. For instance, two motor cars will have the same function as passenger transport, but the symbolism of a Rolls Royce, and what it says about its owner, is very different from that of a Citroën. Ordinary literary analysis will not reveal these myths, for writing and other signs are not transparent, and in our society the full symbolism of our cultural artefacts is not consciously apparent. Nevertheless, it affects the public. So the structural analyst must maintain a distance from mass-culture, and should employ *sarcasm* to subvert these implicit meanings.

Barthes takes a kind of phenomenological approach, bracketing the functional significance of signs before considering their secondary meaning. His work can be seen as combining elements of Marx, **Freud** and others in order to criticise bourgeois culture. Counter-critics of Barthes's structuralism argue that he underestimates the public's ability to discern and reject myths.

See also **Lacan; phenomenological method; structuralism**

Beauvoir, Simone de

Simone de Beauvoir (1908–86). French philosopher, essayist and novelist. Her magnum opus, *The Second Sex* (1949), proved profoundly influential on the feminist movement. It distinguishes between sexual and gender differences, between biology and social identity.

De Beauvoir described herself as a disciple of her friend and lover, Jean-Paul **Sartre**, her philosophy being an extension of his ideas on **freedom** and **responsibility**. Her own writing leans towards a more social existentialism than Sartre's, in which individual freedom is only possible through communication with other free persons, so that everyone has a concern with the freedom of others.

Many feminist philosophers have objected to de Beauvoir's analysis of gender, complaining that she asks women to develop masculine qualities of assertiveness and independence. Certainly she sees the masculine wish to dominate as a way to freedom, and the feminine desire to please others as a renouncing of autonomy, for she sees such behaviour as a matter of choice and not as biologically determined. She analyses social domination and submission, and identifies **being-for-itself** with masculinity, men treating women as the **Other** (a trait **Levinas** betrayed in his philosophy), as fearing woman, and limiting her to her uses to man: that of wife, mother, prostitute, etc. Thus woman becomes an object, a **being-in-itself**, and loses her freedom:

> One is not born, but rather becomes, a woman ... [I]t is civilization as a whole that produces this creature, intermediate between male and eunuch, which is described as feminine. (De Beauvoir, 1949: 295)

But while women may feel themselves to be objects, they also have a sense of themselves as subjects:

> Woman is opaque in her very being; she stands before man not as a subject but as an object paradoxically embued with subjectivity; she takes herself simultaneously as *self* and as *other*, a contradiction that entails baffling consequences. (Ibid.: 727)

De Beauvoir describes how women sometimes resort to **resentment**, the ineffectual blaming of men. Some women become how men define them, so choosing inauthenticity.

De Beauvoir sees action and not contemplation as determining freedom. For a long time she believed that only socialism could liberate women from inequality and oppression; but she hypothesises two kinds of freedom: that of controlling circumstances, and the ability to utilise circumstances to the fullest. And unlike Sartre, she admits that freedom is limited by the contingent facts of one's environment.

See also **ambiguity; authenticity and inauthenticity**

becoming

Existential philosophers and psychotherapists, with all their differences, are united in the importance they assign to **choice** and their belief that identity is constructed through the choices we make. Existential theorists see no fixedness to the human life, except at **death**. Until then, however one avoids it, one is in constant flux, never still, always *becoming*. To maintain one's personality, one has constantly to choose it, and to be in an apparently unchanging situation, one has constantly to commit to it, to choose it again and again. In **client-centred psychotherapy**, *becoming* means the increase of autonomy, but in mainstream existential thinking we are all, always, becoming. It does not imply better or worse, simply that human life is self-manufactured. **Kierkegaard**, drawing from **Hegel's** idea that *becoming* is a synthesis of being and non-being, uses the term in a very specific way, to indicate that as the self is a mixture of the finite and the infinite, so becoming is the synthesis of the two into concreteness. For **Heidegger** the process of becoming is a consequence of the way in which *Dasein* exists in **time** and is always a **project**, or projection. Existential therapists take great interest in the direction that their clients' *becoming* has taken and is taking.

See also **authenticity; being-in-itself; change; finite and infinite; freedom**

Befindlichkeit

Literally, *the state I find myself in*, the term is sometimes translated as *state of mind*, at other times as **disposition**. This term indicates ontologically what **attunement** or **mood** (*Stimmung*) means ontically. For **Heidegger**, *Dasein* finds itself **thrown** into a **world** in which it will inevitably care and therefore be affected. *Befindlichkeit* is the way in which the world matters to the individual. With the concept of *Stimmung*, this is ontically applied to the fact that *Dasein* is always in a mood which, whether good or bad, discloses the world of *Dasein*. Heidegger's argument that mood is revealing is a useful one for psychotherapists, for it treats moods as truthful rather than as distortions of objective reality.

See also **care; emotions; ontological/ontology**

Being

The notion of Being is both fundamental and contentious. Existential philosophers regard it as an issue of prime importance.

In the fourth century BC, **Plato** resolved the question of being in a way we may find strange, namely by contending that physical entities are in a transient place between Being (the place of ideal forms) and non-being. Such entities are in the position of **becoming**.

The rationalist philosopher Leibniz, in *On the Ultimate Origin of Things* (1697) posed the question of why there is any world at all. His answer, a kind of religious calculus, was that essence tends towards existence, and that the world we have allows the maximum possibility for divine creativity. This is not a questioning of Being itself, but of contingent existence. When existential philosophers discuss Being as problematic, they are referring to the state of Being rather than a given physical instance of being.

If Being is an abstraction and beings are merely the embodiment of that abstraction, then there may be few questions to ask of Being. And if Being is that fact which permits of no further reduction, then the question of what Being is may be trivial or it may be profound. **Heidegger** is the philosopher who was most devoted to the **meaning** of Being, and he contends that it is supremely profound. In Heidegger's *Being and Time* there are three important factors to the being of *Da-sein*: facticity, *existentiality* and **falling** (or **entanglement**). *Da-sein* is free but limited by **contingency**. *Da-sein* is self-reflexive, and able to reflect on Being, but *Da-sein* also neglects Being. In his later work he became more preoccupied with Being itself than with the Being of *Da-sein*:

> Yet Being – what is Being? It is It itself. The thinking that is to come must learn to experience that and to say it … Being is farther than all beings and is yet nearer to man than every being, be it a rock, a beast, a work of art, a machine, be it an angel or God. Being is the nearest. Yet the near remains farthest from man. Man at first clings always and only to beings. But when thinking represents beings as beings, it no doubt relates itself to Being. In truth, however, it always thinks only of beings as such; precisely not, and never, Being as such. (Heidegger, 1947: 234)

Critics of Heidegger's philosophy complain that he treats Being as if it were a name, and that as a German Romantic he mistakes the etymological history of the German language for an analysis of the world.

Sartre follows Heidegger when he writes, 'Being has not been given its due' (Sartre, 1943a: xxxvi). He continues: 'Being is. Being is in-itself. Being is what it is' (ibid.: xlii).

For **Jaspers**, with his notion of **limit situations**, Being can be found through analysis of an individual's predicament: 'I must *search for being* if I want to find my real self. But it is not till I fail in this search for intrinsic being that I begin to philosophise' (Jaspers, 1932: 45).

The question of Being is bound up with that of **essence**. For some existential thinkers, there is an essence to Being. **Nietzsche**, for instance, is seen by Heidegger as representing **will to power** as the essence of Being. For others (e.g. **Merleau-Ponty**) there is no intrinsic essence to Being, and any essence derives from the **relationship** of an entity with the **world**.

See also *Ereignis*; **nothing, the**; **spirit**

being-ahead-of-itself

According to **Heidegger**, human being (or rather, *Da-sein*) is always ahead of itself (*sich vorweg sein*), that is, considering its own possibilities, whether towards **authenticity** or inauthenticity. Thus human being considers its future. It can do this in an authentic way by **anticipation** and **resoluteness**. This requires the capacity for loyalty (see **constancy and loyalty**) to one's own **existence**. Otherwise the moving forwards into the future can be seen as the simple quality of **projection**, which is an **ontological** given for *Da-sein* because of its essential **thrownness**. If this thrownness is not anticipated resolutely, it may be experienced as **turbulence**.

being-alongside
See **being-together-with**

being-for-another
The egocentric narrator of 'The Seducer's Diary' by **Kierkegaard**, claims that woman is essentially being-for-another, and that being-for-another is a matter of the moment which does not last:

> The moment may take a longer or a shorter time coming, but as soon as it comes, what was originally being-for-another becomes a relative being, and then it is all over. (Kierkegaard, 1843a: 365)

This is in sharp contrast with Heidegger's use of the term in relation to *Mitsein*, or **being-with**. **Heidegger** claims that being-for-another is one of the deficient modes of being-with, which can be overcome into a more authentic form of being-with-one-another in solicitude.

See also **leaping ahead; marriage**

being-for-itself
(*Être-pour-soi*). This is human **consciousness**, as **Sartre** refers to it, human being as ripe with possibility yet possessed of nothing intrinsic. It is an essentially atheistic definition: no god has defined human being, and human being is not determined by Being itself. Likewise, the individual human being's life remains undetermined throughout his or her life, complete only at **death**, when at last it can be described as fixed, for then it has no **time** and no **choice** remaining. This is the essence of humankind, and the core of Sartre's **existentialism**, for with its assertion of a lack of identity comes the terrible liability of individual **freedom**, a freedom we humans often avoid with **bad faith**: 'The For-itself, in fact, is nothing but the pure nihilation of the In-itself; it is like a hole of being at the heart of Being' (Sartre, 1943a: 617).

Human beings are so afraid of their freedom of being-for-itself that they have a tendency to hide in the pretence of being like an object, a **being-in-itself**.

See also **Beauvoir, de; nothingness**

being-for-man
See **love**

being-for-others
(*Être-pour-autrui*). According to **Sartre**, one's own **self** is an object for others and one tries to make objects out of other people:

> Everything which may be said of me in my relations with the Other applies to him as
> well. While I attempt to free myself from the hold of the Other, the Other is trying to
> free himself from mine; while I seek to enslave the Other, the Other seeks to enslave me.
> (Sartre, 1943a: 364)

In his later work, Sartre came to formulate a more reciprocal theory of being-with others, and referred to this as mutuality and **generosity**.

See also ecstasy; **look, the; masochism; Other, the; reciprocity; sadism**

being-in
See **being-in-the-world**

being-in-itself
(*Être-en-soi*). By this, **Sartre** refers to all objects or to living entities lacking self-awareness. For Sartre, these are simple, fixed things: they have a definite opaque identity, and there is no more that can be said about them. A table is a table, and it cannot of itself be otherwise. It is up to *me* to make it a chair or firewood. Derived from *an-sich-sein*, in the philosophy of **Heidegger**.

See also **Beauvoir, de; being-for-itself**

being-in-the-world
Heidegger's term for *Dasein's* existence as essentially unified with a **world**. Existential theories have in common the view of human beings as bound up with the world. We are not mere spectators to, or actors in, a world from which we could in principle be separated, but are inexorably involved with the world and an inextricable part of it. Nowhere is this mutuality emphasised more forcefully than in the philosophy of **Heidegger**:

> The compound expression 'being-in-the-world' indicates, in the very way we have
> coined it, that it stands for a *unified* phenomenon. (Heidegger, 1927b: 53)

In hyphenating being-in-the-world (*in-der-Welt-sein*), stress is placed on the relatedness of the thinking being and his or her world. We are *Dasein – the being that is there*, and we are **thrown** into a world in which we have a mind and a **body**, a world in which there is **time** and **facticity**, and a world to which we are linked through **care**. Being-in-the-world is having an experience of *mineness* (see **identity**), which may lead to the creation of a **self**; it always involves **being-with** others. Heidegger further points out that the factors of the expression 'being-in-the-world' remain to be investigated. What is this 'being' that is referred to? What is the meaning of being 'in'? And what is the nature of this 'world'? The immense philosophical project that is *Being and Time* is largely taken up with the investigation of these very questions.

See also **disposition; unity**

being-there
See *Dasein*

being-together-with
Heidegger's expression (*sein bei*), sometimes translated as *being-alongside*, refers to the significance of the present to *Da-sein*, of being absorbed with the **world**. It is the way in which *Dasein* is in relation to the things in the world. *Da-sein* is **being-with** other people but it is being-alongside, or together with things.

> [B]eing-in-the-world is essentially care ... taking care of things ... Nor does care mean primarily and exclusively an isolated attitude of the ego towards itself. The expression 'care for oneself,' following the analogy of care and concern, would be a tautology. Care cannot mean a special attitude towards the self, because the self is already characterised ontologically as being-ahead-of-itself. (Heidegger, 1927b: 193)

Being-alongside is what we do in relation to our *Umwelt* (see **four worlds**), which we are absorbed in and therefore close to, that is, being-together-with. Being-with is reserved for our being with other people.

See also **being-ahead-of-itself; being-in-the-world; care; ontological**

being-towards-death
To be mortal is to possess all possibilities for life, including the **possibility** for the end of all possibilities: 'A *constant unfinished quality* thus lies in the essence of the constitution of Da-sein', writes **Heidegger** (1927b: 236), who argues that in everyday life, **They** evade the fact of **death** by always claiming it to be vaguely in the future, whereas as a possibility it is always present:

> Even 'thinking about death' is regarded publicly as cowardly fear, a sign of insecurity on the part of Da-sein and a dark flight from the world. *The They does not permit the courage to have Angst about death.* (Ibid.: 254)

In **authenticity**, the individual accepts death, and faces it as his or her own prospect. And the solitariness of personal death reflects the **care** one must have towards one's life. To stand in authentic awareness of the possibility of one's death is to accept the individuality of one's own existence, to realise that one exists for the sake of oneself, that one must care about life, and that one exists in **time**. It is therefore not death itself that matters, but *Dasein*'s attitude towards the possibility of death which we have to learn to live with. Being-towards-death refers to this attitude of awareness of life and the fact that it is limited in time: 'Dasein does not first die, or does not really die at all, with and in the experience of factual demise' (Heidegger, 1927a: 247).

In **anticipation** we become ready to face the reality of our death and what is possible for us before our death and it is this that leads to the anticipatory **resoluteness** that is being-towards-death.

See also **anxiety;** *Dasein*; **tranquillisation**

being-with

Heidegger coined the term *Mitsein* to indicate that human being (***Dasein***) is essentially being-with-others. We are **thrown** into a **world** that we share with others, and we are inextricably involved with others, so that the self that we consider as *I* is not simple and detached, and is not separable from the world or from the others in this world. We are so directly with-one-another that even if others are physically absent, we still relate to others, and we are inevitably involved with others whether they are present or not:

> Even if the particular factical Dasein does *not* turn to Others, and supposes that it has no need of them or manages to get along without them, it *is* in the way of Being-with. (Heidegger, 1927a: 123)

We are so fundamentally being-with that we are in the first instance taken over by the existence of others: we are fallen with others. And it is our **fallenness** that leads to our inauthentic mode of being, from which we have to extricate ourselves in order to discover **authenticity**. Once we have achieved this, we can be with others in an authentic or inauthentic manner.

See also **leaping ahead; leaping in**

benumbing
See **numbing**

Berdyaev

Nikolai Alexandrovich Berdyaev (1874–1948). Ukranian philosopher. Influenced by **Kant**, Fichte, **Hegel**, **Schopenhauer**, Marx, **Dostoevsky**, **Nietzsche**. With the ending of Soviet socialism, his popularity in Russia grew. His many publications include *The Meaning of the Creative Act* (1916), *The Meaning of History* (1923), *Slavery and Freedom* (1939) and *The Beginning and the End* (1947).

Born of an aristocratic family, Berdyaev enlisted at Kiev military academy where he had the first of two religious conversions. He aligned himself with Marxist ideology, and for this was confined to northern Russia from 1898–1900. After the 1917 Revolution, now Professor of Philosophy at Moscow University, he was at first tolerant of the new socialist regime but his increasing criticisms led in 1922 to his exile by the Soviet government. He left with his wife, first to Berlin, and then in 1924 they settled in Paris.

Berdyaev's philosophy may be characterised as concerning itself with **freedom** and the eternal. He argues that freedom is primary; it precedes **existence**:

> Freedom is the ultimate: it cannot be derived from anything: it cannot be made the equivalent of anything. Freedom is the baseless foundation of being: it is deeper than all being. (Berdyaev, 1916: 145)

The basis of the cosmos is freedom, a state of indeterminacy in which all is mere potential. The fact of actual existence points to a purposeful act of creation, and to God the Creator, who is at the heart of Berdyaev's thought.

For with this initial act of creation came value, and God and humankind's evolving pursuit of it. For Berdyaev, God is less a being than a creative process and a moral principle. Evil is unrealised potential, the neglect of the individual, a divergence from divine purpose – hence Berdyaev's criticism of Soviet life, since its communal spirit was at odds with personal freedom. For Berdyaev, each person must decide for themselves about right and wrong:

> Civilisation promises to emancipate man and there can be no dispute that it provides the equipment for emancipation; but it is also the objectification of human existence and, therefore, it brings enslavement with it. (Berdyaev, 1939: 118)

Human beings are fallen spirits, who have lost the eternal, and now live in bounded **time** and **space**. In consequence, we take a limited and objective view of our existence, an objectifying mentality that splits subject from object. And we believe **truth** to be objective, that it can always be measured or deduced (see **technology and technological attitude**). Yet this is so only of the objective world. Ultimate truth has no verifiability, for it is reality itself, and to search for it is to miss it. It is immediate and present, for it is of the spirit. This is why the individual personality is supreme, for it contains all, it contains the universe, whereas society is an objective fact. This is not individualism, nor is Berdyaev's philosophy opposed to community. On the contrary, for Berdyaev, human beings are inextricably involved with one another.

As for time and space, their transcendence is possible through creative ecstasy. In this way we may commune briefly with the divine, with eternal reality. But eternal redemption will occur only when we become persons – not mere individuals, enslaved by the material world, but beings in communion with one another, in partnership with God.

Compare with **Buber; Heidegger; Marcel; Tillich**

Bergson

Henri-Louis Bergson (1859–1941). French philosopher of Anglo-Polish parentage. His influences include Plotinus, Maine de Biran, Darwin and Herbert Spencer. His own influence has been felt not only in philosophy, but also in literature and psychotherapy, for instance in Proust and **Minkowski**. He also had considerable influence on **Merleau–Ponty**. His published works include *Time and Free Will* (1889), *Matter and Memory* (1896) and *Laughter* (1901). In 1927 he was awarded the Nobel Prize for Literature.

Bergson's philosophy is marked by a peculiar **dualism**, of matter and the life force, the first of which presents resistance to the second. He argues that scientific measurement is reductionist and misrepresents human experience. Human reality, according to Bergson, is **change**, duration, **becoming**. But while science measures discrete phenomena, this does not do justice to how we actually experience reality. For instance, **time** is neither measurable nor divisible, since it is continuous. When we listen to music, we do not hear disconnected sounds, we hear a melodic flow. Only the present is present to experience; *pure memory*, a spiritual device, which generally enforces a **forgetting** of the past, allows it to be present when necessary.

bias
See **countertransference; perception; phenomenology; relationship; transference**

Binswanger
Ludwig Binswanger (1881–1966). Swiss psychiatrist and psychotherapist. Influenced at first by **Jung** and **Freud**, later by **Husserl, Buber** and **Heidegger**. As the first great existential therapist, his own influence is widespread, but especially upon **Merleau–Ponty** and **Boss**. His most important publication is *Grundformen und Erkenntnis menschlichen Daseins* [Basic Forms and Cognition of Human Existence], published in 1942 but not yet translated. His various case studies, including his well-known case of anorexia nervosa, in Ellen **West** (in May et al., 1958), describe how he worked with his patients.

Binswanger trained under Jung and Bleuler, then met Freud. They remained friends to the end, despite Binswanger's dislike of Freud's biological determinism and reductionism. From 1910–56, Binswanger was Director of the Bellevue Sanatorium in Kreuzlingen (as had been his father and grandfather).

Binswanger moved from a psychiatric orientation to one of existential analysis (*Existenzanalyse*). He focused on exploring and understanding his patients' world relatedness and their world-design. From Heidegger's concept of **being-in-the-world**, he elaborated the idea of three modes of being-in-the-world, of three worlds, Umwelt, Mitwelt, Eigenwelt (see **four worlds**), the three together constituting the person's meaning-world. Later still he developed the idea of four modes of world relations, for in common with Buber he saw relationship as profound, and containing great potential for change:

1 *Anonymous.* This resembles I–It relating (see **I–Thou/I–You**). This is the world in which absolutes and material facts dictate.
2 *Plural.* These are formal relationships, in which we dominate or are dominated.
3 *Singular.* Our relationships to ourselves, positive or negative.
4 *Dual.* This is the world of **love** and friendship, of I–Thou relating.

Binswanger made great use of Husserlian **phenomenology**. Similarly, he employed Heidegger's philosophy, although he took Heidegger's description of the conditions of human existence (the **ontological**) for an account of everyday life (the **ontic**), and in consequence he mistakenly judged it lacking. Binswanger also criticised Heidegger's lack of any account of love, and his failure to consider that an authentic, loving relationship might lead to self-realisation.

body
Existential philosophers are divided on the exact nature of the body and its relationship to mind, but they almost invariably – although **Kierkegaard** is a notable exception – regard the body as more than a vehicle for the mind. For the majority of existential theorists, human being is an active participation in the **world**. And many are opposed to the notion that the body is an article somehow owned by the mind. **Nietzsche**, for instance, is eager to overthrow the idea of a soul independent of the body, an idea **Descartes** had argued. For Nietzsche, the body is all there is:

[The] enlightened man says: I am body entirely, and nothing beside; and soul is only a word for something in the body. The body is a great intelligence, a multiplicity with one sense … There is more reason in your body than in your best wisdom. And who knows for what purpose your body requires precisely your best wisdom? (Nietzsche, 1883: 61–2)

Similarly, **Marcel** states that one *is* one's body. And **Merleau-Ponty** argues that perception is not merely the mind at work, but is possible only through the body, a body that is not a passive receptor of sensory data, but is attuned to the **world**. Moreover, there is unity in the senses and an awareness of that unity. Merleau-Ponty explains that whilst we are able to consider our bodies objectively, that is no more than an attitude we choose to take, and that while there is an objective body, before that we have a *lived body*, that we are, as human beings, an embodied point of view. Furthermore, we are a part of the world: we embody the world.

Our own body is in the world as the heart is in the organism … When I walk round my flat, the various aspects in which it presents itself to me could not possibly appear as views of one and the same thing if I did not know that each of them represents the flat seen from one spot or another. (Merleau-Ponty, 1945: 203)

In other words, one possesses a unified point of view through one's body.

Heidegger is often thought to have given scant consideration to the body, yet it had an importance in his philosophy. He insists that the body is not a corporeal thing, and then he asks whether the body as a phenomenon is the same as the objective body that can be measured:

I am 'here' at all times … [T]he body always participates in the being-here, but how? … The corporeal thing stops with the skin. [T]he difference between the limits of the corporeal thing and the body, then, consists in the fact that the *bodily limit* is extended beyond the *corporeal limit*. (Heidegger, 1987: 85–6)

Like Merleau-Ponty, Heidegger asserts that human beings are essentially integrated into the world through their **thrownness**, and that in this way our bodies can be said to extend into the world.

Sartre considers the philosophical and psychological aspects of having a body, that is, that it may become an object for another, and that one may come to see one's body in the way the other perceives it (see **look, the**). Like Merleau-Ponty, Sartre sees the body as a central point from which the world makes sense, and he argues that the body is an embodied **consciousness**. He also argues that we possess a **pre-reflective consciousness** of our bodies, and that they cannot therefore be exterior to ourselves.

See also **being-in-the-world**; **bodying forth**; **mind–body problem**; **sexuality**; **space**

body-subject
See **Merleau-Ponty**; **subject and object**

bodying forth
An aspect of **being-in-the-world**, the participation in the **world** through the **body**, including the use of the senses, and of language, and thinking.

'A bodying-forth always co-participates in the experience of what is present' (Heidegger, 1987: 200). Bodying forth is thus the way in which we are part of the **world** in a bodily way that is meaningful, making our movements into gestures that carry significance. **Boss** takes up this idea from Heidegger and applies it to psychotherapy (see Boss, 1979).

Bonhoeffer
See **theology**

boredom
Boredom usually indicates a lack of interest and thus demonstrates a lack of **engagement** with the **world. Kierkegaard, Heidegger** and **Sartre** have all famously written on boredom. Heidegger's contribution is significant and much of *The Fundamental Concepts of Metaphysics* (1983) is devoted to the subject. He poses the question whether boredom may be the starting point of **indifference** from which we develop authentic and inauthentic modes of relating to the world:

> Do things ultimately stand in such a way with us that a profound boredom draws back and forth like a silent fog in the abysses of Dasein? (Heidegger, 1983: 77)

Heidegger likens boredom to that essential **attunement**, or **disposition** with which we come to the world. He goes on to distinguish several forms of boredom.

For Heidegger, profound boredom discloses a mode of the world, its commonplace nature. But in boredom we miss something important, for we lose sight of past, present and future, and we **care** for nothing. As a mode of disclosure, then, it reveals some truth, but hides other aspects of the truth.

Sartre similarly describes states of boredom, which he often likens to **nausea**, the fundamental awareness of our basic **nothingness**.

For Kierkegaard, boredom is a mood associated with the aesthetic stage of self-actualisation: when we are deeply bored, we are likely to see the meaningless of our everyday pleasures and to question our **values**.

See also **authenticity and inauthenticity;** *Dasein*; **time and temporality**

Boss
Medard Boss (1903–90). Swiss psychiatrist and psychotherapist. He had personal analysis from Sigmund **Freud,** and at first his practice and thinking was psychoanalytic. He studied under various of Freud's disciples as well as with Karen Horney and Kurt Goldstein (both influences on Carl **Rogers**), then collaborated for some years with Carl **Jung**. He then came under the influence of **Binswanger,** but when he wrote a critique of Freud, Jung and Binswanger, it led to a rift between the two.

Boss became increasingly interested in the philosophy of Martin **Heidegger,** developing a lengthy collaboration with the philosopher. In fact Heidegger encouraged Boss's application of his ideas to therapeutic practice and gave seminars to Boss's students for many years in what became known as the **Zollikon**

Seminars. When Boss developed his own form of existential therapy he termed it *Daseinsanalysis* to show its derivation from Heidegger's concern with *Dasein*. He wrote an account of his approach to therapy in *Psychoanalysis and Daseins-analysis* (1957), in the same year publishing *The Analysis of Dreams*. In 1979 *Existential Foundations of Medicine and Psychology* caused consternation with its criticism of the two professions. Boss emphasises Heideggerian concepts like **attunement**, world openness and embodiment. His approach to dreaming consists of seeing the dream as an expression of the dreamer's world-relatedness.

Notwithstanding the gap that Boss had created between his existential therapy and **psychoanalysis**, he saw himself as working with Freud's legacy. For whilst he believed that Freud's therapy lacked a sound theoretical foundation, he was content with Freud's practice of therapy, believing it broadly in accord with existential thinking. Because of this Boss advocated the use of a couch and of free association. With Heidegger's encouragement Boss founded the International Federation of Daseinsanalysis.

both/and
See **either/or**

boundary situations
See **Jaspers**

bracketing
See **phenomenological method**

Brentano
Franz Brentano (1838–1917). German psychologist, philosopher and theologian, whose magnum opus is *Psychology from an Empirical Standpoint* (1874). His principal influences were **Aristotle**, Thomas Aquinas and Francisco Suárez. The influence of his approach is widespread, but especially upon **Husserl** and **Heidegger**, as well as on **Gestalt psychology**.

From his medieval studies, and because he rejected the idea of the mind as a passive receiver of impressions, Brentano reintroduced the notion of *directedness* or **intentionality** as an essential aspect of mental activity. Dissatisfied with the scientific weakness of **psychology**, he argued that the correct approach to investigating the mind is observation not experimentation, for the inescapable problem with self-reflection or introspection is that one cannot observe and participate in one's own mental processes, cannot simultaneously be **subject and object**. And one can only describe mental operations as they occur. He also argued that one cannot know another mind, and that physical causation cannot explain mental phenomena. However, although the fruits of phenomenological investigation are limited, he believed that from particular results general truths can be established, a belief that depends on the subject being representative of all human minds. Of mental activity, Brentano suggested that *presentations* – ideas, perceptions, fantasies, remembering, etc. – are accompanied by judgements and feelings. And like **Descartes**,

Brentano held there are no unconscious mental acts, his argument being that as we perceive, so we have an awareness – albeit perhaps not explicit – of that act of perceiving. As Husserl showed, it is the latter that can be captured through phenomenological investigation.

Buber

Martin Buber was born in Vienna on 8 February 1878 and died in Jerusalem on 6 June 1965.

Notable works: *I And Thou* (1923) and *Between Man and Man* (1929).

Influenced by Jewish mysticism and Hasidic Judaism.

Influence on: Jewish and Christian theology, and throughout existential and humanistic psychotherapy and counselling.

Life and ideas: When he was three, his mother left his father, and Martin was sent to live with his grandparents. His grandfather was a successful business-man and a noted rabbinical scholar. Martin studied **philosophy**, philology and history of art at the Universities of Vienna, Leipzig, Berlin and Zurich, and in 1904 was granted a Doctorate by Vienna. In 1899 he married Paula Winkler (who under the pen name Georg Munk, became a respected novelist), and they had two children. He became Professor of Philosophy of Jewish Religion and Ethics at Frankfurt University in 1924, until Nazi influence saw him first removed from office, and then from lecturing in any way. A prominent Zionist from the 1890s, and an advocate for a binational state for Arabs and Jews, he emigrated to Palestine in 1938. He was appointed Professor of Sociology of Religion at the Hebrew University and was the first President of the Israeli Academy of Science and Humanities. From 1916–22 he worked on his mag-num opus, *Ich und Du* (*I And Thou*, or *I And You*), and for years afterwards elab-orated on its thesis that for human beings there is a holistic and fulfilling way of relating to other people and other spiritual entities – I–**Thou** or I–**You** relat-ing, and that we lose its benefits with our everyday manner of relating, our tendency to speedily objectify phenomena and thus to distance ourselves.

For Buber, dialogue between beings is not mere words: 'The eyes of an animal have the capacity of a great language' (Buber, 1923/57: 144). Dialogue for Buber is an utter openness to the other. A young man once sought Buber's advice, and Buber responded, but in a distracted and unengaged manner. Mulling over the interview, the young man decided to go to war and was killed. Learning of his death, Buber accepted some responsibility for this outcome, that he had related in I–It fashion, and had not given all he could when it was asked.

In later years Buber became interested in psychotherapy. He warned thera-pists to realise that psychotherapeutic theory is limited, and argued that it is the spirit of the encounter which is fundamental to lasting and significant thera-peutic success. 'All actual life is encounter', he wrote (ibid.: 62). His firm belief was that profound relating changes and heals.

See also **encounter; interhuman; relationship; Rogers; Tillich**

Buber–Rogers dialogue

In 1957 Carl **Rogers** had a public discussion with Martin **Buber** at a confer-ence on Buber's work at the University of Michigan. Each with strong beliefs on human relations – the one mystical, the other psychological – their language differed radically. As a consequence, they were read by earlier commentators as being in substantial disagreement – an understandable reading since Buber himself frequently misheard or misinterpreted Rogers. For instance, when Rogers said: 'I have wondered whether your concept – or your experience – of what you have termed the I–Thou relationship is ... similar to what I see as the effective moments in a therapeutic relationship' (Anderson and Cissna, 1997: 29), Buber responds as if Rogers has claimed that therapy is entirely I–Thou relating. Buber then devoted much of the discussion to emphasising the difference between patient and therapist – a difference Rogers had already and explicitly acknowledged – that the patient cannot see the therapist as clearly as the therapist sees the patient. Flawed transcripts of the meeting were for many years all that was available, and these encouraged a view of their divergence. In fact, both agreed how important it is for the therapist to give permission to the client to *be*, and that there is a **being-with** that is profoundly healing. When Rogers says '[I]n those moments when real change occurred ... it would be because there *had* been a real meeting of persons in which ... it was experienced the same from both sides', Buber responds with 'Yes. This is, this is really important' (ibid.: 53).

The meeting influenced both men, each absorbing some of the other's views. Buber soon afterwards wrote an Afterword to *I and Thou*, in which he spoke of the 'person-to-person relationship' of psychotherapy (see **I–Thou**). And Rogers later wrote:

[The] recognition of the significance of what Buber terms the I–Thou relationship is the reason why, in client-centered therapy, there has come to be a greater use of the self of the therapist, of the therapist's feelings, a greater stress on genuinenes. (Rogers, 1974: 11)

Too often, the connection between existential thought and psychotherapeutic practice is difficult to see; but in this important meeting there is a rare opportunity to examine an encounter between an existential philosopher and a psychotherapist.

See also **client-centred psychotherapy**; **existential psychotherapy**; **I–Thou**; **Zollikon Seminars**

Bugental

James Bugental (b. 1915). American existential-phenomenological psychologist with a humanistic background. Notable writings include *The Search for Authenticity* (1965) and *Psychotherapy and Process* (1978).

Bugental sees psychotherapy as a philosophical enterprise, an examination of one's life and the **world**, the search for a realistic attitude to living, and the encouragement of **responsibility**, courage, self-awareness, creativity and encounter with others. He warns against social adjustment where it requires the normalisation of what he sees as negative **values**, such as materialism and competitiveness and separation from others. The quality he prizes most is **authenticity**, by which he means being fully aware in the moment, accepting responsibility and **choice**, and accepting the possibility of **tragedy**, that is, awareness of the contingency of the world, of Fate, that events beyond one's own powers can affect one's life. The greatest of these, of course, is **death**. It is partly from this that existential **anxiety** develops, though it is also informed by condemnation and **guilt** (the knowledge that what we do matters, but that we do not do all we could), as well as **meaninglessness** and isolation. Like **Tillich**, he writes of neurotic anxiety, an anxiety towards mundane matters that is actually an avoidance of facing existential anxiety and a hindrance to developing greater authenticity.

Bultmann
See **theology**

calculative thinking
See **thinking**

call of conscience
(*Gewissenruf*). A Heideggerian term to indicate *Dasein's* summons to its own **guilt**. **Heidegger** frequently complains that individuals lose themselves in **idle talk, curiosity, ambiguity** and the **They**. He claims that for the most part we have not discovered our selves, but instead take up the views and attitudes of the mass. These are inauthentic ways of being as opposed to the authentic owned way of being of which *Dasein* is capable.

For Heidegger, conscience is not moral; it does not speak of deeds good and bad; it is not the result of the approval and disapproval of others. Nor is it biological in origin, but it is an aspect of the fundamental characteristics of being human:

> Conscience gives us 'something' to understand, it *discloses* ... A more penetrating analysis of conscience reveals it as a *call*. (Heidegger, 1927b: 269)

The call (or *voice*) of conscience is a call to oneself. It is a summoning of *Dasein* to become aware of its own possibilities. It has no words and asks nothing specific. But the call of conscience calls *Dasein* back to its ownmost potentiality for being itself.

See also **authenticity; falling; potentiality-for-being-oneself**

camel, the
See **Zarathustra**

Camus
Albert Camus (1913–1960). French novelist, dramatist, journalist, essayist and philosopher. His novels include *The Outsider* (1942b, sometimes translated as *The Stranger*), *The Plague* (1947) and *The Fall* (1956). His plays include *Caligula* (1944), and his essays include *The Myth of Sisyphus* (1942a), *The Rebel* (1951) and *Reflections on the Guillotine* (1960).

He was born in Algeria of poor and illiterate parents, and his father died in the First World War soon after Albert was born. He co-founded an underground newspaper during the Second World War and was friends with **Sartre** until the latter, in *Les Temps Modernes*, published a hostile review of *The Rebel*, accusing Camus of a naïve embracing of the bourgeois **values** of justice and **love** of fellow man. In 1957 Camus was awarded the Nobel Prize for Literature. Three years later, returning home to Paris, he died in a car crash.

Camus rejected the term *existentialism*, and perhaps his work is better described by reference to his notion of the **absurd**, the human demand for order, justice and **meaning** in a meaningless universe indifferent to such demands. The concerns of Camus's philosophy are **alienation** and engagement; responsibility and dignity, **guilt** and innocence in the face of **tragedy**. Camus wrote that there is only one really serious philosophical question, that of suicide and whether life is worth the trouble. His own answer was emphatic, that suicide is self-defeat, surrender to the absurd.

In *The Outsider*, a man indifferent to the death of his mother is brought to trial for the haphazard killing of a stranger. He himself is a stranger in his own world, a passive observer, a man who lets things happen, who has no love of life or man. But in prison, awaiting execution, he at last overcomes his terrible **nihilism**.

Camus's book about Sisyphus develops these themes further. In Greek mythology, Sisyphus had angered the gods and was sent to Hades. There, in hell, he was made to push a boulder up a hill, and to roll it off the farther slope; though the great weight of the stone meant that each time he neared the summit it escaped his hold and rolled back down to the foot of the hill. In this endless futility, and his awareness of its futility, Sisyphus is the absurd hero *par excellence*:

> If this myth is tragic, that is because its hero is conscious. Where would his torture be, indeed, if at every step the hope of succeeding upheld him? ... Sisyphus, proletarian of the gods, powerless and rebellious, knows the whole extent of his wretched condition; it is what he thinks of during his descent. The lucidity that was to constitute his torture at the same time crowns his victory. There is no fate that can not be surmounted by scorn. (Camus, 1942: 109)

Camus imagines that the struggle itself is enough to fill a man's heart, that for such as Sisyphus, the universe would have no master, and be neither sterile nor futile. He imagines that Sisyphus is happy.

care

(*Sorge*, literally: worry). A central idea in the philosophy of **Heidegger**. Human beings always care, because they are nothing unless they reach out towards a world that matters to them. *Da-sein*'s solicitude – care for others (*Fürsorge*) and *concern* for things (*Besorgen*), is an essential aspect of *Da-sein*: 'being-in-the-world is essentially care' (Heidegger, 1927b: 193), and: '*Angst* provides the phenomenal basis for explicitly grasping the primordial totality of being of Da-sein. Its being reveals itself as *care*' (ibid.: 182). This is an aspect of *Da-sein* even when *Da-sein* appears neglectful, for *Da-sein* cannot escape care:

> The *deficient* modes of omitting, neglecting, renouncing, resting, are also ways of taking care of something, in which the possibilities of taking care are kept to a 'bare minimum.' ... Furthermore, we use the expression also in a characteristic turn of phrase: I will see to it or take care that the enterprise fails. Here, 'to take care' amounts to apprehensiveness. (Ibid.: 57)

Heidegger relates an old fable:

> Once when 'care' was crossing a river, she saw some clay; she thoughtfully took a piece and began to shape it. While she was thinking about what she had made, Jupiter came by. 'Care' asked him to give it spirit, and this he gladly granted. But when she wanted her name to be bestowed upon it, Jupiter forbade this and demanded that it be given his name instead. While 'Care' and Jupiter were arguing, Earth (Tellus) arose, and desired that her name be conferred upon the creature, since she had offered it part of her body. They asked Saturn to be the judge. And Saturn gave them the following decision, which seemed to be just: 'Since you, Jupiter, have given its spirit, you should receive that spirit at death; and since you, Earth, have given its body, you shall receive its body. But since "Care" first shaped this creature, she shall possess it as long as it lives. And because there is a dispute among you as to its name, let it be called "homo", for it is made out of humus (earth).' (Ibid.: 198)

See also **relationship**; **sight**

Cartesian dualism
See **Descartes**

causality
The extent to which one event necessarily or contingently determines another. In everyday thinking it seems evident that when one billiard ball strikes another and the second rolls away, that it must be that the first has caused the second to move. Not all thinkers have thought it so evident. David Hume, for instance, speaks instead of the *constant conjunction* of events, thus preferring a looser idea of causality, that is, that although one event is always followed by another, it does not mean the first determined the second. And indeed, modern thinking allows for the possibility that the cause of an event could follow the effect, and further still, for the possibility of randomness. But with human agency the issue is still more difficult, for in what way is a thought, a word, a perception or an experience like a billiard ball? Yet people often cite these as if they were causes. Fred will say that he jumped into the lake because his friend John was drowning, and Susan explains that she left her husband because he was unsympathetic. Listeners to these accounts will usually nod their heads understandingly and pose no question. Existential authors would argue however that each was a free **choice** merely informed – however passionately – by Fred's and Susan's **values**, by their reasons.

Although seldom discussed, it is important that a psychological therapist knows what his or her own beliefs are on this matter, for it affects the way in which clients' words are understood, and how the effects of psychotherapy are explained. Therapists who hold a deterministic theory of causality, such as found in behavioural psychology or psychoanalytic theory, will understand client stories as explicable through causal events. But in **existential psychotherapy**, the client's life will be seen as one of choices amongst contingent facts, and of **freedom** versus restriction. Therapy then is a **dialogue** from which the client or patient chooses to effect **change**. The therapist is no more than a catalyst in such a process.

See also **determinism; facticity; mind–body problem**

certainty
See **doubt; Kierkegaard; nausea; Nietzsche; not knowing; Ricoeur**

change
People who come to psychotherapy or psychotherapeutic counselling are invariably looking for improvement in their lives. Sometimes, of course, they would prefer other people to alter, but have reluctantly accepted that they themselves need to change. However, it is debatable what is meant by change. Is it the loss or gain of distressing symptoms? Is it a change in personality or is it a change in outlook? And does the therapist force these changes? Or must the client find the answers, even though at the commencement of therapy she has no idea what to do? And can the prospective patient expect wholesale change or even a cure? Or is a small gain the most that can be hoped for?

Kierkegaard believed that people do not fundamentally change. From his perspective, personality change is improbable, even though a person can significantly change their perspective on how to live their life. But **Heidegger** would argue that human existence is a continuous process of change and transformation over time. And a Sartrean perspective might be that as we are constituted by our actions, and since our past is substantially irrelevant, so we should henceforth take **responsibility** to re-invent ourselves.

So for a therapist who adopts the ideas of **Sartre**, a positive therapeutic outcome might be an adjustment by the client to her basic **project**, and it might be to realise that however pessimistic or preoccupied she might become with her sorrows and fears, so she has **freedom** and **choice** to shape herself.

For many practitioners of **existential psychotherapy**, the aim of therapy is a gain in **authenticity** or **congruence**, in other words to become more true to oneself and to the realities of the human condition. For others it is to take a **leap of faith**.

Buber writes of the therapeutically transforming quality of the I–Thou relationship, a transformation that may change how the person relates to herself and others.

See also **repetition**

chatter
See **idle talk**

chiasm
See **ambiguity**

child, the
See **Zarathustra**

choice
There are two preliminary features of this subject useful to remark upon. First, philosophers generally distinguish between *decision* and *choice*. A decision is

made after some deliberation, but a choice need not be; it might be made from habit (for example, offered a choice of political candidates, I might abstain from voting, merely because that is what I always do). When existentialists speak of choice, they may seem to imply what is here meant by decision, but it is rather that they reject the notion of choice without intention. Second, there is a psychological question about choice, whether choices are rational or emotional, the result of our fears or desires. This last question is usually resolved by existential authors with an insistence that the passions are as intentional as cool deliberation.

The existential approach is known above all for its emphasis on personal autonomy, insisting that we possess some **freedom** to make choices which shape our lives. It also emphasises how taking **responsibility**, facing up to situations and perhaps making changes, can be daunting. So existential theories explain why sometimes we prefer to cling on to the beliefs, assumptions and behaviour that are often the cause of our unhappiness rather than face the **anxiety** which change can bring, one aspect of which is the awareness we all possess that any given choice is a commitment to one alternative at the exclusion of all others. **Kierkegaard** emphasises this, and makes the point that we cannot be sure that any given choice is the best one. And he argues that choices may not be made from simple self-interest, but may be calculated from ethical or religious principles. More difficult still, important choices cannot always be made from solid and reliable facts, but often require a **leap of faith**.

Sartre places choice at the very centre of his philosophy. Because human beings have no predetermined **essence**, we need to constantly choose our lives, and it is our choices that define us, and our choices that constitute our ever-changing identity. Indeed, the only choice we cannot make is not to choose. He introduces the idea of **project** to explain how our choices are often explicable by reference to an earlier choice, an underlying and still contemporary commitment (perhaps I abstain from voting because my father was a politician, and I want to oppose his democratic **values**). This emphasises our ultimate responsibility. And Sartre answers the question of **passion** versus reason by saying, 'emotion is not a physiological tempest, it is a reply adapted to the situation' (Sartre, 1943a: 445). However, Sartre warns that we frequently avoid the discomfort of freedom, and resort to **bad faith** so as to avoid choice.

Existential theorists remind us that even when we try to avoid choice, we make choices through action or by default, voting with our feet. Our choices affect not only the events that we imagine constitute our lives, but also our *selves*. Yet different theorists sometimes see choice and freedom in different ways. **Camus**, for instance, holds that the foremost philosophical choice for anyone is whether to live or die. Whereas for Sartre, suicide is an act of bad faith.

The existential therapist's client is likely to become aware of their own ways of choosing, and to realise that not choosing is impossible, that avoidance is itself a choice. A problem-solving or solution-focused therapy will consider decision-making and action as the crux of therapy. An existential psychotherapy will typically begin with or somehow include a consideration of choices made or evaded, noticed or kept from direct awareness, and whether any apparent choices made were possible or impossible (that is, were futile efforts to overcome any of the givens of existence).

See also **authenticity; crowd, the; either/or; engage; repetition; thrownness**

cipher

Derived from an idea by Pascal, **Jaspers** describes how we are alerted to the **comprehensive** by ciphers, that is signs or symbols, which represent the **truth** of all that is. To discover their meaning, these ciphers must be *interrogated*, a dialectical process of mutual question and answer.

Examples of possible ciphers include overwhelming aspects of nature, ideas in philosophy or religion, aspects in a work of art, and reflection on **Being**. Jaspers claims that the main purpose of **metaphysics** is to disclose these ciphers.

circumspection

See **sight**

clearing

(*Lichtung*). Literally lightening, this term it has come to mean a clearing in a forest, the place where light can shine. **Heidegger** uses the term to suggest a space where things can come to light and he shows it to be the particular privilege of human beings. It is up to human beings to create a **space** in which things can be revealed. *Dasein* is that which is capable of bringing things to light, it is the place where **truth** can be revealed or uncovered.

The task of human beings, then, is to uncover what has been concealed and to create a clearing:

> Concealment is not the antithesis of consciousness but rather concealment belongs to the clearing ... Clearing is never mere clearing, but is always the clearing of concealment. (Heidegger, 1987: 228–9)

This notion was applied to psychotherapy by Medard **Boss**, who described therapeutic space as one where things were allowed to come to light and be revealed.

See also **being-in-the-world; concealment; disclosure; sight**

client-centred psychotherapy

Also referred to as Rogerian, person-centred, or non-directive psychotherapy. Some Rogerians refer to classic client-centred therapy to distinguish their stricter practice from the great number of integrative or eclectic practitioners who use only elements of Rogers's theory.

Client-centred therapy originated in 1940 with a paper by Carl **Rogers**, 'Newer Concepts in Psychotherapy'. By 1951, Rogers had in place a formal theory of personality, comprising nineteen propositions, the fourth of which is the *actualising tendency*, a development of Kurt Goldstein's theory of self-actualisation. Rogers makes this into a natural science theory. It is not a normative theory, although it has moral implications, for it suggests what might be beneficial, and Rogers supposed that healthy maturation leads to socialisation. Briefly, the hypothesis (evolved over the years) states that organisms and ecological systems strive to maintain and develop their potential, and that an unhelpful environment will thwart such development. Sometimes misconstrued as a claim of humankind's essential goodness, it acknowledges that human beings have both constructive and destructive potential. In later years, Rogers referred to it as the *formative tendency*, emphasising its being a process, one that evolves towards greater complexity. (And in this way, it may be compared with chaos theory.)

The fourteenth of Rogers's propositions refers to *psychological pathology*, stating that when a person denies to awareness significant sensory and visceral experiences, there will be psychological maladjustment. By this is meant a kind of self-censorship deriving from introjected disapproval: a person (and formatively, a child) who is struggling to win love will suppress what seems disapproved of in him or her self.

In the 1950s Rogers described his six conditions of the therapeutic process:

1 That two persons are in psychological contact.
2 The client is incongruent, being vulnerable or anxious.
3 The therapist is congruent in the relationship.
4 The therapist experiences unconditional positive regard towards the client.
5 The therapist experiences empathic understanding of the client's internal frame of reference.
6 The client perceives to some degree conditions 4 and 5.

With this came a therapeutic system designed to provide a reparative environment, in which the maladjusted person learns to accept their psychological and visceral experiences – in short, themselves.

Like **psychoanalysis**, this therapeutic system endeavours to bring into conscious awareness what through psychological defensiveness has been kept unconscious – or out of awareness. It does not place direct value on the personal philosophical investigation that characterises **existential psychotherapy**, but insofar as it allies a **phenomenological method** with a belief in the unfixedness of personality, it is existential. For if the ambition of client-centred therapy is to uncover the real person, it does not imply a determined and unchanging person:

> To some it appears that to be what one is, is to remain static ... Nothing could be further from the truth. To be what one is, is to enter fully into being a process. (Rogers, 1961a: 176)

Rogers does not believe that an unchanging way of being is right or natural:

> It seems to me the good life is not any fixed state. It is not, in my estimation, a state of virtue, or contentment, or nirvana, or happiness. It is not a condition in which the individual is adjusted, or fulfilled, or actualized. To use psychological jargon, it is not a state of drive-reduction, or tension-reduction, or homeostasis. (Ibid.: 185–6)

What Rogers demonstrates here is that **existence precedes essence**:

> One way of expressing the fluidity which is present in such existential living is to say that the self and personality emerge from experience, rather than experience being

translated or twisted to fit preconceived self-structure ... It means instead a maximum of adaptability, a discovery of structure in experience, a flowing, changing organization of self and personality. (Ibid.: 188–9)

Lastly, both client-centred and existential therapy share a commitment to **being-with** the client rather than solving their problems.

See also **Buber–Rogers dialogue; congruence; encounter**

Climacus, Johannes
Pseudonym used by **Kierkegaard** for *Philosophical Fragments* (1844a) and *Concluding Unscientific Postscript to the Philosophical Fragments* (1846a).

close off
According to **Heidegger**, one can open oneself up to the primordial fact of **being-with**, or one can close it off (*Verschliessen*). These are aspects of **authenticity and inauthenticity**. And closing off what is actually out in the open results in one not being authentically aware of the **world**, oneself or others. There are other ways in which it is possible to close off, including in one's stance towards the present, the **forgetting** of **existence**, one's **thrownness**, and of one's ownmost potentiality of being. Heidegger claims it is **alienation** from authentic modes of being that produces this closing off:

This alienation closes off from Dasein its authenticity and possibility, even if only the possibility of genuinely foundering. (Heidegger, 1927a: 178)

See also **awaiting; cover up;** *Dasein***; entanglement; potentiality-for-being-oneself; time and temporality**

coefficient of adversity
In **Sartre's** analysis of the human **situation**, the coefficient of adversity is constituted by the limitations of one's plight versus one's aspirations:

I am not 'free' either to escape the lot of my class, of my nation, of my family ... I am born a worker, a Frenchman, an hereditary syphilitic, or a tubercular. The history of a life, whatever it may be, is a history of a failure. The coefficient of adversity of things is such that years of patience are necessary to obtain the feeblest result. (Sartre, 1943a: 481–2)

The analysis of how one's plight is of advantage in achieving one's aspirations is the *coefficient of utility*.

See also **freedom**

cogito
See **Descartes; pre-reflexive consciousness**

collective unconscious
See **Jung**

commitment
See choice; leap of faith; love; Ortega; passion; truth; Unamuno

common understanding
Heidegger distinguishes at length between his own ontological understanding (*Verstand*) and the *vulgär*, or common understanding (he also refers to *Verständigkeit*, or common sense). He argues that all too often the common conception of things is a misunderstanding of things. Giving conscience as an example, he demonstrates the difference between the popular conception of conscience as a moral response to a specific situation, and the profundity of the call of conscience, in which a powerful but non-specific call is felt by an individual to more fully become him or herself. The common understanding, the beliefs of the They, can be insidious, undermining the full truth of the nature of Being. This is similar to Husserl's notion of the *natural attitude*, an attitude which must be suspended by the *epoché* (see not knowing and phenomenological method), in order that our assumptions can be set aside and the world viewed as it really is.

communication
See Jaspers

competition
See generosity; intersubjectivity; seriality

comprehensive, the
Also translated (from *das Umgreifende*) as *the encompassing*. Jaspers uses this term to mean that which goes beyond the limits of being as we experience it. It can be taken in its limited form of consciousness or *Da-sein*, or it can be taken in its wider form as that which is the source of truth. We human beings understand that our freedom is a gift from something beyond us: this is *the encompassing*, something which is all that is beyond ourselves, but includes ourselves, a transcendent something that is all of being, including all its constituent entities. It can be understood to be there, but can only be gestured towards; it cannot be fully known or described, and so our own selves cannot be fully known. Thus it is an act of faith to believe in it, an act of philosophical faith (*philosophische Glaube*) to hold that human beings need and are open to transcendence. Jaspers believes that we all have a fundamental striving to reach the comprehensive. And so for Jaspers, who rejects conventional organised religion, but not religious faith, the comprehensive can be referred to as God.

concealment
(*Verborgenheit*). Literally, this means to protect something by hiding it away. Hiddenness is opposed by Heidegger to unhiddenness, or truth (*Unverborgenheit*, or *aletheia*). All unhiddenness depends on human beings. It is only *Dasein* that can unconceal, or unhide the truth or equally conceal or hide it. The

world starts out as being concealed and hidden and *Dasein* has to uncover truth.

> Truth (uncoveredness) is something that must always first be wrested from entities. Entities get snatched out of their hiddenness. (Heidegger, 1927a: 222)

The term is also used by Heidegger in his account of **phenomenology**:

> [W]hat remains *concealed* ... or what falls back and is *covered up* again, or shows itself only in a *distorted* way, is ... the *being* of beings ... Essentially, nothing else stands 'behind' the phenomena of phenomenology. Nevertheless, what is to become a phenomenon can be concealed. (Heidegger, 1927b: 35–6)

See also **disclosure and disclosedness**

concern
See **care**

congruence
A term from **client-centred psychotherapy**, and central to its practice, which may or may not be practised by existential therapists. Despite the fact that a few client-centred or humanistic authors use the term *authentic* as a synonym for congruence, it is not the same as **authenticity**. Its opposite, *incongruence*, concerns what for client-centred therapists is the main form of psychological defence, that is, denial. Congruence is, variously, a person's awareness of his or her experience without attempt to distort or minimise it; accuracy of perception – judged by how well it corresponds with external reality; a close match between a person's *ideal self* (the self they believe is or would be approved of by others) and how they perceive themselves to be.

In this way, a connection between the notion of congruence and authenticity is clear: each is concerned with **truth**; but whereas congruence is concerned with psychological honesty, authenticity is about acceptance of the degree of one's responsibility and power as well as of one's inevitable existential limitations.

In client-centred psychotherapy, congruence and incongruence are used to describe the client or the therapist's mental processes, not their behaviour, and therapeutic practice does not require the congruent therapist to communicate his or her thoughts or feelings without reason:

> [T]he aim is not for the therapist to express or talk out his own feelings, but primarily that he should not be deceiving the client as to himself. (Rogers, 1957: 224)

The therapist expresses his inner experiences when necessary, to promote a truthful **encounter** with the client. For **Rogers**, communicated congruence encourages congruent responses in the client, and congruency being psychological wellness, is psychotherapeutic.

See also **alienation; immediacy; interhuman, the**

conscience
See **call of conscience**

consciousness and unconsciousness
What consciousness is and how it arises remain amongst the most puzzling and difficult of questions for philosophers, psychologists and cognitive scientists, each of whom tends to see it as their domain. The answers to these questions impinge on issues in philosophy of mind, psychotherapy, **metaphysics**, religion and science, and so are of great importance.

For those physicalists who believe that immaterial phenomena are reducible to material phenomena without loss of explanatory power, these are pseudo-problems. For others, consciousness just cannot be explained by science, because it is transcendental and mysterious.

Consciousness is sometimes considered an emergent property, arising from brain activity, where mind supervenes upon the possession of a neural system. But if this is so, and if it is not reductionistic, it still does not explain what consciousness *is*.

It is often assumed that by *consciousness* is meant a single phenomenon, but different theories describe consciousness in different terms, including cognitive consciousness, intentional consciousness, self consciousness, and phenomenal consciousness. It is therefore clear from an existential perspective that consciousness is a complex and diverse phenomenon.

Definitions of consciousness tend to be circular, employing unilluminating synonyms like *awareness* or *experience*. Nonetheless, sensation, perception, emotion and thought seem to be directly connected with the experience of consciousness. Some scientists and philosophers write of consciousness as no more than neural activity, but this reduces a subjective experience to an objective biological process and loses the original phenomenon. Not all neural activity is consciousness. A computer can process information, but there is no evidence to suppose it possesses consciousness. So not all of what we consider in ourselves to be thought is itself evidence of consciousness or constitutes consciousness.

If consciousness is not completely amenable to objective investigation, then the techniques of **phenomenology** are invaluable as a scientific means of studying its subjectivity. This is contentious, as many theorists maintain that not all mental phenomena are available to consciousness. It is commonly accepted that not all mental processes are conscious, but for the psychoanalyst or anyone who holds a theory of a distinct unconscious (an idea systematised by **Freud** but anticipated by amongst others, Leibniz and **Nietzsche**), there must be a part of the mind not directly susceptible to everyday examination, for its contents can only be inferred from the conscious outpourings of symbolised ideas, these symbols deriving from censored instincts. In contrast, the phenomenologist holds that the mind is in principle entirely open to analysis.

For **Sartre**, consciousness is not a passive receiver, but arises from engagement with life (see **project**). It is intentional, out in the world. Sartre argues that the notion of the unconscious is superfluous and illogical. How can the unconscious respond to the conscious if it is unconscious? The censoring agency (the superego) must at some level be aware of what it is repressing. Instead, Sartre describes different levels of **intentionality**, where the person's focus of intention lies; and he makes the distinction between reflective and non-reflective consciousness. His concept of **bad faith** shows that self-deception allows consciousness to be more or less sharp and more or less self-reflective according to circumstances and personal **choice**.

Many others have disputed Freud's theory of the unconscious and its concomitant need for symbolic interpretation of what is hidden in the unconscious. For instance, the notion of **disclosure** by **Heidegger** does away with the necessity for a biological model of the mind, for it allows that there are degrees of awareness, degrees of illumination, as well as different points of focus. Heidegger's concept of **attunement** indicates the disclosure of mood, a focus of attention to what is mentally happening – rather like the idea of selective attention (how in a hubbub of noise one can attend to a conversation). Heidegger's concepts of **authenticity and inauthenticity** allow him to develop a more complex account of a person's different levels of consciousness. The idea of **incongruence** in client-centred therapy is a related idea.

See also **being-for-itself; body; mind–body problem; pre-reflexive consciousness**

considerateness
See **sight**

constancy and loyalty
Heidegger speaks of constancy (*Beständigkeit* and *Selbständigkeit*) in a variety of contexts to refer to what is constant amidst change. For instance:

> Da-sein is in principle different from everything objectively present and real. Its 'content' is not founded in the substantiality of a substance, but in the '*self-constancy*' of the existing self whose being was conceived as care. (Heidegger, 1927b: 303)

For Heidegger, *Da-sein*, the human being, has no substance, only **existence**. **Being** may be constant, but the **self** is not a fixed thing. Being-for-oneself is created and its constancy rests only in its existence and in a continuous commitment to it.

A similar concept is loyalty (*Treue*). Resoluteness is the loyalty of existence to its self and requires an engagement with **anxiety** and **death**. It is only in resolutely anticipating death whilst recollecting the past that a historical constancy is created that can constitute a sense of self. Such constancy has to set itself continuously against the potential of distraction and requires a steadiness of *Da-sein* which incorporates **fate**. Gabriel **Marcel** had a similar concept of fidelity, which is a loyalty to existence, the other and God.

See also **anticipation; identity; resoluteness**

Constantius, Constantine
Pseudonym used by **Kierkegaard** for *Repetition* (1843c).

contingency
Amongst the many metaphysical questions of humankind is whether we are central to the cosmos. Perhaps the most discouraging of the many possible answers is that we are merely contingent, that there is no necessity to our existence or our character. This is taken by **Sartre** emphatically to be the case and it is examined frankly in his philosophy (as it is explored more indirectly in the work of other existential writers). In Sartre's philosophy, the fact of our contingency brings **freedom**. As free entities (we are **being-for-itself**) we depend upon the solid and dependable things of the **world**, upon **being-in-itself**, that which behaves according to the laws of nature. Our freedom manifests through **consciousness**, which is the capacity of being-for-itself to be aware of its freedom and its infinite possibilities. Apprehension of this may induce **nausea**, such is the steadiness of the world about us and the unsteady, free and contingent nature of ourselves.

See also **facticity; possibility**

contradiction
See **dialectic; paradox**

co-presence
See **Laing**

Cooper, David
David Graham Cooper (1931–86). South African psychiatrist who came to England where at Shenley Hospital he established an experimental psychiatric ward, Villa 21. He then worked with **Laing** in establishing a therapeutic community at Kingsley Hall. An existentialist and a Marxist, Cooper originated the **anti-psychiatry** movement, with which Laing later denied involvement. Cooper's works include *Psychiatry and Anti-Psychiatry* (1967), *The Death of the Family* (1971) and *The Grammar of Living* (1974).

countertransference
In psychoanalytic theory, this is **transference** on the part of the analyst. It is thus a form of therapist bias, and accordingly **Freud** regarded it as something to be overcome. But by the 1950s, psychoanalytic theorists were arguing that it could be positive, that feelings and thoughts aroused in the therapist may be a direct transfer of the psychic state of the patient.

The existential analyst takes a different view. Analysis is of the totality of the client's way of being, as he or she actually *is*, but while this includes the past insofar as it is present, and the future insofar as it is present, the emphasis is on what *is*. Existential therapists assume that in common with other human beings, they will experience strong and often significant feelings towards their clients, an awareness of which is an essential part of the therapeutic enterprise, and requiring the clarification of the dynamics of the therapist–patient relationship. The therapist's bias will sometimes be based on the therapist's own past experiences, sometimes on recent or current events, opinions or prejudice; sometimes they will be a direct response to something the client evokes or reveals. The therapist will consider exploring this personal response with the client in order to uncover what is occurring, for it may disclose something important about the client, the relationship or the bias of the therapist, which needs to be addressed and resolved. Discussions of personal bias will be taken to supervision.

See also **existential psychotherapy; interpretation; psychoanalysis**

covering up
We all live for the most part in an inauthentic way, writes **Heidegger**, for we obey without **thinking** the prescriptions of what we imagine society (the **They**) expects of us. In this way we conceal the **truth** of our **Being** and evade **authenticity**. Examples of what we cover up (*Verdecken*) or conceal for ourselves include **time** and **death**. For instance, we may tell ourselves that death is inevitable for everyone, and so understand it as a fact of the **world**, yet regard it as something out there in the world, not with us. Indeed, if we think of our own death at all, it is lodged in the vague future and not as an ever-present possibility we carry within us from the moment of our birth. Thus we cover up death. Heidegger claims that as long as we continue to cover up and conceal **reality**, we will continue to be in inauthenticity. To become authentic, we have to be prepared to allow the world to disclose itself to us as it is (see **disclosure and disclosedness**) and to uncover things with resolute **anticipation**.

critical theory
See **Frankfurt School, the**

crowd, the
A term used by **Kierkegaard** and sometimes translated as *the public*. Allowing oneself to be taken over by the crowd is to take an easy option and forsake the possibility of becoming an individual. It has a similar meaning to Nietzsche's the **herd** and Heidegger's the **They**. **Nietzsche** is as much an individualist as Kierkegaard and both these authors believe it is important to remove oneself from the influence of the crowd or the herd. **Heidegger** stresses that the **relationship** of the individual with the mass is inevitable and is in fact part of the human tendency to relate to others and to ourselves in an anonymous fashion. Heidegger's term *the They* therefore has a specific and different meaning and applies to the individual's anonymous relationship to themselves.

Kierkegaard is more simply concerned that the individual will be lost in the mass, will forget his own existence:

> The fact that several people united together have the courage to meet death does not nowadays mean that each, individually, has the courage, for even more than death the individual fears the judgement and protest of reflection upon his wishing to risk something on his own. The individual no longer belongs to God, to himself, to his beloved ... (Kierkegaard, 1846b: 261)

curiosity

This word is used in a narrow sense by **Heidegger**, to describe an aspect of everyday **Being** in an inauthentic mode. It is related to **ambiguity** and **idle talk**:

> When curiosity has become free, it takes care to see not in order to understand what it sees, that is, to come to a being toward it, but *only* in order to see. It seeks novelty only to leap from it again to another novelty ... Curiosity has nothing to do with the contemplation that wonders at being. (Heidegger, 1927b: 172)

This is the opposite of the usual sense of *curiosity*. Instead, this state of curiosity restlessly seeks novelty and distraction. It thus avoids disclosing Being.

See also **disclosure; fallenness**

cypher
See **cipher**

daimonic

Etymologically related to *spirit*, this term is used by **Nietzsche** and has been elaborated on by **May**. It is also influenced by the **will to live** concept devised by **Schopenhauer**. May describes the daimonic as: 'the urge in every being to affirm itself, assert itself, perpetuate and increase itself' (May, 1969b: 123). He adds: 'The daimonic is any natural function which has the power to take over the whole person' (ibid.), and that the absence of the daimonic is apathy.

May describes the daimonic as the power of nature, beyond **good and evil**, and with the potential either for destruction or creativity. If integrated into the personality, it is creative. If it takes over the self and becomes excessive, it can become evil (ibid.: 124). It thus requires balance:

> In its right proportions, the daimonic is the urge to reach out towards others, to increase life by way of sex, to create, to civilise ... It is the joy ... of knowing that we matter ... that we are valued. (Ibid.: 146)

This idea is not without difficulties. The implication that it is an external quality, and the claim that a human being can be taken over by it run counter to most existential theories of **freedom**.

Nietzsche makes the distinction between the **Dionysian and Apollonian** forms of daimonic power in *The Birth of Tragedy* (1872). Dionysus is the god of chaos, fruitfulness, creativity and ecstasy, whereas Apollo is the god of order and dreaming. It is profoundly important to Nietzsche that account is taken both of comedy and tragedy as constituents of human life.

The notion of the daimonic can be compared with self-actualisation (see **client-centred psychotherapy**) and **will to power**.

See also **choice**; **essence**

daimonic possession
See **May**

Dasein/Da-sein

Literally 'being there'. A term **Heidegger** uses to indicate *human being*. Often *Dasein* is translated from the German as *existence*, and this is usually adequate. But when Heidegger began to explore the question of **Being**, he wanted, in his precise way, to jettison the ordinary connotations of existence or human being, and use a more neutral and abstract term. What appealed to him about *Dasein* is that more exactly it means being-there, for it comprises *da* and *sein* (*there* and *being*). Often it is written *Da-sein*, to emphasise that it is to be understood as being-there, which suggests that it begins as a **being-in-the-world**, that it is not and cannot even in principle be a pure spirit or consciousness (as **Descartes** had supposed). Neither is it a pure object, capable of objective inspection: it is not simply subject or object. For Heidegger there is no substantial **self**. Being in the **world**, and essentially a part of the world, means *Da-sein* is always in **relationship**. And thus *Da-sein* lives in an anxious state between **freedom** and **thrownness**, unfixed and always changing, ever **becoming**. Heidegger also describes *Da-sein* as 'being-open' (Heidegger, 1987: 225). Other characteristics of *Da-sein* include that it is **care**, and that it is prone to **falling**.

Many other existential writers have taken up this term, including **Jaspers**, **Boss** and **Binswanger**. But in his later writings, Heidegger uses *Dasein* less often, preferring *human being* or *mortal*.

See also **clearing; everydayness; existential; identity; presence**

Daseinsanalysis

(*German: Daseinsanalyse*, and often half-translated as *Daseinsanalysis* meaning analysis of human being.) A form of **existential psychotherapy** associated particularly with **Boss** (but see also **Binswanger**, for his *Existenzanalyse*). It retains some of the practice of **psychoanalysis**, such as free association and use of the couch, whilst replacing almost all of its theory. Inspired by the philosophy of **Heidegger**, the investigation of *Dasein* is at its heart.

A human being is not merely an apparatus, physical or mental, since an apparatus cannot relate itself in a meaning-disclosing manner to the **world**. We find **meaning** in our relationships with the world, and this is because we are not just involved in such relationships, we are never without them, they constitute us. We are essentially out in the world, amongst what matters to us.

Daseinsanalysis disposes of the notion of the unconscious (see **consciousness**), replacing it with the Heideggerian idea that whilst *Dasein* illuminates **Being**, it may not fully illuminate a particular phenomenon – in other words, there are degrees of awareness, but nothing is altogether outside of awareness. And because *Dasein* always discloses Being, there is no need of a theory of **transference**, as all relating is genuine. Thus, the *Daseins*-analyst refrains from symbolic interpretations. Instead, therapeutic interventions are derived from **phenomenology**. The *Daseins*-analyst rejects all preconceived categories, even those of 'self', 'person' or 'psyche'. Instead, openness is cultivated so as to be receptive to how the patient appears in his or her full immediacy. For the *Daseins*-analyst, the phenomena that emerge in a therapeutic session need no interpretation, only careful description and understanding. Similarly, the *Daseins*-analyst, seeing **Freud's** mechanical causality as inappropriate to *Dasein*, refrains from attributing causal connections to the past.

As to practice, just as Freud asked his patients to be honest and truthful with themselves and with the analyst, so Boss requests his patients to let things be (*Gelassenheit*). He makes use of free association, and like Freud, he provides his clients with a couch, believing that the body should be as relaxed as the mind (the fact of embodiment leads to the idea of **bodying forth**, the way in which our bodies interact with the world), and then the therapist, relieved of the distraction of being observed, may more easily maintain an evenly hovering attention to emerging phenomena. However, drawing attention to emerging phenomena does not mean only considering that of which the patient is already well aware:

> [T]he patient's being includes, apart from overtly admitted and accepted modes of behavior, a great many other modes of being, some of which the patient is trying hard not to become aware of ... (Boss, 1957b: 235)

Dreams are treated in similar way to waking-life experience, that is, without supposition of symbolism or the idea of wish fulfilment, instead considering what the patient's **dreams** illuminate about their *Dasein*.

> *Daseinsanalysis* admits all phenomena on their own terms. Hence the therapist avoids a second danger – that of 'curing' the patient's initial symptoms then inducing a new neurosis called 'psychoanalytis.' This syndrome (by no means rare) leads its sufferers to ritualistic thinking and talking in psychoanalytic terms and symbols. (Ibid.: 236)

Boss's approach has a complex and abstruse theory-base, founded upon Heidegger's philosophy. Nonetheless, various *Daseinsanalytic* societies and institutions have been established since the 1970s, including an International Federation created by Boss.

See also **body; person; releasement; self; Zollikon Seminars**

death

In the popular imagination, existentialism is 'all about death'. However, it is less about considering our physical demise than considering the effect that mortality has on our being, how we deal with the apparently obvious knowledge of our finiteness, and what then follows: how we face our lives.

If we admit our personal **temporality** to ourselves, we see our lives in a different light than when, in our everyday manner, we obscure death from sight. We make life more meaningful when we accept that death is always impending and that we are always mortal. **Heidegger** emphasises that although our death is certain, our non-existence is a **possibility** (an afterlife is still a further possibility). But we should, he says, face up to mortal death. For him, **anxiety** is an alertness to our death, revealing our **care**. For Heidegger, the fact of our inevitable demise allows us to shape our lives in a way that immortality would not, for with immortality we would have no care.

Levinas opposes Heidegger in that he does not believe the **meaning** of death resides in our own death, but is in that of the **Other**.

Sartre opposes some of Heidegger's ideas, and does not accept his assertion that a person's death is uniquely personal. For Sartre, all subjective experience is personal, including one's experience of life and **love**. While Heidegger claims we cannot anticipate our death because we do not know for certain when it will be, and all we can do is to be aware of the reality death has for us now, Sartre rejects this. For Sartre, death is the removal of the possibility of possibility. It is about the loss of our **freedom** and it is freedom that imparts uniqueness and meaning to life. It is not, as it is for Heidegger, something that gives inspiration to living. Death opposes freedom, it does not contribute to life.

Contrary to such agnostic or atheistic views, religious existentialists see death differently, since for them there is beyond physical demise **transcendence**, immortality. For **Marcel**, for instance, the existence, in love, of an **I–Thou** relationship means that the object of one's affections is physically lost in his or her death, but the transcendental relationship, the Thou, remains, so fidelity remains possible.

See also **anticipation; authenticity; being-towards-death; cover up; resoluteness**

deception
See **delusion**

deconstruction
A philosophical method of analysing texts, associated with **Derrida**, who insists there is no definition of deconstruction. As others commonly define it as a profound scepticism towards coherency of **meaning**, his insistence shows an ironic consistency. Derrida acknowledges the influence of **Heidegger**, and his idea of *Destruktion*, or destructuring. But if in Heidegger's philosophy there is a continual questioning of **truth**, in Derrida's there is a continual refutation of any truth. Deconstruction has been influential most of all in literary criticism.

Akin to deconstruction is *post-modernism*, with its scepticism towards **science**, political institutions, traditional **philosophy**, objectivity and ideals, and an enthusiastic and often playful willingness to experiment with style.

de-distancing
When **Heidegger** writes of distance, he does not mean physical distance, but the space that *Da-sein* needs to grasp things. He also speaks of the distance that we create rather than the distance that actually exists. A person can be closer to us when several miles away than when living next door to us, for instance. So when he writes of *Entfernung*, de-distancing, or *deseverance*, bringing near, he means that *Da-sein* is capable of bringing things within reach:

> Da-sein is essentially de-distancing ... As the being that it is, it lets beings be encountered in nearness ... *An essential tendency towards nearness lies in Da-sein* ... With the 'radio,' for example, Da-sein is bringing about today de-distancing of the 'world' which is unforeseeable in its meaning for Da-sein, by way of expanding and destroying the everyday surrounding world. (Heidegger, 1927b: 105)

Humankind's pursuit of power over the **world** (see **technology**) means we are in danger of losing touch with our ability to understand **Being**. Technology brings everything so close that our space becomes obstructed and we lose touch with the fourfold of earth, sky, gods and mortals. We need to find the right distance in relation to the world.

defences, psychological

Psychological defences are the means by which people seek to protect themselves against threatening thoughts, emotions, events or impulses. Because existential thinking places existential concerns as fundamental and foremost, not all existential practitioners accept the notion of defence. Those who do deem psychological defences to be employed in order to cope with the otherwise overwhelming **anxiety** arising from awareness of (for example) **freedom, choice, death** and **nothingness**.

The main styles of defence are seen to be *denial* and *displacement*, defences which result in the state known as **inauthenticity**. These defences are seen by existential theorists as being as much metaphysical as psychological. In fact, because the source of this existential anxiety is so powerful, relief can be obtained by displacing existential angst onto mundane matters, a condition known as **neurotic anxiety**. It has to be stressed that only some existential authors use this language of defence. Others, such as **Heidegger** and **Sartre**, do not use such psychoanalytic language. They prefer to speak in terms of **closing off, covering up** or of being in **bad faith**.

Whereas in **psychoanalysis**, defences are seen as arising and residing in the unconscious, in **existential psychotherapy**, with its very different notion of **consciousness**, it is thought that awareness of these defences is always to some extent conscious.

See also **guilt; incongruence; projection; shame**

delusion

Also translated (from *Täuschung*) as *deception*. **Heidegger** writes that both a person's **attunement** and the **call of conscience** are subject to two kinds of distortions, one useful, the other unhelpful. In the first place, because **mood** discloses the environment in different ways on different occasions, this variability can be judged to be the product of delusion, but existentially it is the disclosure of different aspects of the **truth**. Heidegger tends to see this kind of deception as an inevitable part of being human. People are led astray and in this process they find out about the **world**. On the other hand, the individual is affected by the opinions of society, of the **They**, and in consequence the individual's They-self can delude the authentic **self**. We are for instance taken over by **idle talk** and deceive ourselves into finding important what is untrue or of no significance.

See also **authenticity and inauthenticity; falling**

denial

See **bad faith; congruence; defences, psychological; good faith; no-saying; projection**

depersonalisation

See **Laing**

depression

See **despair**

dereflection
See **Frankl**

Derrida
Jacques Derrida (1930–2004). French philosopher and originator of **decon-struction**, born in Algeria and teaching both in Paris and the United States. Influenced by **Nietzsche, Freud, Husserl, Heidegger** and **Levinas**. His own influence has been widespread, but especially in literary criticism, and his many publications include the three that in 1967 introduced his theories of **decon-struction**: *Of Grammatology, Writing and Differance*, and *Speech and Phenomena*.

Like **Ricoeur**, Derrida believes the **world** is not experienced directly, but through language. Therefore, to understand understanding we need to exam-ine language. Derrida further argues that language refers only to other lan-guage, that there is an interdependence of words, and each word has a trace in other words, so each by its **presence** implies the *absence* of others. This *play* (or *differance*) in language means that **meaning** is always postponed and differ-ent. The way in which overt meaning can be subverted by incidental aspects of language – like rhetorical flourishes, gives complete freedom of **interpretation**. Derrida claims that the spoken word is no more immune from re-interpretation than the written text, and that the intention of the speaker or writer should be ignored, for they are not the originators of their linguistic expressions, lan-guage being already replete with meaning. There is thus no fixed point of ver-ifiability, and as signs are arbitrary there is no absolute **truth**. Complaining that Western philosophy is based on presence, on rationality (or *logocentrism*), Derrida's philosophy is consequently one of extreme relativism.

This rejection of the ownership of expression challenges the purpose and viability of psychotherapy, for Derrida's ideas appear to question the validity of any conversation, and any attempt to understand another. However, he follows Heidegger's notion of **being-in-the-world**, of the essential insepara-bility of human being from the world. Applied to linguistic expression, or any use of signs, it warns against treating the individual as utterly distinct, as entirely novel. Instead, **individual** is a concept to be considered cautiously, and **relationship** is all-important.

Descartes
René Descartes (1596–1650). French philosopher, generally seen as the father of modern philosophy. His influence is pervasive, and although in the phe-nomenological and existential fields his conclusions are considered erro-neous, his ideas are often seen as the starting point for a bold philosophical departure (see **Husserl** and **Sartre**).

In some ways Descartes was a metaphysician, concerned with the **reality** behind appearance; his modernity lay in his belief that rationality could pro-vide a reliable foundation for knowledge. Although, like the later existential philosophers, he did not personally doubt the existence of the **world**, he carried out a thought experiment in which he did so, and concluded with the intuition *Cogito, ergo sum*: I think, therefore I am (a 1200-year echo of St. Augustine's *Si fallor, sum*: If I am deceived, I exist).

It is this fundamental capacity for doubt and therefore for fresh thinking that Husserl took as the starting point for **phenomenology** (see Husserl's *Cartesian Meditations*, 1928). But unlike Descartes, Husserl does not conclude that we know how the universe is arranged. Descartes assumed that thought requires a thinker, and he continued to argue for God's existence and for the fact of God's existence as a guarantee of the trustworthiness of human cognition. The existential proposition contained in Descartes's *cogito* does not imply mind–body dualism (that mind and **body** are mutually irreducible), but Descartes goes on to argue that while matter has extension (that it occupies space), thought lacks this property, and therefore they must be distinct substances. Moreover, the mind or soul must be able to survive without the body since it does not depend on it.

However, as well as Cartesian dualists, there are other mind–body dualists who see embodiment as a requirement for mind. And dualists do not always insist on absolute differences of the mental and the physical. *Emergentism*, for instance, suggests that mental qualities are emergent properties of brain processes.

Both mind–body dualism and physicalism (or materialism) are problematic. The former can give no satisfying account of how mind and body interact. The latter has no way of explaining phenomenal experience. Therefore, some existential theorists are dualists, and some are monists, but neither party can claim superiority.

For Descartes, all thinking is conscious. This and his scientific scepticism paved the way for phenomenology.

See also **idealism; mind–body problem; transcendental ego**

description
See **phenomenology**

deseverance
See **de-distancing**

desire
See **emotions; Lacan; lack; look, the; love; masochism; sadism; Schopenhauer; sexuality**

despair
(*Fortvivlelse*). For **Kierkegaard,** this is more than an emotional state, it is an intense loss of **meaning,** an awareness of the hollowness of life. Nor is it necessarily the result of disappointment. It may follow failure, but it may follow success, where success is revealed as doomed to eventual failure. For instance, a man might win a woman's heart, but despair when he realises he loves another mortal being more than himself and more than God. In Kierkegaard's philosophy, only the dutiful love of God is a guarantee against despair:

Despair consists in laying hold on an individual with infinite passion; for unless one is desperate, one can lay hold only on the eternal with infinite passion. Immediate love *is* thus desperate; but when it becomes happy, as we say, it is hidden from it that it is desperate. (Kierkegaard, 1847b: 303)

Despair, for Kierkegaard, is inevitable. It is in many ways the opposite of angst, or **anxiety**, which is similarly inevitable. Despair is a sign that one is avoiding the demands of either end of the spectrum of life, in the same way in which anxiety is a sign that we are exposed to them:

Possibility and necessity belong to the self just as do infinitude and finitude. A self that has no possibility is in despair, and likewise a self that has no necessity. (Ibid.: 35)

See also **introversion; sickness unto death**

destiny
See **fate**

determinism
See **freedom and free will**

diagnosis
See **psychopathology**

dialectic
From the Greek for conversation, *dialektike*, which literally means to talk through something. The term has over the centuries been used in a wide variety of ways. **Socrates** used it to mean a kind of philosophical debate (see **Socratic method**) in which an interrogator, through methodical questioning, attempts to find the contradictions in his adversary's claims in order to arrive at the **truth**. **Aristotle** distinguished between dialectical and demonstrative reasoning, the former referring to a process of critical thinking, the latter proceeding from facts that can be observed. **Hegel**, following a tradition going back to Heraclitus, saw a dialectical process in the history of ideas, a process he not only agreed was a means of progress, but insisted was a necessary process. Dialectics for him was a necessary means of overcoming opposites. His dialectic is usually represented as a three-stage model, with *thesis* (or statement) followed by an *antithesis* (or counter-statement), and their contradictions being resolved by means of a *synthesis* of the two. This synthesis then becomes the new thesis, and is then contradicted by a new antithesis, and so on, resulting eventually in the perfect **truth**, the Idea. Actually, it was Fichte who devised this thesis–antithesis–synthesis model, although he did not use it in the way just outlined. Hegel, going beyond Fichte's terminology, believed in the inevitability of contradiction and the transcendence of contradiction.

Whereas Hegel had been more interested in the history of ideas, Marx adapted the Hegelian dialectic (into what others called *dialectical materialism*) to describe the material history of humankind. And **Sartre**, with his *Critique of Dialectical Reason* (1960), fused Hegel and Marx together with influences from

Kant, and developed the idea of a dialectical process at work in human affairs in both thought and action, and argued for its being a model for reasoning.

Dialectical reasoning is a process eminently adaptable for use in psychotherapy and in **philosophical counselling**. It comfortably allows the apparent **paradox** that one statement (or state-of-affairs) may contain as much truth as its opposite, for it holds that everything contains or develops contradiction – contradiction which can be developed into a more profound insight. Thus it discourages the demand for immediate and simple truth and encourages examination of the complexity of things. And it takes a person well beyond potential ambivalence or conflict into the realm of creativity.

See also **either/or**

dialogical
See **interhuman, the**

dialogue
Literally meaning *talking through*. Two or more people committed to getting to the bottom of something may discuss the matter quietly in order to clarify it. Existential therapy uses dialogue as a preferred method of working, so establishes a conversation where all parties are equal, whilst the therapist is uniquely available to focus on the client's issues.

See also **Buber; encounter; interhuman, the; intersubjectivity; relationship; Rogers**

différance
See **Derrida**

Dilthey
Wilhelm Dilthey (1833–1911). German philosopher, historian and literary critic. He was influenced especially by **Kant**, and his ideas on **interpretation** and his development of a **hermeneutics** had a great influence on **Jaspers** and **Heidegger**. He wrote extensively, much of it published posthumously in his *Selected Works* (1985). His philosophy is wide-ranging, dealing with history, biography and the social sciences.

Dilthey's philosophy may be seen as starting from a new theory of categories. Kant, following **Aristotle**, had argued that there are absolute and universal categories: *quantity, quality, relation* and *modality*, and that our judgements are made according to these. Dilthey argues that there are indeed categories, but they have no absolute existence, and are the contingent product of human being. His own list includes: *power* – how we understand our experiences in terms of their helpfulness or obstructiveness; *meaning* – which is the past; *purpose* – the future; and *value*, the present. These then are ways of instantly sorting and assessing our experiences in terms of what is important to us as individuals. Dilthey holds that each person has a *Weltanschauung*, a worldview or general perspective, and that to understand another person, one must imaginatively re-create their *Weltanschauung*. And he differentiates the study of the natural world, which can be studied in a detached and objective fashion – employing causal explanations (*Natur Wissenschaften*, or natural sciences) – and the works of humankind which have to be studied in a different way (*Geistes Wissenschaften*, or human sciences). He insists that to study people or their art, culture, history, religion, we must employ our own human experience to understand, for there is something peculiar about the study of human beings by human beings, and we can only see it from inside, as we are all within the area of study. But as we all share the common human elements of life, its **meaning** and purpose, so it is possible to understand others. And if we wish to do so, our method is to attempt to relive their mental states, employing our own inner familiarity with love, fear, anguish, yearning, and so on. In later years, Dilthey added other, more objective components to his system, claiming that after subjective understanding of a human being or human expression one should consider too the context, that is, the culture and language.

dimensions
See **four worlds**

Dionysian and Apollonian mentalities
According to **Nietzsche** (and before him, **Schopenhauer**), the ancient Greeks saw human life as terrible and tragic. In *The Birth Of Tragedy* Nietzsche discusses the implications of this view. By his analysis, the Greeks were able to transform life and affirm it through their art, but with two distinct approaches. The Dionysian mentality is an unrestrained and spontaneous desire for excess whereas the Apollonian mentality aims for restraint and harmony. Each is a way to affirm life through art, the Apollonian through the production of a veil of beauty, the Dionysian through embracing the entirety of life itself, including its horrors. Of the Dionysian way, Nietzsche writes:

> We are to recognise that all that comes into being must be ready for a sorrowful end; we are forced to look into the terrors of the individual existence – yet we are not to become rigid with fear ... We are really for a brief moment Primordial Being itself, feeling its raging desire for existence and joy in existence. (Nietzsche, 1872: 17)

However, when in later years Nietzsche wrote of the Dionysian approach to life, he had synthesised the two mentalities.

See also **daimonic; yes-saying**

directedness
See **intentionality**

disalienation
See **alienation**

disclosure and disclosedness

(*Erschliessen* and *Erschlossenheit*). Terms used by **Heidegger** in his analysis of what it is to be a human being, and how human **Being** reveals itself. These terms mean to open and to be open, to reveal and to be revealed. Human beings, that is, *Dasein*, are essentially manifestness. They disclose the **world** and Being. *Erschlossenheit* is the basic mode of being of *Dasein*, which means that *Dasein* is essentially in **truth**:

> Disclosedness is constituted by state-of-mind, understanding, and discourse, and pertains equiprimordially to the world, to Being-in, and to the Self ... Disclosedness is part of Dasein's ownmost being and belongs to its existential constitution. (Heidegger, 1927a: 220–1)

> Da-sein is ... distinguished by the fact that in its being this being is concerned *about* its very being ... It is proper to this being that it be disclosed to itself with and through its being. (Heidegger, 1927b: 12)

See also **concealment**

discourse

A fundamental aspect of *Dasein's* everyday **being-in-the-world** as described by **Heidegger**. One of the three **existentials** (**disposition, understanding** and **discourse**). It does not mean speech or communication, but *Dasein's* making-sense of the **world** to itself using **attunement** and **understanding**. It is the precursor of **language**, and if expressed, is expressed in language:

> When something no longer takes the form of just letting something be seen, but is always harking back to something else to which it points, so that it lets something be seen *as* something, it thus acquires a synthesis-structure, and with this it takes over the possibility of covering up. (Heidegger, 1927a: 34)

dispersion

The nature of *Dasein* is to be dispersed or distracted. Our **being-in-the-world**, in its **everydayness**, is that of an absorption with practical necessity and a following of the dictates of society. In these ways we lose sight of **Being**. This is a consequence of our fundamental mode of Being as **care**. We are always outside of ourselves, projected into a **world** and **fallen** with others. Because of this, our attention is distracted and dispersed in the world. We cannot see the wood for the trees, and the centrality of Being is dispersed by the diversity of our activities. But the disconnectedness in the events of life does not reflect the **essence** of what it means to be human, for our experiences are connected and we are unified.

See also **fallenness; self; thrownness**

displacement

See **defences, psychological**

disposition

Heidegger speaks of disposition (*Befindlichkeit*) when he explains that *Dasein* is always related to the **world** in a certain way. To be a human being is to be in **attunement**, to be in orientation or **relationship** to the **world**. *Dasein* is always disposed to the world in a particular way, it is therefore in a specific **state of mind**. It cannot escape from finding itself in a particular modality of Being in relation to its situation. Ontically, this reveals itself as **mood** (*Stimmung*). Disposition is one of the fundamental **existentials** of being human, alongside **understanding** and **discourse**.

distantiality

(*Abständigkeit*, from *Abstand* meaning distance). In the philosophy of **Heidegger**, this is a form of inauthentic behaviour (see **authenticity**), but it is an aspect of being-with-one-another. In its everydayness ***Da-sein*** constantly compares itself with others, caring about **averageness**, about difference and distance from the mass of human beings. This means that we are always trying to catch up with others or measure ourselves against them. In this, Heidegger highlights a theme common in existential philosophy: that human beings seek the safety of the **crowd**, and in so doing evade individuality and **choice**.

See also **being-with; care; de-distancing; everydayness; individual, the; levelling down; publicness**

distraction

See **dispersion**

Dostoevsky

Fyodor Mikhailovich Dostoevsky (1821–81). Russian novelist and essayist. When he was sixteen his mother died, and two years later his bullying, alcoholic father was murdered by his own serfs. At about this time Dostoevsky developed epilepsy. Sympathetic to socialism, in 1849 he was arrested for subversive activity and sentenced to death. The sentence was commuted to imprisonment in a labour camp in Siberia, but only at the last moment before execution: an event that stayed with him, and which he used, together with his experience of epilepsy, in *The Idiot* (1868). During his incarceration he constantly read the only permitted book, the *New Testament*. He rejected vehemently his earlier secular politics and turned to religion. In 1857 he married, but unhappily; in 1864 his wife died (and so too his beloved brother Mikhail). Three years later he remarried, this time contentedly. In 1886 he wrote *The Gambler*, using the experience of his own gambling sprees. His other novels include *Notes from Underground* (1864), *Crime and Punishment* (1866), *The Possessed* (also translated as *The Devils*, 1871–72) and *The Brothers Karamazov* (1879–80). Dostoevsky's influence on other writers is widespread, and includes **Nietzsche** and **Freud**.

The overt themes in Dostoevsky's writing include **freedom**, evil, sin, **guilt**, and religious faith versus rationality. More implicit themes include **authenticity** and **love**. He believes that rationality is inadequate to explain human life, and that if human life were entirely explicable through rationality, there could be no **free will**. And thus he rejects **science** and **psychology** as dangerously reductionistic. Struck by the restraints on freedom imposed by the church, society and law, he is just as certain that the nature of humankind is free and that we yearn to be untrammelled. And for Dostoevsky, revolt itself is disproof of the universality of reason. Therefore, in his fictions, those protagonists who experiment passionately with their freedom are criminals and revolutionaries. Consequently the action in his stories is replete with murder, suicide and other violence. Few writers have explored as thoroughly the destructive urges of the human spirit. Without belief in God and an afterlife, freedom allows evil, for the individual's will is their own law and anything is permitted. There can be no truth in romantic ideals; thus Dostoevsky reaches **nihilism**.

But with religious faith comes **meaning**, the possibility of redemption through sacrifice, as well as an inhibition on the freedom of the **self**. Dostoevsky's view of salvation is through faith, and love of life and others.

Compare with **Kierkegaard; Unamuno**

double bind
See **mystification**

doubt
Ordinarily, this means uncertainty or scepticism. But in philosophy it is often a deliberate method of examining what has previously been taken for granted, so as to arrive at greater certainty. This hypothetical suspension of certainty is best exemplified in the philosophy of **Descartes**:

> I shall proceed by setting aside all that in which the least doubt could be supposed to exist, just as if I had discovered that it was absolutely false. (Descartes, 1641)

Critics have complained that this kind of doubt is an affectation, and that it is so purely logical that it ignores the everyday certainties that derive from experience, for instance, that the sun will rise tomorrow.

Husserl, though, takes his inspiration from this Cartesian doubt, claiming that philosophical investigation should begin with an absolute lack of knowledge, a setting-aside of assumptions. However, unlike Descartes, Husserl never doubts that there is an embodied thinker amidst others. Thus his **phenomenology** is a systematic process of philosophical doubt that is nevertheless founded upon a given of **existence**.

The more analytical existential philosophers, notably **Heidegger, Sartre** and **Merleau-Ponty**, make great use of this **phenomenological method**, but they also utilise another aspect of doubt – they question assumptions. Heidegger, for instance, takes the fact of **Being** and (in *Being and Time*) examines it in extraordinary depth. It is a fact usually unquestioned, normally eliciting no doubt, but in Heidegger's hands, what is ordinarily beyond doubt is submitted to such scrupulous examination that surprising new conclusions result.

dragon, the great
See **Zarathustra**

dread
See **anxiety**

dreams
The cause of dreaming is still not fully understood, and while some writers believe that dreams have a purely psychological origin, others hold that their origins are physiological. Few would dispute that dreams are revealing, but debate continues over what it is that is revealed, and how it should be discovered and understood. **Freud**, in *The Interpretation of Dreams* (1900), describes dreams as the royal road to the unconscious, for he holds that dreams are driven by unconscious wishes disguised within the dream. He believes that while dreams have a manifest content, they also have a latent content: the latter only discoverable through free association to the elements of the former. **Jung**, on the other hand, believes dreams not to be disguises but communications. What he calls *big dreams* he claims to be expressions of the collective unconscious. *Little dreams*, however, are mere expressions of personal preoccupation. Adler saw dreams as efforts to problem-solve.

The existential approach to dreams makes none of these assumptions. Indeed, **Boss** rejects Freudian assumptions of the symbolism of dreams. In *The Analysis of Dreams* (1957a) he writes of how dreams should be taken at face value, as illuminations of the dreamer's experience of existence. Making use of the philosophy of **Heidegger**, Boss claims that dreams concern experience not well understood by *Da-sein*. Recent studies of dreams seem to bear this out, finding little divergence between the preoccupations of dreams and waking life, and showing that people dream about much the same thing from one year to another. So, taking a phenomenological approach (see **phenomenological method**), dreams, daydreams and fantasies have **meaning** for the person just as much, and in the same way, as everyday experience. In this way, Boss does not distinguish between objective and subjective levels of a dream.

Dreams throw light on the waking world of the person, and the technique for investigating dreams is phenomenological exploration. In this way we uncover the dreamer's current mode of being as exposed in the dream. Of course, even for the existential phenomenologist, there are many ways to elucidate dreams. Amongst these is to see if the dreamer is in control or is passive, and also to note the pervading mood of the dream. Use can be made of the notion of the **four worlds**, to see what is revealed of the dreamer's **relationship** respectively to the physical world, to other people, to him or herself, and to ideals and **values**.

drives
See **lack**; **Sartre**; **sublimation**; **Yalom**

dual mode of relating
See **Binswanger**

dualism
See **Descartes**

dwelling
In *Being and Time*, **Heidegger** uses this term (*Aufenthalt*) to imply that human beings are not in the **world** in the way that objects are in the world, but that our lives are meaningfully related to the world. In his later writings, he develops this further, in a poetic and mystical way:

> Mortals dwell in that they save the earth ... To save properly means to set something free into its own essence ... Mortals dwell in that they initiate their own essential being ... (Heidegger, 1954c: 352)

Dwelling is our attitude to life, the way we **care**. In-dwelling is our way of **being-in-the-world**.

early Heidegger
See **turn/turning**

ecstasy
From Greek, *ekstasis*, meaning to stand out, and linked etymologically to **existence**. In existential philosophy the term is used in a similar way to **transcendence**, not meaning a trance-like state but referring to an essential aspect of human **Being**, and a reference to its being beyond the mere physical facts of its place:

> *The existential and temporal condition of the possibility of the world lies in the fact that temporality, as an ecstatical unity, has something like a horizon* ... The unity of the horizontal schemata of future, having-been, and present is grounded in the ecstatic unity of temporality. (Heidegger, 1927b: 365)

Thus ecstasy is possible because of **temporality**:

> *Temporality is the primordial 'outside of itself' in and for itself.* Thus we call the phenomena of future, having-been, and present, the *ecstasies* of temporality. (Ibid.: 329)

Sartre employs similar usage, adding that *ekstasis* is possible through **being-for-others** and in objectifying oneself.

See also **Moment, the; possibility**

ego
See **self; transcendental ego**

eidetic reduction
See **phenomenological method**

Eigenwelt
See **four worlds**

Einfühlung
See **Jaspers**

einspringen
See **leaping in**

either/or
Kierkegaard's concept of the necessary **choice** between radical alternatives. The hedonist will discover **despair** when he sees how empty is the pursuit of pleasure. He may then want to escape his despair by adopting an ethical life. This requires a definite choice; but how will he choose? For Kierkegaard the contradictions and paradoxes of the **world** are not resolvable through mere logic. In **Hegel's dialectic**, contradiction and **paradox** are resolvable through statement of thesis and antithesis and the generation of a synthesis of the two. This was anathema to Kierkegaard, and he derided Hegel's scientific approach as *both/and*, a lack of commitment:

> My either/or does not denote in the first instance the choice between good and evil, it denotes the choice whereby one chooses good and evil or excludes them ... That some-one who chooses good and evil chooses the good is indeed true, but this becomes evident only afterwards, for the aesthetic is not evil but indifference ... Here, again, you see the importance of choosing, and that what is crucial is not so much deliberation as the baptism of choice by which it is assumed into the ethical. (Kierkegaard, 1843a: 486–7)

Kierkegaard's either/or is a commitment to choice itself. We become truly individual only when we are willing to make deliberate decisions and opt for one or other of our possibilities.

embodiment
See **body**

emergentism
See **Descartes**

emotions
A remarkable feature of emotions, one of intense interest to psychotherapists, is that one can have an emotion and not be fully aware of it; or that, aware of some mental or physical agitation, one may wrongly ascribe it, for instance claiming to be in a state of pleasant anticipation when it is evident to others that one is afraid.

There are many other questions concerning the nature of emotions. Do they have a natural function? How do they arise, and how are they maintained or extinguished? Are they mental, physical, or behavioural, or some interactive combination? And what counts as an emotion? Is disgust an emotion? Is **love**? Are emotions passive, like sensations, or are they active, like perceptions? Is emotion different in any important way from **mood**? There seem to be many different emotions, but is this so or is there a very small number of pure emotions from which these others are mixed, as all colours result from red, blue and green?

In psychology there are numerous competing theories of emotions, none of which has yet won the day. Physical scientists too have shown an interest in emotions. For Darwin, emotions are vestiges of what was once functional in an earlier, primitive life. And philosophers who have discoursed on emotions include **Plato, Aristotle, Spinoza, Descartes,** Hobbes and Hume.

It is popularly held that emotions are beyond reason. Ann may be angry with Bill, thinking herself insulted, but her anger may vanish at once when the apparent insult is revealed as a misunderstanding. This suggests the part of rational computation in the arousal and extinguishing of emotion. But in the case where Carol loves David even though he is indifferent to her, there is no sign that reason plays any instrumental part in the matter. Plato judged emotions to be distinct from reasoning and from desire. Philosophers in general have usually regarded emotions as dangerous because, unlike reason, emotions are inclined to inspire us to rashness. But the idea that emotions are essentially active and participatory, that they cannot be separated from us, fits well with the existential notion that we are utterly involved with the **world** in our very being.

Heidegger takes the view that *Dasein* is always related to the world in a certain tonality: we always find ourselves in relation to things and other people in a particular state of mind. We are attuned to the world in a particular way and we can only get out of a mood by getting into another mood. *Befindlichkeit*, or state of mind or disposition, is one of the fundamental existentialia, one of the principles of our way of being.

Sartre is the existential theorist with the most substantial theory of emotions. He takes his lead from Heidegger and sets himself against Pierre Janet, who sees emotionality as a behaviour of defeat, and Tamara Dembo, who sees emotions as actions of last resort. Sartre argues that each neglects the importance of **intentionality** of **consciousness**: that emotions are not reflective, that while it is possible to be aware of an emotion, emotion is not itself an awareness of **self**:

> [F]ear does not begin as consciousness *of* being afraid, any more than the perception of this book is consciousness of perceiving it. The emotional consciousness is at first non-reflective, and upon that plane it cannot be consciousness of itself. (Sartre, 1939: 56)

According to Sartre, emotions are always directed towards an object, but when there are obstacles to our desires, then we employ emotions to act as magical routes to our desires. Emotions are an escape from predicaments. They are transformations of the world, a world which is *difficult*:

> When the paths before us become too difficult, or when we cannot see our way ... and nevertheless we must act. So then we try to change the world; that is, to live it as though the relations between things and their potentialities were not governed by deterministic processes but by magic. (Ibid.: 63)

Sadness is a means of avoiding facing difficult facts, for instance, the bankrupt who chooses to dwell mournfully on his misfortune rather than to sell his beloved motor car and travel henceforth by public bus. The man who in terror faints at the sight of a ferocious beast thus denies the animal's very existence.

And the joyful lover, dwelling in celebration of the possession of his beloved, is avoiding the difficult fact of keeping her love.

Sartre adds that there are two kinds of emotion. One is the use of magic to overcome a deterministic world, and the other is a response to a world that itself seems unpredictably magical.

For the existential thinker, emotion is a mode of grasping the world. Without emotion, the world would be an undifferentiated mass. Emotion is an aspect of consciousness itself. But whether using Sartre's theory or not, the existential therapist will see emotion and mood as signs of **care**, of what is powerful in the person's **relationship** with the world.

See also **anxiety; attunement; boredom; existentials/existentalia; guilt; hodological space; nausea; passion; shame; slime; Unamuno**

empathy
See **client-centred psychotherapy; Dilthey; Husserl; intersubjectivity; Jaspers; other minds; point of view; resonance; subject and object**

empiricism
See **Heidegger; metaphysics; pragmatism; rationalism**

encompassing, the
See **comprehensive, the**

encounter
In **existential psychotherapy** this usually refers to the meeting between therapist and client. It indicates an openness of **self** by the therapist and is distinct from the common division between therapist and client as observer and observed, or subject and object. Instead, it is an active and wholehearted participation with another person as a human being. **Buber** speaks of the *in-between* (*das Zwissenmenschlichen*) which is the space created by mutuality in the reciprocal **relationship** between two people willing to meet in I–Thou mode. It is in this way that real **dialogue** is created, encountering the whole of someone else's being with the whole of one's own. Such an encounter does not necessarily require words and has a sacred quality:

> Where un-reserve has ruled, even wordlessly, between men, the word of dialogue has happened sacramentally. (Buber, 1929: 3–4)

Used in this way, the term, not exclusively existential, is nevertheless typical of the approach.

Heidegger uses *encounter* (*Begegnis*) to describe how human beings confront the world:

> [T]he world is always already the one that I share with the others. The world of Da-sein is a *with-world*. Being-in is *being-with*-others ... They are not encountered by first looking

at oneself and then ascertaining the opposite pole of a distinction. They are encountered from the *world* in which Da-sein, heedful and circumspect, essentially dwells. (Heidegger, 1927b: 118–19)

See also **being-in-the-world**

enframing

Enframing is a particular way of shaping and regarding the state of the world. **Heidegger** argues that the technological attitude precedes the physical development of **technology**, the production of machines and industry; it is an attitude towards the **world**, a way of revealing the world as a source of materials, which tools may shape. It is a mastery of the world through tools. This enframing (*Ge-stell*) is the essence of technology (though not, Heidegger insists, of **science**). In itself, it is revealing, for it shows aspects of **reality** through its means of order, measurement and pragmatism. However, it possesses danger in its exclusion of other ways of revealing, other ways of thinking, other ways of **Being**. With the impression it creates that all relations are pragmatic, it conceals the full range of ways of Being.

Thus the challenging enframing not only conceals a former way of revealing (bringing-forth) but conceals revealing itself and with it that wherein unconcealment, i.e. truth, propitiates. Enframing blocks the shining-forth and holding sway of truth. (Heidegger, 1954a: 333)

engagement

This term is used by **Sartre** in a twofold way: to describe the inescapability of the individual's involvement in the **world**, and to indicate that **freedom** is only possible through personal commitment to a **project**. In the process of engagement the world becomes meaningful and **values** emerge: 'In this world where I engage myself, my acts cause values to spring up like partridges' (Sartre, 1943a: 38).

engulfment

See **Laing**

entanglement

Verfangenheit – literally, being caught up in. In **Heidegger's** philosophy, entanglement is an aspect of **fallenness**. In a state of **anxiety** at **Being**, a person may absorb or entangle themselves in the world of things or of other human beings, and letting themselves be taken over by them, so avoiding Being and consequently leading to an inauthentic mode of existing.

See also **authenticity**; **close off**; **rapture**

environment

See **four worlds**

epistemes
See **Foucault**

epistemology
see **knowing and knowledge**

epoché
See **not knowing; phenomenological method**

equalisation
See **phenomenology**

equipment
See **world**

Erbe
German term meaning *heritage*. For **Heidegger**, human beings exist in community and in **time**. We have a common history, a cultural heritage. However, we choose what we take from the past to construct our own future:

> The resoluteness in which Da-sein comes back to itself discloses the actual factical possibilities of authentic existing in terms of the heritage, which that resoluteness takes over as thrown. Resolute coming back to thrownness involves handing oneself over to traditional possibilities, although not necessarily as traditional ones. (Heidegger, 1927b: 383)

Some commentators see in this a political conservatism, even a leaning to authoritarianism. Others see it as the offer of personal autonomy.

See also **authenticity;** *Da-sein*; **facticity; repetition; resoluteness; thrownness**

Ereignis
A German term, meaning *event* but used in a technical way by **Heidegger**, especially in his later philosophy, when he describes **Being** as unfolding in *Ereignis*. Going back to the roots of the word, he shows how it originally means *appropriation*. To *be*, then, is to take ownership. It is an activity, an event, the ownership of one's life-world. And as an activity, it takes place in **time**.

See also **care**

Eremita, Victor
Pseudonym used by **Kierkegaard** for *Either/Or* (1843a).

essence
The inner nature and what is fundamental about a thing. Arguments abound in philosophy seminar rooms and public bars alike as to the identity of

human nature. Often the answers are formulated in terms of physical or psychological or behavioural terms, for instance that we are animals, that we are rational, that we are territorial. But the existential thinker usually believes that these qualities are too contingent to be essential. The existential theorist is more interested in philosophical categories, in what it *means* to be a human being. Because of this, existential philosophers usually speak of the human condition, rather than of human nature. In other words, the essence of human beings is to have to exist in certain conditions.

Kierkegaard, for example, believes that human being is essentially in tension between the **finite and infinite**. But Nietzsche argues that the **will to power** is at the heart of being human, and that the main challenge is to overcome ourselves and make a bridge between animal and superman. How one faces the **world** and the part one has to play in the world concerns many philosophers. **Heidegger**, for instance, argues that *Dasein* has as its ontological essence, **care, time, attunement, understanding** and **discourse**. Some existential philosophers claim that **existence** is an essence. At times, Heidegger does this. But for **Sartre**, human being is essentially **freedom** and **nothingness,** and everything else remains to be determined by the individual and how he or she responds to their experience.

From the essences we accept as being fundamental can be deduced general principles of human engagement with life. For instance, Sartre's essence of freedom implies that **choice** will be a significant aspect of everyday life. The existential psychotherapist will have philosophical beliefs concerning what is essential to human being, and from this underlying theory will explore how the individual lives his or her life. **Husserl** claimed that essences could be observed directly through **intuition**, through the so-called W*esenschau*.

See also **existence precedes essence; intuition; phenomenology**

eternal return

> What if a demon … said to you, 'This life, as you live it now and have lived it, you have to live again and again, times without number … And everything in the same sequence and a series …' (Nietzsche, 1882: 341)

Eternal return or *eternal recurrence* is an idea, not originally by **Nietzsche**, that in a universe of infinite possibility, there must be **repetition** – indeed, cycles of repetition. Nietzsche's use of this idea is to see it as a test of one's life, for it raises a moral questioning of how comfortable one is with one's own actions: what if we had to forever relive what we are doing now? (In this, perhaps, is Nietzsche's vision of Hell – echoed in **Sartre's** play, *No Exit.*) It is also echoed in the notions of **repetition** by **Kierkegaard** and **Heidegger**.

See also **yes-saying**

ethical life
See **Kierkegaard**

ethics of ambiguity
See **ambiguity**

eudaimonia
A Greek term, literally meaning the possession of a good daimon, or guardian spirit, it refers to the good life – not merely a life one personally **values**, but a life that would be thought good by all right-minded or rational people. What constitutes the good life and how it can be obtained was a preoccupation of the Athenian philosophers, and each of their different schools of philosophy had an answer to each of these questions. For some, the supreme good was sensual pleasure; for others it was an untroubled state of mind. For some, such as **Aristotle**, the way to gaining such well-being came from the exercise of virtue, for others, such as **Plato**, it was through the use of reason. The Epicureans sought the solution in the pursuit of happiness, while the Stoics, by hardening themselves to pain and discomfort.

All these approaches share a tendency to control the passions. For the existentialist, this can be judged to be a means to lessen the **anxiety** that accompanies the arousal of **passion**, its concomitant aspirations and its potential for disappointment.

For the existential psychotherapist, it is important to examine the **meaning** of a person's passions – those values, or things or other people that an individual desires or detests wholeheartedly. But further than this, an existential therapist will not encourage the suppression of deep feelings and will enable a person to come to terms with the opposites of pain and pleasure, good and bad.

See also **care; emotions**

event
See *Ereignis*

everydayness
Human beings must necessarily absorb themselves with everyday matters, and live practical lives through the adoption of a pragmatic attitude. **Heidegger** argues that to understand *Dasein*, we have to begin by describing everyday experience so as to capture the basic states of human **Being**: 'And this means that it is to be shown as it is *proximally and for the most part* in its average *everydayness*' (Heidegger, 1927a: 17).

Heidegger describes how this everydayness (*Alltäglichkeit*) overlooks all but the mundane. He points out that what is the most familiar is the most overlooked and unexamined. For instance, everydayness judges **anxiety** as no more than muddlement. Overall, then, it is an inauthentic way of living. On the other hand, however limited it is, it is the world of first-hand experience, whereas **science** and **philosophy**, although they are questioning activities, are intellectual examinations, and distinct from immediate experiencing. So it is in everydayness that we spend most of our time, and in which we have contact with what is real; yet it is in that state that we fail to be aware of and question the nature of Being.

evil
See **good and evil**

evil, banality of
See **Arendt**

existence
The Latin *existere* means to stand out or to emerge. Commonly there is a contrast between the existence and the **essence** of an entity. But for many existential philosophers there is little difference between existence and essence. **Heidegger** applies it only to *Dasein*: 'The "essence" of Dasein lies in its existence' (Heidegger, 1927a: 42). He shows that *Dasein*'s mode of being is to exist. **Sartre** takes this idea further and based most of his writing on the notion that Heidegger had put forward, namely that **existence precedes essence**.

Existential philosophers have from the start been preoccupied with the nature of human existence: 'Existence itself, existing, is a striving and is just as pathos-filled as it is comic' (Kierkegaard, 1846b: 92). **Kierkegaard** did not believe human existence can be defined in the manner of objects; the mere physical presence of *homo sapiens* is not existence. Thus he set the tone for the existential attitude towards existence. Further than this, existence is mysterious, perhaps even beyond human comprehension:

> Existence itself is a system – for God, but it cannot be a system for any existing spirit. System and conclusiveness correspond to each another, but existence is exactly the opposite. (Ibid.: 118)

However, God does not exist in the way that human beings exist. God is simultaneously outside and inside existence (this is termed *transcendent immanence*). Human beings are different in that their existence has to be transcended and created at all times. Most existential authors speak about existence without reference to God. Sartre asserts the importance of the human challenge to make something of our own existence, since none of it is given from the outset:

> What do we mean by saying that existence precedes essence? We mean that man first of all exists, encounters himself, surges up in the world – and defines himself afterwards ... [T]here is no human nature, because there is no god to have a conception of it ... Man is nothing else but what he makes of himself. (Sartre, 1946: 28)

existence precedes essence
This is the fundamental basis on which all existential writing is founded. **Heidegger** contends that *Dasein* has no **essence** like other entities: 'The essence of Dasein lies in its existence' (Heidegger, 1927a: 42). Similarly, **Sartre**

claims it as a fundamental tenet of existentialism that a human being has no predetermined character, that there is no innate human nature. Thus, all that may be said of a human being is that it exists. However, Sartre goes on to specify that human beings have **consciousness**, and it is this that allows us to determine our actions through **choice**, and it is our actions that describe us. So as for our essence, we are constantly leaving in our wake the facts of what we have done. As history, this is fixed, and so becomes a kind of essence through the process of **mineralisation**. But our future is always free, because the immediate implication of consciousness in combination with lack of character is **freedom**, and the unavoidable fact of choice. Indeed, Sartre says that the one choice we lack is the option not to choose. Freedom is thus inseparable from human being.

An obvious complaint against Sartre's axiom is that human beings are generally consistent and even predictable, and that we have enduring characteristics, or personality. Sartre replies with the concept of **project**, that what gives consistency of character to a person's behaviour is the project they have themselves already in broad terms chosen, and their further choices are in accord with those initial choices. Nevertheless, the human being, the **being-for-itself**, is always leaving behind that which is already made, its own *past*, and it is always moving towards its possibilities. A human being is thus free until **death**, when choices can no longer be made, and at last that person's entire existence is fixed, for there are no more possibilities. Similarly, for Heidegger, human beings are always **thrown** and projected towards a future. The challenge is to become aware of one's ownmost **potentiality-for-being-oneself**.

See also **bad faith; causality; determinism; facticity; possibility; projection; time and temporality**

existent
See **ontic**

existential
Of **existence**, especially human existence. To be distinguished from *existentialist*, which refers to the specific philosophical movement of **existentialism**. Existential issues are the issues thrown up by human living. Applied to philosophical reasoning, it implies that existence cannot be set aside from consideration of the human condition. Non-existential philosophers like **Descartes** sometimes hypothesise there to be no **world**, but in existential thinking it cannot, even hypothetically, be removed from human existence. The world is presupposed and is essential and integral in all existential philosophising, since human beings exist fundamentally in a world.

existential anxiety
See **anxiety**

existential guilt
See **guilt**

existential psychotherapy

The aim of existential psychotherapy is to clarify, reflect upon and understand life as each person in practice experiences it in order to overcome particular problems or resolve dilemmas. Different forms of psychotherapy have different theory, practice and focus. While the various approaches derived from **psychoanalysis** claim incomplete psychic development as the subject of the therapist's attention, behavioural psychology cites maladaptive learning as the problem, and **client-centred psychotherapy** views a lack of psychological **congruence** as the central issue, so existential therapy views the person as fundamentally in **relationship** with the difficult factors of **existence**, especially **freedom** and **facticity** (the limits of freedom). Very briefly, the objective of existential psychotherapy is to develop the person's truthfulness with themselves – **authenticity**, and an openness to **Being**.

It is an essentially philosophical approach, one that sees the problems and issues that give rise to distress as the consequence of difficulties encountered in living rather than indicators of mental heath and illness. In fact, it calls into question many of the assumptions that underpin the more medically informed approaches. Thus it tends to reject, partly or wholly, notions of **psychopathology** in favour of **choice**.

One aim of existential therapy is to help people become better acquainted with themselves, to help them clarify their *worldview* through exploration of the contradictions, discrepancies and paradoxes that make attempts at self-understanding so difficult. With increased clarity comes a better chance to resolve problematic issues.

Existential therapy is scientific, in that it is methodical (through its use of the **phenomenological method**). But it rejects the Newtonian determinism of psychoanalysis and behaviourism in favour of a reciprocity that, for instance, includes the person's will as an agency. And it is holistic in that it includes the entire context of the person's life and **world**. Because existential philosophy describes the person as living between the chance circumstances of the world and their own decisions in response to that world, an existential therapist will try to aid the patient in therapy to see the choices they have actively made, as well as how elements of their life are beyond choice.

In practice, existential psychotherapy and counselling is characterised by the examination through dialogue of how a person lives his or her life, considering the **meaning** they give to their experience and what they value and disvalue. Special attention is given to signs of **alienation** and to indications of the pursuit or avoidance of personal choice and power. But the healing power of the therapeutic relationship itself is also considered to be extremely important.

According to existential thinking, people are always in relation, so therapist and client face each other and engage in active conversation, and not – as in classical analysis – with the therapist observing the client in a detached manner. It is a mutual dialogue, an **encounter**, albeit one where the focus of attention is constantly on the client's experience, and often on the client's **emotions**, for emotions are seen as a barometer of the person's **values**, and **anxiety** is seen as a healthy and natural reaction to life.

This is a therapy that not only examines subjective experience, but never tries to reduce it or objectify it, and so it is radically different from those therapies that claim objective knowledge. It is primarily concerned with exploring the world of individuals on their own terms, allowing them to arrive at their own insights and to make the choices and decisions which they feel are right for them rather than attempting to cure or change behaviour which may in fact be fundamental to their existence. It emphasises the need each of us has to find our own inner equilibrium and to live life in accordance with our own deeply held **values** and beliefs rather than those of others.

Not all existential therapists work in the same way or hold the same views. For example, existential practice is usually phenomenological, but how much use is made of this method varies from one therapist to another. But in all cases, existential therapists work with the live experience of their clients and not their own ideas and formulations.

There is a wide range of theoretical influences that an existential therapist may draw upon, especially **Kierkegaard, Nietzsche, Jaspers, Heidegger, Buber, Sartre** and **Merleau-Ponty**. But there is a division, if not a sharp one, in the use of existential philosophy in psychotherapy. There are those who believe that existential philosophy is an influence, that it can be added to an already more-or-less complete psychotherapeutic theory, for instance, Irvin **Yalom**, an existentially informed psychoanalyst. Then there are those who see the possibility of a complete existential psycho-philosophical approach, for instance, Ludwig **Binswanger**, Medard **Boss** and others, including the authors of this book.

existentialism

Existentialism is a philosophical movement that arose largely in consequence of the work of Jean-Paul **Sartre**. Existentialism flourished on the continent of Europe from the Second World War to the 1960s and was then replaced with other fashionable movements such as **structuralism**, post-structuralism, and later **deconstructionism** and post-modernism. Existentialism as a philosophical or a social movement has to be sharply distinguished from *existential philosophy* or *philosophy of existence*, which is a more far-reaching approach that encompasses all philosophies whose main concern is to describe human existence. The primary concern of existential philosophies is with the clarification of human **Being**, or **existence**, whereas the primary concern of existentialism is to establish a particular approach to human **freedom**.

Existentialism provides a theory of how human beings are fundamentally free and how human existence has to be lived before it can be defined. Sartre made a distinction between human **being-for-itself** and objects **being-in-itself** and he declared that the challenge of being-for-itself was to choose itself and become what it will be. Existentialists reject both simple subjectivity and simple objectivity as inadequate to understanding the human experience. Instead, the existentialist usually makes use of **phenomenology** to understand human experience. Existentialism is thus probably the most psychological of philosophies, and this is one reason for the development of an **existential psychotherapy**.

There are very many writers who are described by commentators as existential but who themselves reject the term. In order to distinguish those philosophers and practitioners who base their work on a broad consideration of existence rather than on a narrow existentialist theory, it is better to abandon references to existentialism and speak instead of existential philosophers or existential psychologists.

The themes of existential philosophy include **alienation, anxiety, choice, conscience, death, freedom, guilt, responsibility** and **shame**. The major existential philosophers include **Kierkegaard, Nietzsche, Heidegger, Sartre** and **Merleau-Ponty**.

Compare with **pragmatism; rationalism; Stoics and stoicism**

existentials/existentialia

Existenzialen – **Heidegger's** term for the fundamental characteristics of *Dasein*.

See also **care; disposition; judgement; language; understanding**

existentiell

If *existential* pertains to the nature of **existence**, then *existentiell* (*existenziell*) pertains to the individual's own existence. It applies to the whole range of possibilities open to human beings as well as to the limited choices *Dasein* makes in making use of these possibilities or neglecting them. And the latter is the starting-point from which to investigate the former:

> We come to terms with the question of existence always only through existence itself. We shall call *this* kind of understanding of itself *existentiell* understanding. (Heidegger, 1927b: 12)

Such personal knowledge is limited, yet analysis of existence in general, of **Being**, must root itself in human experience.

See also **choice**

Existenz

See **Jaspers**

Existenzanalyse

See **Binswanger**

existing individual

See **individual, the**

extraversion

See **introversion**

face
See **Levinas**

facticity
Both **Heidegger** and **Sartre** use this term to refer to the facts of life that restrict our **freedom**. For Sartre there can be no freedom without it being considered within the context of a particular **situation**. Facticity refers to those aspects of the situation not set by ourselves. It includes our past, other people's decisions, the laws of physics, and so on. It provides the limits of human existence, what is not open to **possibility**. For Heidegger it is related to **thrownness**, and relates to the fact that *Dasein* finds itself in a world that is already constituted:

> The concept of 'facticity' implies that an entity 'within-the-world' has Being-in-the-world in such a way that it can understand itself as bound up in its 'destiny' with the Being of those entities which it encounters within its own world. (Heidegger, 1927a: 56)

See also **contingency**

faith, religious
See **Kierkegaard; Marcel; passion; sickness unto death; theology; Tillich; Unamuno**

falling, fallenness
In *Being and Time*, **Heidegger** writes:

> [T]here is revealed a basic kind of Being which belongs to everydayness; we call this the *'falling'* of Dasein. This term does not express any negative evaluation, but is used to signify that Dasein is proximally and for the most part alongside the 'world' of its concern. (1927a: 175)

Heidegger's notion is of falling into *inauthenticity* (see **authenticity and inauthenticity**). And as with inauthenticity, falling is a fact of human existence: 'Falling is a definite existential characteristic of Dasein itself' (Ibid.: 176).

There seems an echo of Christian theology in Heidegger's choice of term – although he denies a connection – since he links the notion of falling with temptation. Falling is a very basic way of being human, since it involves us in being with others and being taken over by the *They-self*:

The alienation of falling – at once tempting and tranquillising – leads by its own
movement, to Dasein's getting *entangled* in itself. (Ibid.: 178)

To fall is to lose sight of all but everyday concerns. This is particularly common when an individual is tempted to give up his or her individuality and
instead merge into the **They**. Thus, in fallenness, we are less able to question
and consider the world or our lives. But fallenness is the usual mode of existence for *Dasein*; because we are **thrown** into the world, we must attend to
our everyday life in it. And if fallenness suggests a permanent fall from grace,
it is not so, according to Heidegger. For in a life predominantly inauthentic,
it is possible to capture moments of authenticity. At the same time we always
have to take into account our moments of falling into **idle talk, curiosity** and
ambiguity.

See also **curiosity; entanglement; everydayness; lostness**

fascination
See **numbing**

fate
Psychotherapists, psychologists and counsellors are generally hostile to talk of
fate, for it seems to suggest a renouncing of autonomy. But the existential
therapist believes a balanced outlook is one that understands the limits of personal control. **Nietzsche**, for instance, recommends the love of one's fate,
amor fati. **Kierkegaard** on the other hand, considers the two enemies of individuality to be fatalism and fanaticism: the first consisting of not caring
enough and the second of caring too much.

In *Being and Time*, **Heidegger** distinguishes between fate (*Schicksal*) and destiny (*Geschick*). They each refer to the limits of **freedom**, in which history and
culture delimit an individual or a society, but *fate* refers to the individual
whereas *destiny* is the shared fate of a community.

Da-sein can only be reached by the blows of fate because in the basis of its being it *is*
fate ... Da-sein is disclosed as being-in-the-world for the 'coming' of 'fortunate' circumstances and for the cruelty of chance. (Heidegger, 1927b: 384)

However, as well as being what is imposed, fate is also that which is chosen.
Sartre's view that man is condemned to be free does in some ways constitute
a vision of an inescapable human fate, or at least of an inescapable reality of
the human condition.

See also **being-in-the-world;** *Da-sein*

fear
For **Heidegger**, every mood is disclosive, that is, mood reveals something
about our **world**. In the case of fear, it discloses the individual's vulnerability
to a threat that is near (see **de-distancing**). Fear is distinct from **anxiety** in
that it is a response to a specific threat whereas anxiety is the fear of nothing:

'Fear is Angst that is fallen on the "world", inauthentic and concealed from itself as Angst' (Heidegger, 1927a: 189).

fellow-feeling
See **intersubjectivity**

fidelity
See **loyalty; Marcel**

finite and infinite; finitude and infinitude
For **Kierkegaard**, human being lies in the tension between the finite and the infinite. Between the limits of everyday life on earth and eternal God in endless Heaven is where the human self battles to find balance, to synthesise its elements of finitude and infinitude:

> Whoever does not wish to sink in the wretchedness of the finite is constrained in the most profound sense to struggle with the infinite ... From finitude one can learn much, but not how to be anxious, except in a very mediocre and depraved sense. On the other hand, whoever has truly learned how to be anxious will dance when the anxieties of finitude strike up the music and when the apprentices of finitude lose their minds and courage. (Kierkegaard, 1844b: 160–2)

Kierkegaard links the infinite with the idea of **possibility** and the finite with the idea of **necessity**. He sees the **self** as having to maintain the tension between possibility and necessity in order to find its equilibrium. The self is a **freedom** which has to live in the **dialectic** between possibility and necessity, infinite and finite aspects of existence:

> Possibility and necessity belong to the self just as do infinitude and finitude. A self that has no possibility is in despair, and likewise a self that has no necessity. (Kierkegaard, 1849: 35)

See also **anxiety; facticity**

fleeing
Human being, or *Dasein*, finds it hard to face its own nature. This is a consequence of our **thrownness** into a **world** of things and of our **fallenness** with other people, each of which allows us to escape from ourselves:

> Dasein's falling into the 'they' and the 'world' of its concern, is what we have called a 'fleeing' in the face of itself. (Heidegger, 1927a: 185)

Heidegger describes how in the face of our own **Being**, we often take flight (*Flucht*) from our potential to be ourselves:

> As a being which is delivered over to its being, it is also delivered over to the fact that it must always already have found itself, found itself in a finding which comes not from a direct seeking, but from a fleeing. (Heidegger, 1927b: 135)

Paradoxically, this very turning away indicates an **attunement**; it shows that from which we take flight. In **fear**, we may flee from direct threats, but in angst, we fly from the indefinite nature of our own Being, as well as from the inevitability of our own **death**: 'As falling, everyday Being-towards-death is a constant *fleeing in the face of death'* (Heidegger, 1927a: 254).

See also **entanglement**

flesh
See **Merleau-Ponty**

flight
See **fleeing**

forgetting
Martin **Heidegger** complains of the neglect, of the forgetting (*Vergessen*) of **Being**, and contends that since **Plato** and **Aristotle** it has been cast into oblivion (*Vergessenheit*). He also discusses forgetting and remembering, taking issue with the accounts of forgetting provided by **psychology** and **psychoanalysis**. In psychoanalytic thinking, acts of forgetting are commonly hypothesised as deliberate actions calculated to meet with unconscious wishes. For instance, a woman leaves her purse with a man: this is evidence that she wishes to return to him. Heidegger disagrees, offering instead a phenomenological account: forgetting, he says, is not a displacement or a mislaying, but a **concealment**. Remembering is a making-present, and forgetting is not considering something as present, not belonging to a current undertaking. So the woman who leaves behind her purse has left it amidst a current occupation, for she is still present with her admirer. What in psychoanalytic theory is repression of memory is in Heidegger's thinking a decision to attend to other matters, so that the painful memory is let go.

Heidegger considers one form of forgetting to be particularly important and that is *self-forgetting*. This is a way of withdrawing from authentic ways of being and therefore leads to inauthenticity:

> But when one projects oneself inauthentically towards those possibilities which have been drawn from the object of concern in making it present, this is possible only because Dasein has *forgotten* itself in its ownmost *thrown* potentiality-for-Being. This forgetting is not nothing, nor is it just a failure to remember; it is rather a 'positive' ecstatical mode of one's having been – a mode with a character of its own. (Heidegger, 1927a: 178)

See also **authenticity**; *Dasein*

formative tendency
See **client-centred psychotherapy**

Foucault
Michel Foucault (1926–84). French writer trained in **philosophy**, sociology and **psychology**. His influences include **Hegel**, Marx, **Heidegger** and **Merleau-Ponty**. Works include *Madness and Civilization* (1961), *The Order of Things* (1966),

The Archaeology of Knowledge (1969), and *The History of Sexuality* (envisaged as six volumes, just three completed and published: 1976, 1984, 1984). His earliest writing was on psychological matters, and at one time he was associated with the **anti-psychiatry** movement.

A structuralist (that is, one who believes that underlying semantic structures shape the identity of thought), Foucault later distanced himself from the movement, although he continued to see texts as existing in a context of linguistic and socio-political structures which are different at different times of history (epistemes). He views human being in the same light, claiming that the very notion of Man is the result of an epoch of rationality, an epoch now in decline after belief in the human being as independent and rational has been fatally undermined by, for instance, notions of the unconscious (see **consciousness/ unconsciousness**). His description of the different epistemes of human culture are the result of his search for an understanding of history. His early writing, which he refers to as 'archaeology', tries to excavate the implicit knowledge that is fundamental to the sciences, for he holds that apparently independent thought (for example, **science**) is actually shaped by unconscious and invisible factors. According to Foucault, it is through the elevation of cultural norms such as reason that those judged in opposition to those norms, such as the mad, are criminalised. It is for this reason that Foucault is opposed to reason.

Foucault also abandoned Marxist theory, objecting to its materialistic notion of human life whilst he held that human beings transcend the physical. But his thought is guided by an ethics, a passion for the rights of the oppressed. And just as Marx explains that an **alienation** from the means of production results in an unsatisfactory life, so Foucault argues that all social relationships are relationships of power, a power he believes is frequently sadistic. Thus in his later writing he considers the individual as a **subject**, as subservient, and he examines the ways in which individuals are objectified.

See also **being-in-itself; Derrida; Lacan; Ricoeur; technology and technological attitude; thrownness; will to power**

four worlds

It was **Binswanger** who devised the notion of three worlds or dimensions to human living: *Umwelt, Mitwelt* and *Eigenwelt*. He devised these three worlds out of **Heidegger's** description of *Umwelt* and *Mitwelt* and his implied *Eigenwelt*. Many other existential psychotherapists have since taken up the idea, finding a number of uses for it. One of the authors (EvD) has argued the case for a fourth dimension, the *Überwelt*, since the dimension of a spiritual world is described in Heidegger's later work, which refers to the fourfold human relation to earth (*Umwelt*), **world** (*Mitwelt*), man (*Eigenwelt*) and gods (*Überwelt*) (van Deurzen, 2002).

The existential therapist wants to avoid intra-psychic classifications that restrict or bind the client, and the idea of existential dimensions allows that, permitting a way of plotting a person's position in the world that is descriptive rather than prescriptive, that is subjective rather than attempting to be objective. It is also a means of reference from which the exploration of the client's relationships can be made, for each of the dimensions is an area of **relationship**.

- *Umwelt.* This is the physical dimension. It involves the senses and the **body.** The basic facts of our **existence** are physical, that we have bodies, that our environment physically touches us. Many of these facts are given, are not the result of **choice,** but just how we respond is often indicative or parallel to the third dimension. For instance, our satisfaction or dissatisfaction with our own bodies will influence our position in the other dimensions (and vice versa).
- *Mitwelt.* This is the social or public dimension. It is our everyday encounters with others. Our modes of interpersonal relating are within this dimension, whether we are dominant or submissive with others, or whether we withdraw. Within this dimension we react to our culture, its mores and expectations. We align ourselves to it, or oppose it, or are alienated from it.
- *Eigenwelt.* This is the psychological or private dimension. It is the dimension most associated with psychotherapy, for it involves the person's relationship to him or her self, and to intimate others (whether actively present or not, thus it includes parents, even if never seen, and it includes any relationships with deceased loved ones). Exploration of this dimension can reveal how intimate the person is with others, and with his or her self.
- *Überwelt.* The spiritual dimension. This is the world of meaningfulness, of ideas, religious beliefs, ethical **values.** The *Überwelt* is the attitude one takes to life. It is not necessarily explicit or reflective, and elucidation of a person's spiritual dimension means clarifying what their implicit beliefs are, although the person may not be overtly aware of these beliefs (and which they may themselves challenge as they come to light).

The idea of these dimensions should not be taken as definitive. It is a device for thinking and exploring. It is typical of the freedom of **existential psychotherapy** that there is no requirement for the therapist to use it.

Frankfurt School
The Frankfurt School of Social Criticism was a group begun in the 1920s, influenced by the theories of **Hegel** and Marx. It reconstituted itself after the Second World War and was highly critical of **Heidegger's** ideas, whilst at the same time being much influenced by them. The development of *critical theory* by the sociologist (and composer) Theodor Adorno (1903–69) showed a typical distrust of **science** and **technology,** as well as offering a critical examination of the thinking behind many social practices, as well as many analyses of faulty **interpretation.** Later members, such as Jürgen Habermas (b. 1929), who argue for **psychoanalysis** as a form of liberation, are less anti-rationalist.

Frankl
Viktor Emil Frankl (1905–97). Psychiatrist and psychotherapist who was born and died in Vienna. Influenced by **Nietzsche, Freud,** Adler, Max **Scheler.** Author of several widely read books, including *Man's Search for Meaning* (1946), *The Doctor and the Soul* (1955) and *Psychotherapy and Existentialism* (1967).

As a Jew, Frankl was interned in four Nazi concentration camps. His father and mother, his wife and his brother all died, leaving him and his sister as survivors. He later described three stages he had observed in camp survivors: on admission, shock and disillusionment; during incarceration, a protective apathy and dulling of emotions; on liberation, a sense of unreality and depersonalisation, and then the re-emergence of emotions. It occurred to him that life had lost its **meaning** for most camp inmates, but that even a life of privation and fear could still have meaning. The psychotherapy he developed from this experience he called *logotherapy* (from *logos, word or meaning*) literally meaning therapy of meaning.

Logotherapy is sometimes referred to as *existential analysis* and used to be referred to as the Third Viennese School of Psychotherapy (the others being the approaches of **Freud** and Adler). Frankl contends that human beings have to create meaning for themselves and have a fundamental **will to meaning**. Meaning can come from three sources of value:

1 *experiential values*, where we enjoy the good things that are available to us, for instance in nature, or through love
2 *creative values*, where we generate good things through our personal deeds or our creativity
3 *attitudinal values*, where we learn to endure pain, guilt or death (which Frankl termed a *tragic triad*).

Suffering itself can be seen to be an achievement, and **guilt** utilised for self-reform. And awareness of **death** can be used to take responsibility for one's life. So whilst acknowledging that human beings are subject to various unalterable conditions, we are nevertheless free to choose our attitude towards those conditions.

This creative and forceful approach to meaning meant that Frankl was often directive in his remarks to his patients, for instance, when he suggests that life should be lived as if one were living already for the second time and one had acted the first time as wrongly as one was about to act. The paradoxical flavour of these words (see *amor fati*) was evident in his behavioural interventions, where he refined the paradoxical intention or paradoxical injunction, where an anxious and avoidant patient is asked to do what they believe is beyond their control. This is a case of prescribing the symptom so as to make a person aware of their own ability to control it. For example, the person who believes they will faint in a restaurant is asked to *try* and faint, in order to remove their anticipatory anxiety. Apart from appealing to meaning and paradoxical intention, Frankl was fond of using the **Socratic method**, in helping a person uncover what they know but have forgotten, as well as *dereflection*, which is a way of encouraging a person to turn their attention away from their problems in a more positive direction.

Frankl was criticised by some for making no reference to his Jewishness in his account of his ordeals, but he answered that he did not want to capitalise on being a Jew. In 1992 he founded the Viktor Frankl Institute for Logotherapy and Existential Analysis.

See also **contingency; freedom; paradox; will to meaning**

free association
See **Boss**

free will
See **freedom and free will**

freedom and free will
The concept of freedom is prominent in all existential philosophies. In the ordinary sense, freedom is a lack of constraint. It does not imply the power to achieve anything. A man is free to fly like a bird, but lacking feathers and wings, is unable to do so.

Free will is a more specific issue. A robot may be free in the sense that it has no hindrances, but nevertheless it is impelled by the orders inherent in its programming. To have a degree of free will, whether great or small, is to determine one's own behaviour. A billiard ball cannot determine its own behaviour, but we humans have minds, and we can imagine that somehow the mind causes and directs behaviour.

But determinism is often considered to be opposed to free will, for it implies physical causality, and even if thinking is a behaviour, what causes that? And if thinking is the cause of action, is there not anyway a chain of causes (of motive and **choice**) that results in any given action? Nonetheless, neither research nor argument has proved or disproved the existence of free will. And so the arguments continue.

Contemporary defenders of personal freedom sometimes look for support in the theories of quantum mechanics, in Werner Heisenberg's *uncertainty* or *indeterminacy principle*, and the further ideas of Niels Bohr and Erwin Schrödinger. The uncertainty principle says that some pairs of physical measurements of subatomic particles, for instance, position and momentum, cannot with accuracy be made simultaneously. Some commentators take this to imply more than the ambiguity of measurement in quantum mechanics, but as implying randomness. But if this is so, and if it is possible to apply this to human action, though it might allow for freedom, it could not account for free will.

Sartre agrees that there is no act without a cause. But freedom comes about through **nothingness**, for nihilation is freedom and human beings are nothing, are pure freedom. More than any other writer, Sartre emphasises the tendency of human beings to turn a blind eye to the freedom they possess. Yet he further claims the very denial of freedom can only come about from recognition of it. Still we try to ignore freedom by treating ourselves as though we were mere objects, hiding in our **bad faith**.

> Psychologically, in each one of us this amounts to trying to take the causes and motives as *things*. We try to confer permanence upon them. We attempt to hide from ourselves that their nature and their weight depend each moment on the meaning which I give to them; we take them for constants. (Sartre, 1943a: 440)

Thus we pretend to be something rather than nothing, and end up believing we are not free to change.

An earlier writer, **Berdyaev**, takes a similar position, arguing that to discuss freedom as if it were a question is to objectify it. Berdyaev argues that freedom cannot be an object for it is prior to existence, it is a condition of being.

Sartre is painfully aware that much of the human condition is contingent. But **choice** and action are seen as ways of transcending the **facticity** of one's situation. **Merleau-Ponty** complains that Sartre confuses choice and freedom, and that we do not always actively choose ourselves. He insists that while we have the capacity to choose, we often, through neglect or ignorance, let things happen.

In existential psychotherapy, the pursuit of freedom can emerge from seeing and accepting one's ability to choose, not necessarily in the heat of **emotion** (see **care**), but when we consider our choices.

> We are *true* through and through, and have with us, by the mere fact of belonging to the world, and not merely being in the world in the way that things are, all that we need to transcend ourselves. We need have no fear that our choices or actions restrict our liberty, since choice and action alone cut us loose from our anchorage. (Merleau-Ponty, 1945: 456)

See also **being-for-others; being-in-itself; coefficient of adversity; contingency; probability; transcendence**

Freud

Sigismund ('Sigmund') Schlomo Freud (1856–1939). Viennese founder of **psychoanalysis**, and an influence on **existential psychotherapy**, especially in *Daseinsanalysis*. Other references to his ideas can be found under: **Binswanger; Boss; consciousness/unconsciousness; countertransference; dreams; Lacan; phenomenology; project; projection; psychology; Schopenhauer; sublimation; will to power; Yalom; Zollikon Seminars.**

friendship

According to the pessimistic Danish philosopher **Kierkegaard**, friendship is something one must guard against, for although we sometimes wish another person to mean much to us, other human beings can only be in each other's way. Moreover, both romantic **love** and friendship reveal partiality, and are therefore an offence to the ideal of love. Worse still, love by one human for another is a disguised self-love, and we should consider whether there is a love that is not self-love. Only God deserves to be loved as much, and only in the love of God can there be salvation.

Sartre's view that 'Hell is other people' illustrates the challenge of being with others and puts into question what friendship may provide. However, in his later work, speaking of co-operation and **generosity**, Sartre's outlook is more positive.

See also **marriage; solitude**

future
See **time and temporality**

Gadamer

Hans-Georg Gadamer (1900–2002). A student and follower of **Heidegger**, but also influenced by **Dilthey** and **Husserl**. Author of *Truth and Method* (1960). His reputation rests on his teachings in **interpretation**, in particular his *reader-response theory*, the idea that the historical context of the reader is a crucial factor in the meaning of a text. Gadamer's work has had a wide influence, and has stimulated renewed interest in **hermeneutics**.

Gadamer's central thesis may be taken as saying that we cannot reconstruct the original meaning of a text – the author's intentions – because we have been **thrown** into a particular culture, and our ideas and means of inter-pretation are inevitably grounded in our historical milieu. There can be no neutral ground from which to understand human expression. Instead, we interrelate with a written text from the perspective of our own time. All inter-pretations are informed by prejudice or pre-judgements. There is thus no final and authoritative reading of a text, and there is no objective **truth**. Gadamer thus occupies a middle ground – relativism – between the subjectivism of Dilthey and the objectivism of Heidegger. This cultural relativism means that judgement of whether an interpretation is accurate or inaccurate can only be made by mutual agreement. Having rejected objectivity, Gadamer is opposed to subjectivism. He dislikes this in Dilthey's philosophy, and more especially in the writings of **Nietzsche**.

Understanding, for Gadamer, is socially constructed; it comes about in dialogue. Language is the medium in which **Being** manifests itself, so it is through conversation that we acquire **meaning**.

A psychotherapist using Gadamer's ideas would see her clients as essentially of their time, and would bear in mind that a person cannot create meaning alone, and cannot expect to find absolute and final meaning.

Gelassenheit

See **releasement**

gender

See **Beauvoir, de**

generosity

For **Sartre**, generosity derives from the pleasure of ownership. In offering a gift to another person, one is actually enjoying the satisfaction of possession. In the realm of literature, Sartre describes how writing and reading require a *pact of generosity*. Reader and author must each trust the other, for each needs the other. The writer generously provides his or her freedom of imagination, and the reader in turn offers his or her time and heart to bring it to life. Without this mutual generosity, literature could not live.

Since this is an account of narrative-telling, it might be compared (though Sartre does not make such a comparison) to psychotherapy, in which one person relates the **truth** of his or her life to a listener who provides attention and understanding. In this light, psychotherapy may be seen as an active partnership which thrives on the reciprocal nature of the exchange. The more the client gives of her **reality**, the more it is possible for the therapist to give her **totalisation** of the situation. The co-essentiality of the other is thus confirmed. We move from instrumentality (using the other as an object) to **praxis** and to relations of reciprocity instead of **seriality**, and this leads to feelings of solidarity.

> [E]very creation is a form of giving and cannot exist without this giving ... There is no other reason for being than this giving. And it is not just my work that is a gift. Character is a gift. The Me is the unifying rubric of our generosity. Even egoism is an aberrant gift. (Sartre, 1983: 129)

See also **Other, the**

Gestalt psychology

Gestalt psychology arose in Germany in the 1930s out of dissatisfaction both with behavioural psychology and **psychoanalysis**. Its main protagonists were the psychologists Wertheimer, Koffka and Köhler, who were inspired by **phenomenology**. As **science** in general was increasingly appreciating organisation in nature, so the Gestaltists argued for consideration of the whole. Whereas it was previously believed that in human perception the whole is built from the parts, Gestalt theorists believed the whole is grasped at once, and that perception is essentially organised. From this they argued that to understand human behaviour, the entirety of the individual in his environment needs to be considered as a whole.

Gestalt psychology later declined as a single approach, and its claims to have a physiological basis remain unproven, but its holistic approach was and remains highly influential. In psychotherapy it has directly influenced the formation of Gestalt psychotherapy and **client-centred psychotherapy**. And with its emphasis on interconnectedness, it has much in common with twentieth-century existential theorists like **Heidegger** and **Buber**. **Merleau–Ponty's** work leans heavily towards Gestalt psychology.

Ge-stell
See **enframing**

givens of existence
See **essence; facticity; limit situations; ontology**

God
See **absurd, the; alienation; anxiety; availability; Berdyaev; comprehensive, the; despair; Dostoevsky; existence; friendship; guilt; Kierkegaard; Levinas; love; sickness-unto-death; theology; Tillich**

God, death of
See **Nietzsche; nihilism**

good and evil
Discussions of the basis of morality often begin with this distinction, and the question: Is there intrinsic good and evil? For the religious thinker the answer will usually be affirmative. Good is seen to derive from what is godly and evil from what is not.

Many existential writers are reluctant to speak directly of good and evil, yet all promote certain **values** as intrinsically good, for instance, the recognition and exercise of **freedom**. **Nietzsche**, however, approaches the issue directly and forcibly:

> One knows my demand of philosophers that they place themselves *beyond* good and evil – that they have the illusion of moral judgement *beneath* them. This demand follows from an insight first formulated by me: that *there are no moral facts whatever.* (Nietzsche, 1889: 93)

Nietzsche offers an explanation for the use of the terms *good* and *evil* in a manner predating the attribution theory of modern social psychologists:

> What really are our reactions to the behaviour of someone in our presence? – First of all, we see what is in it for *us* ... We take this effect as the intention behind the behaviour – and finally we ascribe the harbouring of such intentions as a permanent quality of the person ... (Ibid.: 69)

Thus we erroneously conclude whether a person is essentially good or not. Nietzsche goes further, and in anthropological spirit, distinguishes between two uses of *good* and *evil*, from what he calls **master morality and slave morality**.

The modern **relativism** we are so familiar with results from this overthrow of the **absolute**, leading to the conclusion that *good* is no more than a term of approval, that a good thing is simply what is good in its own terms, instrumental to any given purpose, e.g. a good child, a good battle, a good cry, a good spanner, or a good painting, and that the terms *good* and *evil* apply only in relationship to what is of human advantage and disadvantage. Such a view easily results in an ethical **nihilism**. But Nietzsche is adamant that new values must be sought from which to judge what is good and what is evil.

See also **revaluation of values**

good faith
From **Sartre**. If **bad faith** is the tactical disbelief of what one believes, then good faith is full belief in one's beliefs. However, this is to fix the **world** and forget its possibilities.

> To believe is to know that one believes, and to know that one believes is to no longer believe. Thus to believe is not to believe any longer ... The ideal of good faith (to believe what one believes) is, like that of sincerity (to be what one is), an ideal of being-in-itself. (Sartre, 1943a: 69)

Thus good faith is a denial of **freedom**, and is actually another form of bad faith.

See also **being-in-itself; possibility**

good life, the
See *eudaimonia*

gravity, spirit of
See **laughter**

guilt
Guilt is the sense of having earned condemnation through transgression of the rules or through sinning. (Sin refers to being wrong, but it does not necessarily mean personal transgression.) Guilt and **shame** sometimes overlap, although most existential authors carefully distinguish the two. The discomfort of guilt may result in remorse, confession and reparation – or acceptance of punishment. Or it may result in self-deceptive denial. Yet the feeling of guilt is in itself no proof that one is guilty.

There are many different kinds of guilt, not always set apart: there is legal guilt and moral guilt, and of the latter there is individual guilt and collective guilt. Existential authors, especially when from Nordic or Germanic background, connect guilt with indebtedness, since the German word for guilt is *Schuld*, also meaning being in debt.

Kierkegaard holds to a version of collective guilt, or original sin, as well as recognising the inevitable potential for the transgressions of individuals. The **good** is but one thing (see **point of view**), and to be an individual is in itself sinful, evidence of separation from God.

Nietzsche gives a legal account of guilt as indebtedness. The guilty party is in debt to another. Nietzsche further believes that there is satisfaction in punishing.

The distinction between normal guilt, neurotic guilt and existential guilt can be found in several authors. **Boss** is known for distinguishing existential guilt from neurotic guilt. By his definition, normal guilt follows from an act that goes against the rules; neurotic guilt results from excessive preoccupation with an act that is not reprehensible but which one's parents might reject; whereas existential guilt is the experience of not having acted when one ought to have done so.

Existential guilt is also an idea from the philosophy of **Tillich** and has been taken up by his followers **May** and **Yalom**. Everyday guilt, according to Tillich, is a way of distracting us from our existential guilt, which is the fact of our estrangement from God.

Like Nietzsche, **Heidegger** makes use of the idea of debt. But Heidegger argues that there is in humankind a pre-ethical, primordial guilt, and that *Da-sein* is guilty because it is in the world in a state of incompleteness:

> [B]eing-guilty *does not result from an indebtedness, but the other way round: indebtedness is possible only 'on the basis' of a primordial being guilty* ... And that means that *Da-sein as such is guilty* if our formal existential definition of guilt as being-the-ground of a nullity is valid. (Heidegger, 1927b: 284–5)

Guilt is thus primordial and is a consequence of *Da-sein's* owing something to existence: *Da-sein* is such that there is always still something outstanding, something that needs to be completed in the future. Guilt is a fundamental state and it requires the **call of conscience** to pay attention to it and act on it. This is the key to **authenticity**.

The existential psychotherapist works with the discomfort of guilt by paying attention to what that discomfort reveals of the client's **values**.

See also **Bugental; falling; Frankl**

Habermas, Jürgen
See **Frankfurt School, the**

Haufniensis, Vigilius
Pseudonym used by **Kierkegaard** for *The Concept of Anxiety* (1844b).

Hegel
Georg Wilhelm Friedrich Hegel (1770–1831). German philosopher. An influence on many existential theorists. References to his philosophy can be found under: **alienation; becoming; dialectic; either/or; individual, the; Kierkegaard; love; master–slave dialectic; spirit.**

Heidegger
Martin Heidegger was born in Messkirch, Germany 26 September 1889, and died in Messkirch 26 May 1976.

Notable works: *The Concept of Time* (1924); *Being and Time* (1927); *An Introduction to Metaphysics* (1935); *The Question Concerning Technology and Other Essays* (1954a); *What Is Called Thinking?* (1954b); and *Zollikon Seminars* (1987).

Influenced by: Pre-Socratic philosophers (especially Parmenides); **Aristotle; Plato;** Duns Scotus; **Kant; Dilthey; Hölderlin; Kierkegaard;** and **Husserl.**

Influence on: **Boss; Binswanger; Sartre; Gadamer; Bultmann; Tillich; Derrida;** and **Merleau–Ponty**

Life: Heidegger's father was Sexton of the local Catholic Church, St Martin's and Martin's boyhood was spent in the small town of his birth, a quiet and conservative place. In 1909 he entered a Jesuit seminary, but left after a few weeks. In 1911 he enrolled on a philosophy course, and by 1916 was assistant to Husserl. He became Professor at Marburg in 1923, and then at Freiburg in 1928. From 1933–4 he was Rector at Freiburg University, and – as a National Socialist – gave his inaugural lecture on 'The Role of the University in the New Reich'. He renounced his allegiance to Husserl, at least publicly, and seemed to sympathise with much of Nazi ideology. He supported Hitler, and strove to make Freiburg University fit into the National Socialist order. Perhaps he was guilty of no more than political naïvety, believing that his romantic ideals met with those of the Nazis, for instance, that National Socialism was opposed to **technology**, but not all critics are able to forgive him. After the War he remained almost silent on his membership of the Nazi party, merely calling it a 'blunder'. He was at first forbidden to teach, and fell into some kind of emotional crisis, for which he was treated by the psychotherapist Medard **Boss**. In 1949 he was granted permission to teach, and gave seminars to Boss and his students (see **Zollikon Seminars**). All through his life he retained rustic ideals, and loved spending time walking in the Black Forest.

Major ideas: His philosophy is characterised by its concerns with fundamental problems. Because he is concerned with the significance of these ideas for social and interpersonal consequences, he at times seems a metaphysician, at others a political philosopher or a philosopher of morals. His principal concerns are with **Being, existence** and **time**, and what these mean to human beings.

Earlier European philosophers had usually been rationalists or idealists, believing in the capacity of the intellect to discover **truth**, or holding that **reality** is basically mental. But Kant had added to his **rationalism** a portion of *empiricism*, the idea that we are first informed through our senses, and not just from introspection (as, for example, **Descartes** believed). Like those before him, Kant believed that human beings share the same experience of the world, implying the possibility that general and universal truths are discoverable. But Heidegger, like **Nietzsche** and **Husserl**, rejects the applicability of general principles. For Heidegger, life and the mystery of existence cannot be explained, only experienced. Instead, he tries to formulate the fundamental ontological principles governing human experience.

Heidegger frequently complains that **philosophy** has stopped thinking, that it has greatly declined since the time of the Pre-Socratics. He declares, 'we must be ready to learn thinking' (Heidegger, 1954b: 369). And thinking, for Heidegger, is equivalent to *thanking*, in that it is an appreciation of the **world** for what it really is. Modern philosophy prefers logic and assertion to what Heidegger calls thinking – that is, making the effort to understand existence (or **Being** and the **Nothing**). If Husserl is interested in how we understand, Heidegger is concerned with how we *are*. He constantly pursues the most fundamental questions, the very most basic of which he claims has been overlooked by his predecessors in the past two thousand years of philosophy. In *What Is Metaphysics?*, he expresses it this way, explaining that the basic question of **metaphysics** is: 'Why are there beings at all, and why not rather nothing?' (Heidegger, 1929: 110). Parmenides had said we cannot speak of Nothing, but Heidegger has a passionate concern with the significance to the human spirit of the **possibility** of **nothingness**. According to Heidegger, the human spirit senses the potential to be Nothing, for there to be Nothing, and this impinges on and forms our very nature, our **essence**.

Heidegger's phenomenological investigations conclude that what differentiates human beings from other beings is that existence – or Being – is a fundamental and intrinsic concern for us. We are aware of our Being, we *care* about it. Thus Heidegger refers to human beings as *Da-sein* (or *Dasein*) – 'being-there' or 'being-in-the-world'. And this care runs through all his analyses of *Da-sein*. He also emphasises how time is an important fact to be considered in the analysis of what it means to be human, what it means to *be*. At any instant in our lives we are incomplete, there is always future potential, and a '*constant unfinished quality* thus lies in the essence of the constitution of Da-sein' (Heidegger, 1927b: 236).

We are all born into a world that is not of our making. In Heidegger's terms, *Da-sein* is **thrown** into the world, and we share our **fate** with all others. But our awareness of this may obscure the fact that nonetheless we possess **choice**. Such a misunderstanding, or psychological evasion, is referred to by Heidegger as inauthenticity, which is the way in which we initially are in the world, when we live our lives as though we were one of a mass of causally determined others. We fall into merely going with the flow, accepting received judgements, choosing according to habit, or social norms – what is done, what **They** do (e.g. to consider in any given situation, that this is what one *does*), and this **falling** with others means we have lost our humanity, or rather, that we have not yet fully gained it. To become capable of **authenticity**, we have to relinquish our tendency to shirk and evade reality and release ourselves from the **idle talk**, **curiosity** and **ambiguity** through which an inauthentic stance is perpetuated. It is when we allow ourselves to experience **anxiety** in the face of our essential nothingness and aloneness that we can achieve authenticity. Such anxiety (or *Angst*) illuminates the everyday quality of living when we are prepared to be aware of our mortality – this leads to the experience of **uncanniness**, *Unheimlichkeit*. Heidegger often refers to authenticity as a **resoluteness** in the face of death, or an anticipation of our ownmost potentiality-for-being-ourselves. It is the **call of conscience** that will wake us up to this possibility. We may suffer **guilt** at our lack of power over our past, but the call to conscience alerts us to become authentic, to see that peculiar mixture of freedom and constriction that is humankind's (or *Da-sein's*) lot. 'And to what is one summoned? To one's *own self*' (Heidegger, 1927b: 273).

Opinions differ not only on the value of Heidegger's ideas, but on their nature. Bertrand Russell perhaps typified the view of the British philosophical establishment of the mid-twentieth century in remarking of Heidegger's writing that in it there is 'psychological observation made to pass for logic' (Russell, 1959: 303). Existential thinkers may complain this fails to accept the close relation of **psychology** and philosophy, and that philosophy is not served merely by logic.

Contribution to psychotherapy: Heidegger's philosophy provides a model for how to live. It also offers an examination of what is wrong with modern life, for he is not neutral, and his passions are everywhere in evidence, for example, in his approval of authenticity, and his disapproval of the **technological attitude**. There are technical implications in his writing, for instance that our moods are a **disclosure** of our understanding of our existential position. Like Husserl, Heidegger's philosophy justifies a phenomenological approach, describing rather than explaining. There is also a thorough-going, if incomplete, explanation in his philosophy of human nature. Another important Heideggerian contribution to psychotherapy is his understanding of two different ways of being with others, either in a **leaping in** for the other or a **leaping ahead** of the other's possibilities, the latter being a help to the other in opening a new perspective.

Other Heideggerian and related entries: *Befindlichkeit*; **being-toward-death**; **being-with**; *existentiell*; **falling**; **freedom and free will**; **hermeneutics**; **Moment,** the; ontic; ontological/ontology; phenomenology; potentiality-for-being-oneself; turn/turning

herd, the

The mass of people, seen by **Nietzsche** as unthinking and cowardly. Most people find it easier to follow others and do what the herd does. This is similar to Kierkegaard's **crowd** and Heidegger's **They**. For Nietzsche, modern society has a **resentment** of the noble type of person, those free-thinking individuals who are strong and powerful, and who challenge convention. The herd instead responds by producing moral and religious constraints on the noble man, and in this way mediocrity triumphs over nobility. That the weak have their own interests would not be so bad if they did not spoil the potential of the master spirit with the imposition of their self-serving rules. But it is as if sheep had tamed lions through their sheer numerical superiority.

In a Nietzschean-based **psychotherapy**, an analysis of the patient's unexamined **values** should result in a **revaluation of values**, and a rejection of unexamined moral codes in favour of individual thought and decision-making. The individual would instead consult his or her ideas, instincts, aesthetic passions – the entirety of their **self**, physical and mental – before judging how to act. This does not mean selfishness, but rather, a more personal and deliberate decision-making.

According to Nietzsche, just as Christianity has a dislike of the **body**, and makes it subservient to the mind, so the herd dislikes instinct and **passion**, preferring obedience and formulaic living. The Nietzschean **philosophy** integrates what the herd, in its fearfulness, has made disparate. In this way, it is a movement from **no-saying** to **yes-saying**.

heritage

See *Erbe*; **history; legacy; repetition**

hermeneutics

Originally, the theory of interpreting the Bible, later broadened to all texts, and since **Dilthey** to the understanding and **interpretation** of the psychology and works of humankind, including art, history, **philosophy** and religion, as well as the individual's state-of-mind.

Friedrich Schleiermacher believed that through sympathetic reading a person could come to understand a text as well or better than the author, providing use is made of the *hermeneutic circle*, that is, by looking at the parts of a text, then the text as a whole, then with better understanding to reconsider the parts, then to reconsider the whole, and so on. Following Schleiermacher, Dilthey concerned himself with the subjective states of others. But **Heidegger** took hermeneutics to another level, investigating the being who interprets, *Da-sein*. Heidegger's efforts are to make explicit what is actually present but unnoticed, to cast light on human **existence** and through an examination of *Da-sein* to explore the nature of **Being**. But while Dilthey attends to the subjective, Heidegger believes it is possible to uncover objective **truth**.

Hermeneutics is a distinct kind of interpretation, an analysis of what is present rather than a search for what in unconsciousness (see **consciousness and**

unconsciousness) is symbolised by a word or image. It assumes that whilst not everything is immediately visible, everything that can be known is already present. Mere semantic analysis is not sufficient, for it ignores the context of an expression, and it ignores the intention of the author of that expression. In the field of aesthetics, there is a perennial debate whether a work of art should be judged against the artist's intentions or treated as a found item, to be judged by its independent value (for instance, whether an unintended joke is a joke). In a hermeneutic form of psychotherapy, care is taken not to pursue theoretically *possible* meanings; instead, the client and therapist work together to disclose what *is* there. And although in contemporary **psychoanalysis**, the patient is treated very much as a text to be understood, in **existential psychotherapy**, the patient and his expressions are seen not in isolation, but always and only in relation to the **world**.

See also **Gadamer; phenomenology; Ricoeur**

history

Existential philosophers are generally opposed to the notion of history as a factual account of the past. While it is the lives and accomplishments of human beings that are the subject-matter of history, it is human beings who are the historians. The observer – the historian – is necessarily within the field of study, and can never be outside it. For instance, Jean-Paul **Sartre**, in his *Critique of a Dialectical Reason*, argues that we use **totalisation** to summarise what we retain from personal or world history. A history is always a subjective account, and only one of many possible accounts of events.

Like **Kierkegaard** before him, **Nietzsche** sees history as a process of diluting and spoiling great, noble and passionate ideas. He distinguishes between three types of history:

1   *Monumental history* depicts the past as a series of great persons and great actions. This kind of history may be inspirational, but it is false, and an absorption with it can be an avoidance of the present.
2   *Antiquarian history* reveres the past with little concern for the present.
3   *Critical history*, on the other hand, examines and judges the past.

Nietzsche emphasises that a concern with history may be instructive, but may hide the fact that it is in the present that action is required and the past overturned.

Ortega argues that the history of humankind is an account of human beliefs, but that human history reveals the error of living by reason. We are freer than reason and **science** suggest, free to create our own lives. And he argues that although the past is fixed, this should not be taken as evidence of fixedness in human nature.

Heidegger objects to history being regarded as a sequence of events, and argues that it is actually about possibilities, those possibilities derived from our heritage. He further argues that in this way history is primarily a concern with the future. As *tradition*, history is an account of the past that we make our own and that we carry forward, preserve and renew. Individuals tend to live their history either in an inauthentic way by **forgetting**, or in an authentic way by **repetition**. Philosophers need to look critically at these traditions and deconstruct them in order to become authentically historical.

See also *amor fati*; **authenticity and inauthenticity; eternal return; legacy; possibility; praxis; repetition; time and temporality; transference**

hodological space

Explanations of human behaviour often suppose the central significance of personality or instinct – that is, of inner predispositions to act in certain ways. The existential approach differs in viewing human beings as always in active relation to the **world**, so that explanation of human actions cannot derive merely from what is intrapsychic. Some writers provide specific holistic descriptions of the way in which the individual is always and necessarily in a dynamic **situation** (see for instance Kurt Lewin's 1935 *Dynamic Theory of Personality*, and his discussions of *life space*). **Sartre** makes similar use of the notion of hodological space. *Hodos* being Greek for *path*, and hodology a branch of geometry, the notion of hodological space as applied to human behaviour is a borrowing of the mathematical notion of vectors, of forces operating in a direction, or path. A person's space may thus be described in relation to his or her instrumental needs, and the hierarchy of those needs, but also importantly in relation to the possibilities open to the person and the constrictions currently limiting their freedom of movement. In the pursuit of a **project**, a person finds his way through the life space and traces his own particular pathway.

Sartre takes this idea and integrates this into a theory of **emotions**. He argues that rational life recognises hodological space, but that when our hodological plans are frustrated, we frequently deceive ourselves, and instead of facing ourselves in our situations, we employ the seemingly magical transforming power of emotion to overcome our obstacles.

Hölderlin

(Johann Christian) Friedrich Hölderlin (1770–1843). German poet, whose intensely subjective poetry was inspired by the cultures of ancient Greece and Rome, as well as by Christian ideals. His genius was unrecognised in his lifetime, and he struggled financially. Like **Kierkegaard**, Hölderlin rejected common conceptions of happiness, describing pleasure as merely tepid water. And he seems to have foreseen that his life would be tragic. He was greatly inspired by a passionate though Platonic relationship with his employer's beautiful and highly intelligent wife, Susette Gontard, but she died in 1802, and Hölderlin soon became quite mad, and wrote little more. Hölderlin provided a poetry for an impoverished time, after the departure of the gods and before the arrival of a new god. He was a visionary, who saw himself as resembling Oedipus, having an eye too many to survive in a sane manner.

Hölderlin's poetry was an inspiration to **Nietzsche** and a fascination for **Heidegger**, whose own philosophical style changed (see **turn/turning**) from the technical to the poetic as he came to see **Being** as not only mysterious but inexpressible in ordinary **language**. Heidegger claimed that poetry (*Dichtung*) is **ontological**: through the use of words it somehow establishes Being. He quotes from Hölderlin's 'The Celebration of Peace':

> Much, from morning onward,
> Since we became a conversation and hear from one another,
> Have human beings undergone; but soon (we) will be song.

Then he remarks:

> Language was once called the 'house of Being'. It is the guardian of presenc-
> ing, inasmuch as the latter's radiance remains entrusted to the propriative
> showing of the saying. Language is the house of Being because, as the saying,
> it is propriation's mode. (Heidegger, 1959: 424)

See also *Ereignis*; **presence**

homelessness
See **alienation; numbing; uncanniness**

Hoogendijk, Ad
See **philosophical counselling and consultancy**

horizon
See **ecstasy**

horizontalisation
See **phenomenology**

humanistic psychology
Humanistic psychology began in the United States in the 1950s and 1960s as
a reaction against the then prevailing psychological paradigms of behavioural
psychology and **psychoanalysis**, each of which favoured a causal **determinism**. To assert its significance, it was dubbed by Abraham Maslow as the *third
force*. Along with Maslow, its originators included Gordon Allport, George
Kelly, Rollo **May** and Carl **Rogers**.

Previously, behaviourists had judged subjective experience to be utterly
unreliable, possessing no scientific validity, but these new writers emphasised
the significance of subjectivity and its usefulness for the psychological inves-
tigator. And as distinct from what they saw as the pessimism of psychoanalysis, they affirmed the human potential for growth. Thus it was that they saw
their duty as the encouragement of human development. Maslow and Rogers,
for example, rejected explanations of human behaviour as deriving from and
limited by social norms. The psychotherapies that developed from this kind
of thinking stress the importance of human **encounter**, and are opposed to a
technical, manual-driven approach, although in general perhaps less opposed
than existential-phenomenological therapy. Another difference between the
humanistic approach and a fundamentally existential approach is the view of
the self. Whereas for humanists this is seen as an important entity, needing

to be developed to its full potential, existential philosophers generally consider the self to be an illusion.

Humanistic psychologists believe their approach has had a modifying effect upon mainstream psychology and psychoanalytical thinking. This may be so, but cultural changes – of which humanistic psychology is but one – have certainly softened the previously hard determinism of the sciences in general. And, whilst it may not be true of all humanistic psychologists, there has been a strong tendency in humanistic psychology to emphasise the triumphant and ignore the tragic. Perhaps this is because the cultural background to the movement was post-war America, with its immense self-belief in the power of the individual to overcome opposition. **Nietzsche** may rightly be seen as a forefather of humanistic psychology, but in his writing there is both optimism and pessimism, a holistic acceptance of the creative and the destructive, the **will to power**, and contradiction and **paradox**.

There are a number of therapies that identify themselves as existential-humanistic, including Gestalt psychotherapy and some Californian-based forms of humanistic **existential psychotherapy**.

Husserl

Edmund Husserl was born in Prossnitz, Moravia (then part of the Austrian Empire), on 8 April 1859, and died in Freiburg im Breisgau, Germany in April 1938.

Notable works: *Philosophy of Arithmetic* (1891); *Logical Investigations* (1900); *Ideas* (1913); *Cartesian Meditations* (1928); *Formal and Transcendental Logic* (1929); and *The Crisis of European Sciences and Transcendental Phenomenology* (1938).

Influenced by: **Brentano**.

Influence on: Early existentialists, especially **Heidegger** and **Merleau–Ponty**.

Life: Born into a middle-class Jewish family, Husserl received a secular education. He studied astronomy, mathematics and philosophy at the University of Leipzig, gaining a doctorate in mathematics in 1881. He then moved to Vienna, where for two years he attended lectures by Brentano, and made the decision to devote himself to philosophy. Indeed, it is this devotion to philosophy that characterises his life, for philosophy became a vocation to him, in which he placed his hopes and the value of his life. His whole endeavour was always to investigate the most fundamental, the most essential, to question everything, even his own conclusions. Thus, it was with a sense of contrary pride that he described himself as 'a perpetual beginner'. But though he liked to examine matters from many perspectives, he disagreed with the perspective taken by an early assistant of his, Martin **Heidegger**.

Husserl married and had three children. Like his Jewish-born wife, he became a Christian. In 1933 the Nazis came to power and life became difficult. He worked extremely hard, and sometimes suffered spells of depression. He left unfinished or incomplete much of his research, some 45,000 manuscript pages. After his death, his manuscripts were hidden, for fear the Nazis would destroy them. His widow hid in a convent until the end of the war. Husserl's assistant, Edith Stein, died in a concentration camp.

Major ideas: Husserl disputed the empiricist belief that knowledge comes only from direct observation, and one of his most important ideas is that of **intuition** (*Wesenschau*). It is not clear precisely what he meant by this, but in general terms it refers to apprehending what is evident, not merely what is perceived through the senses, but for instance the self-evident truths of logic or arithmetic and the presence of another being.

Husserl regarded **philosophy** as a **science**, a science more exact and reliable than natural science, and his ambition was for philosophy to uncover the fundamental and objective truths on which all other truths are dependent, thus gaining what he called the 'Archimedean point' (as Archimedes had claimed that with a lever and the right place to stand, he could move the world). If modern science attempts to overcome and replace subjective experience, so Husserl believes it should reveal the already present **truth**.

Husserl claims that scientific knowledge is comprehensible only if we first understand the *Lebenswelt* – the **lived world**. He argues that even the objective truths of arithmetic and logic must be grounded in human experience. In *Logical Investigations*, an essay on inconsistency in logic and mathematics, he writes of **phenomenology** as a way to explore the origins of knowledge through looking at the phenomena of **consciousness**, a return to the things themselves (*Zu den Sachen selbst*, a phrase he used again and again), and to see how the **world** is an experience first, and only then an object. Thus, living proceeds **knowing** (compare this with **Sartre's** dictum that **existence precedes essence**); that is, we have experiential relationships with the world before we objectify our experience. But the subjective and objective perspectives are not contradictory, for they are inseparable. Consciousness is always of the world. This idea contrasts with the notion that consciousness is mere self-awareness. Instead, consciousness reaches out to the world and this **intentionality** means that a person is always a **being-in-the-world**.

Husserl's method is phenomenological, intending to avoid the errors of realism and **idealism**, and he argues that immediate meaning arises from interaction between the intentional mind and the world. Husserl was passionately opposed to what he called *the natural attitude* – the use of the natural sciences to understand human consciousness. Thus, his objection to **psychology** is its aspiration to the natural attitude. Husserl holds that psychology tries to objectify that which cannot be objectified, namely, consciousness. Psychologists believe their abstractions are neutral, but such abstractions are already interpretations. Psychologists are naïve realists, assuming an objectivity they do not possess.

What distinguishes the mental from the physical is, according to Husserl, that mental phenomena contain an object intentionally within them. In this way Husserlian phenomenology is opposed to the common supposition that the human mind is a passive receptor of meaningless sense-data.

Critics of Husserl hold that his method relies only on intuition, and that he rejects theory and hypothesis, so that his ideas are untestable. Some critics say he takes a Platonic line (see **Plato**), that knowledge requires seeing things as they are, and that his intuition is mere certainty of belief, of self-conviction. They also claim any supposed transcendental domain cannot be observed (because it is transcendental). But Husserl believes we can grasp **Being** directly through intuition. If psychology is concerned with mental processes as objective facts, then phenomenology is concerned with what is essential in things – and such things need not even exist. From individual experiences, according to Husserl, it is possible to contemplate general essences (Wesenschau).

Phenomenology concentrates on subjective experience. It is uncertain where this leaves the experiencing of others, of other egos, and his philosophy risks **solipsism**. It is also uncertain where this leaves the existential therapist who wants to understand his client, for it cannot be through direct experience. For Husserl, it is through empathy that we intuit the other's experience, just as from particular experiences we intuit general truths.

Contribution to psychotherapy: Husserl's **phenomenological method** of questioning prejudices and assumptions is an essential foundation for existential practice.

Intentionality, as Husserl uses it, says all thought, all conscious experience, is a reaching out to what is or could be in the world. It is, in this way a refutation of the psychoanalytic notion of the unconscious, for it says that all mental processes are conscious, though they may not be clearly seen by the thinker.

I
See **identity; self**

I and Thou
See **Buber**; I–Thou

ideal self
See **congruence**

idealism

Philosophical view that emphasises the significance of ideas or which considers mind (or soul or spirit) to be the most fundamental principle. Coined originally by Leibniz, the term has been used in a variety of ways, so making its relationship to existential philosophy uncertain. By *ideas*, some philosophers mean mental representation; some mean what is spiritual; some (like **Plato**), mean what is ideal. Whatever it is, idealism is certainly opposed to *materialism*, the view that everything can be reduced to the physical (for instance, that all thoughts are reducible, with no loss of meaning, to brain processes). But whilst Berkeley famously pressed the doctrine to its logical extreme, seeming to say that nothing exists but perceptions, other idealist philosophers have merely emphasised the unreliability of sense-data, arguing that we cannot be certain of the physical world, but only of our sensations.

In general, then, idealism promotes the fundamental importance of subjective experience. **Schopenhauer** holds that there can be no object without a subject; existential philosophy in effect adds that there can be no subject without an object, that **Being** is always located in the **world**. Existential philosophy is commonly taken to be opposed to idealism. But when idealism is defined as no more than an emphasis on sense-perception, it is less easy to be sure of the opposition. **Sartre's** work was clearly based in historical materialism, but **Heidegger's** later work has distinct idealist tendencies.

See also **Descartes; mind–body problem; rationalism; solipsism**

identity

Usually defined as those personal features, or personality, that continue over time in the face of outward changes. Human beings exist in **time**, and are subject to change. Our bodies, our behaviour, our attitudes towards life, all may alter. And it is difficult to say how we retain our identity despite what might be radical transformations. Philosophically, this matters because if an individual's identity is not constant, then assigning entitlement and **responsibility** is difficult. The woman who yesterday murdered her husband in a fit of vengeful passion cannot be held responsible if she no longer exists, because the now bewildered woman in the police cell is not the same woman. And if our nature is fixed, if our inheritance or personality is unchanging, then we have little or no **freedom** with which we can be accountable. But perhaps there is something about us that remains constant, that provides us with a continuous **self**. Some writers think so, and suggest that the continuity is our soul; others suggest the **body**, or mind, or personality, or (as Locke argues) **consciousness**. Existential theorists tend to say it is that we maintain our **existence** and therefore have to take responsibility for how we maintain this.

For **Sartre** it is **bad faith** to consider oneself as possessing a personality. It is false, for we are always ourselves choosing to be ourselves. The identities people adopt are therefore no more than games they play in order to give themselves a sense of solidity, something which is ultimately illusory. **Heidegger** writes of *mineness* (*Jemeinigkeit*), by which he means that we are always ourselves and nobody else and that in **authenticity** one accepts ownership of one's own **Being**, and takes **care** of it: 'The being which this being is concerned about in its being is always my own' (Heidegger, 1927b: 42). This is quite different from having an identity. Indeed, according to Heidegger, our selfhood is initially defined by the **They**, or the *They-self*, which shows *Dasein* to be taken over by the world of other people. It is only gradually that a self can be extracted from this absorption in the They.

All this is pertinent to the field of psychotherapy, where identity is invariably an issue, either directly or by implication. Issues of identity may often be founded on misunderstanding of what a self is.

idle talk

From the German *Gerede*. Sometimes translated as *chatter*. **Heidegger** uses this term to describe an everyday aspect of *Dasein's* inauthentic being. Like **ambiguity** and **curiosity** it is an aspect or a phase of **fallenness**, but Heidegger emphasises it is not a term of disparagement. It is however an inauthentic form of discourse:

> Idle talk is the possibility of understanding everything without previously making the thing one's own. If this were done, idle talk would founder; and it already guards against such a danger. Idle talk is something which anyone can rake up; it not only releases one from the task of genuinely understanding, but develops an undifferentiated kind of intelligibility, for which nothing is closed off any longer. (Heidegger, 1927a: 169)

See also **authenticity and inauthenticity; discourse; language; possibility; reticence; They, the; undifferentiated**

I–It
See I–Thou/I–You

illusion
See **bad faith**

imagination
In *The Psychology of Imagination* (1936a), **Sartre** opposes the idea that imagination is much like **perception**, being different only in that it produces mental pictures that are unusually lively and colourful. Instead, with his characteristic concern with **nothingness**, he argues that imagination is an aspect of **consciousness** in which **intentionality** is directed towards what is not. Imagination thus creates an alternative view of the **world**, a way of negating what *is*.

I–Me
See **I–Thou/I–You**

immediacy
As used by **Kierkegaard**, this means a lack of reflection, and a reliance instead on instinct or aesthetic sense. He claims that people are originally immediate in their relation to the **world**, that is, without mediation by reflecting, and with no sense of the infinite (see **finite and infinite**). There is thus at first an *immediate man*, someone like a child, naïve and unquestioning, who judges by appearance. Later on we become capable of a more reflective attitude, one which leads to the recognition of different stages of life.

Contrast with **introversion; reflection.**

implosion
See **Laing**

inauthenticity
See **authenticity**

in-between
See **encounter**

incongruence
See **congruence**

indebtedness
See **guilt**

indeterminacy principle
See **freedom and free will**

indifference

Heidegger argues that *Dasein* must choose to live in **authenticity** or inauthenticity, and claims that it arises in its **everydayness** from a state of neutrality, or indifference (*Indifferenz*). Indifference is the first state that *Dasein* finds itself in, from which authenticity and inauthenticity arise. This is not unlike **Kierkegaard's immediacy**.

Sartre uses the term differently in regard to his theory of human relations, as described in *Being and Nothingness*. He claims that human beings may relate to others in a sadistic and dominant fashion, in a masochistic or submissive manner, or by withdrawing into indifference.

See also **masochism; sadism**

individual, the

Kierkegaard rebels against philosophies like those of **Hegel**, where human beings are seen as the product of a culture, incapable of **transcendence**. For Kierkegaard, this is both a logical and a moral error. The proper basis for **philosophy** is the *existing individual*, who constitutes him or herself through **choice**. Kierkegaard believes it is vital for each human being to claim the right to become a true individual and to stand out from the **crowd**.

Existential philosophy in general tends to examine the individual, for it is the individual who experiences. In the early philosophy of **Sartre**, there is an individualistic position, but later, reflecting Sartre's embracing of Marxism, his philosophy takes a more socially based stance.

individuation

This refers to any situation in which an entity or a reality is constituted as a singular member of a species.

Carl **Jung** uses this term for the task a person faces in middle age of developing a sense of individuality, of personal distinctness. **Heidegger** uses the term in a similar but more complex and philosophical way when he describes how **anxiety** discloses the separateness of the individual:

Angst reveals in Da-sein its *being toward* its ownmost potentiality of being, that is, *being free for* the freedom of choosing and grasping itself. (Heidegger, 1927b: 188)

When a person – *Da-sein* – sees and accepts their essential isolation, they must necessarily see and accept that they have responsibility for their **identity** and their life. Accepting personal individuality also means that the **existence** of the **world** is highlighted, and that it is both distinct and yet always there in relationship to *Da-sein*, and that *Da-sein* is related to the world not as one of a mass (the **They**), but as an individual.

See also **authenticity and inauthenticity; identity; individual, the**

infinite

See **finite and infinite, finitude and infinitude**

initial choice
See **project**

insanity
See **Foucault; Laing; Szasz**

insecurity, ontological
See **Laing**

intentionality
This concept originated with **Aristotle**, and continued in use into the Middle Ages. In the nineteenth century, **Brentano** revived the concept of intentionality or *directedness* as the defining characteristic of **consciousness**, arguing that as thought has content so consciousness is always *of* something. Examples include wishes, beliefs, desires and feelings. Brentano contends that all mental states and only mental states are intentional.

Husserl further developed the idea, arguing that we are conscious through our intentionality, our reaching-out towards the **world**. He adds that the object reached for need not exist in reality, but may as well be an illusion or a fancy. This was his justification for the techniques of **phenomenology**, for he held that consciousness cannot be gauged from objective measurement, from treating it as just another thing.

For Husserl, intentionality overcomes the subject–object dichotomy, the Cartesian division between mind and the world (see **Descartes**). **Heidegger** attempts to apply the concept of intentionality to human beings through a description of human beings as *Da-sein*. His analysis of **Being** is intended to demonstrate how the sentient being is always involved with and inseparable from the world.

However, physical acts and perceptions are arguably more basic than mental acts, and Heidegger diverges from earlier philosophers, those who take intentionality as a quality only of the mind, and instead speaks of the embodiment of experience and argues that action too is intentional. **Merleau-Ponty** further emphasises the significance of the **body**, describing how in everyday life we physically reach out to things and thus connect with the world.

Intentionality, then, is a reaching-out of consciousness. It implies that consciousness is always reaching-out to something, to objects or states. It is in this way that the existential thinker sees human beings as essentially in relation (see **relationship**), never separable from the world. And it shows the distinction between **subject and object** is untenable. We are always partial, always participating in our world. Objectivity, neutrality and isolation are impossible.

But intentionality is not conscious will. Indeed, one's conscious intentions and one's intentionality may be at odds. So it is that intentionality may be an important focus of investigation in **existential psychotherapy**. The existential therapist may use the concept of intentionality in a like manner to the way the psychoanalyst uses the notion of the unconscious, except that intentionality is in principle directly discoverable, whereas the psychoanalytic unconscious is not. But in the consulting room similar means might be used. For instance, **May** recommends free association in order to reveal the patient's intentionality.

See also **pre-reflexive consciousness**

interhuman, the

(*Das Zwischenmenschliche*). Also translated as *the in-between*. According to **Buber**, the interhuman is the **I–Thou** relationship between two people as distinct from human–nature, human–art, or human–God; and it is present to some extent in all person–person relating. Some existential thinkers, for instance, **Sartre**, argue that the human individual is always trying to make an object of the **Other**, but Buber believes that this is neither desirable nor possible. This is not for psychological reasons, for the interhuman is not merely a psychological process but is the confronting of one person by another, the unfolding of which Buber calls the *dialogical*. People are often false, but sometimes a person may be *authentic*, may grant another a 'share in his being' (Buber, 1965: 67). On such an occasion, the authentic person can accept and affirm and be aware of others for what they are, without reduction or abstraction. Thus it is to perceive another's wholeness as a person, and is absolutely unlike objective analysis, for it reveals the uniqueness of the other:

> [W]e must develop in ourselves [what some call] intuition ... I prefer the name 'imagining the real', for in its essential being this gift is not a looking at the other, but a bold swinging – demanding the most intensive stirring of one's being – into the life of the other. (Ibid.: 71)

See also **congruence; dialogue; encounter; relationship**

interpretation

In psychotherapy in general this is the explanation or the process of explaining the deeper significance of the client's words, experiences or actions. In **psychoanalysis** it is an account offered by the therapist to the patient, explaining the symbolic meaning of the patient's words or actions in relation to their unconscious wishes. And the object of this provision of insight into the patient's unconscious processes is to promote integration of the patient's **self**.

A major objection to this kind of interpretation is that it is based on unproven theory, that it may be an imposition of an alien perspective onto the patient's experience, and that it is authoritarian. Such interpretations might be misleading, and could disable the patient rather than give them greater understanding. This sort of interpretation depends on the notion of the unconscious and the concurrent belief that the analyst or therapist has a privileged access to it.

Therapists whose theories dispense with the notion of the Unconscious (see **consciousness/unconsciousness**) will take a different approach to interpretation. The existential or phenomenological counsellor or therapist will not see words or behaviour as symbols from a hidden unconscious. Nor will they assume that rational errors are to blame for psychological distress. They will instead investigate the things themselves – that is, the perceptions of the client of these things (whilst being aware that all perceptions are interpretations of experience). The therapist will use descriptive or hermeneutic interpretations, working with the client to examine their experiences, philosophically and psychologically, to illuminate the fuller extent of their meanings, their ramifications and their consequences. The existential-phenomenological therapist will not allege that overt meanings have covert significance, but will stay within the client's framework of **meaning**. It is the client's worldview, not that of the therapist, that is the focus of attention. Rather than the closing down of experience through definitive interpretation, the object is to understand and open up the client's experience.

See also **ambiguity; apophantic speech; dreams; hermeneutics; intuition; understanding**

interrogation
See **cipher**

intersubjectivity
To understand others as more than objects is both a practical and a theoretical problem. As **phenomenology** deals with the experience of the individual by close investigation of the individual's experience, so it leaves unanswered how an individual can know the experiences of others. Perhaps it is through empathy (*Einfühlung*), as **Jaspers** has argued. Empathy, which is central to the practice of **client-centred psychotherapy,** is the subjective experiencing inspired by the expressions of another person. We apprehend the internal states of others by comparison with the **knowledge** we possess of our own experience. Our personal history of experiencing is the prototype from which we derive this secondary experiencing. The question will always remain as to the reliability of such apprehensions. Two people may agree on the loudness, softness, attractiveness, or painfulness of a phenomenon, but this does not prove the accuracy of their intersubjective knowledge. **Scheler** uses the term *fellow-feeling* to indicate the notion of intersubjectivity, and he argues that this is the way we establish and maintain our mutuality with others. In his later work **Sartre** recognises that reciprocity is an important principle for good human relationships, so as to overcome the competitiveness of seriality. **Marcel** makes intersubjectivity an important part of his explanation of human relations. **Husserl** and **Merleau-Ponty** take the view that human beings are essentially inter-related and never separate. The community we are a part of is as important as our individuality.

See also **being-with; encounter; individual, the**

intertwining
See **Merleau-Ponty**

introversion
Søren **Kierkegaard** uses this term to mean a withdrawal from the **world**, a withdrawal that is both the result of and an encouragement to reflection. So it is a form of introspection, and actively opposed to **immediacy**, the unquestioning immersion in everyday experience. And it may carry with it **despair**, for it is:

a real door though kept carefully closed, and behind it the self sits, as it were, keeping watch on itself, preoccupied or filling time with not wanting to be itself, yet still self enough to love itself. (Kierkegaard, 1849: 94)

This introversion is founded upon a self-perception of weakness, but it is also a kind of pride. It may, says Kierkegaard, be unbearable for the sufferer to unburden his heart to another, and doing so may only increase his despair. If Kierkegaard is right, this raises awkward questions for the psychotherapist.

Carl **Jung** uses the term introversion in opposition to extraversion, to indicate a tendency to be withdrawn into oneself rather than outgoing. This distinction formed an important part of his personality theory and was taken up by psychologists.

intuition

From Latin *intueor*, meaning to look at or scrutinise. For **Husserl**, this does not refer to a guess, a hunch or any kind of parapsychological process, but the action of gaining **knowledge** without the intervening use of inference. This is not mystical or mysterious. It is immediate apprehension of what is immanent. Indeed, Husserl, for whom intuition is the foundation of the practice of **phenomenology**, saw himself as a radical empiricist. Following **Kant**'s belief that sensations, **space** and **time** are known intuitively, he argued that essential intuition is possible, that essences (such as mathematical and logical conclusions) can be known at once, without inference or calculation. He referred to this as *Wesenschau*, the direct observation of essences. To intuit in this way requires a bracketing of the world and oneself (as **Descartes** had done earlier), for to reach certain knowledge requires the phenomenological approach to question all presuppositions. One can then see the **essence** or givenness of a **phenomenon**, and because there has been no mediation by the intellect, such knowledge is incorrigible.

Husserl's phenomenology rather resembles **Plato**'s theory of Forms (or Ideas), in which worldly objects and qualities are said to more-or-less resemble an ideal perfection, so that from what we see we can deduce ultimate reality. The difference is that for **Husserl**, phenomena are in the real world, part of human experience.

Heidegger, however, did not share Husserl's aspiration to such an abstract and scientific phenomenology. From his study of Aristotelian philosophy, Heidegger intended instead to study **Being** through the **interpretation** of what is intuited by *Dasein*. This is possible, according to Heidegger, because *Dasein*, being constituted of Being, has an innate understanding of Being.

Sartre offers a psychological perspective when he agrees with much of what Husserl says but argues that intuition is knowledge that requires the use of inferences, processes of deduction which are at once effaced. And Heidegger, with his notion of things being **ready-to-hand**, argues that we grasp at once the significance of a useful object. One sees a hammer as a hammer, not as an inexplicable long piece of smooth wood attached to a block of steel. And if intuition can be of things that human beings have made functional, that – like hammers and nails – have no essence except that thrown onto them by *Dasein*, our intuitions and our Being must be inseparable. It is for this reason that Heidegger insists that *Dasein* has and knows the nature of Being.

Husserl's views on intuition are accepted by few people today, because his conclusions are generally unacceptable. For instance, he assumes that what is immanent to one person will be the same for another. For the purposes of pure research this is problematic, but for the very personal research that is phenomenological psychotherapy, it is not so, as there is no pursuit of universal **truth**. Another criticism of Husserl's theory comes from **Derrida** who insists that Husserl is wrong to assume language is logical and fails to see that it can be symbolic or loaded with cultural meaning. But again, and for the same reason, this does not present difficulties for the psychotherapist.

For those who take heed of post-Husserlian ideas on intuition, care must be taken over what seems evident, over what appears to be obvious, whether it is the therapist monitoring his or her own mental processes or assisting the patient or client to examine theirs. For all intuitions contain suppositions. That these suppositions are rich with **meaning** is the very stuff of psychotherapy.

See also **interhuman, the**

Irigaray

Luce Irigaray (born 1939). Belgian feminist philosopher. Trained at Louvain, she took her Doctorate at the University of Paris, published as *Speculum of the Other Woman* (1974). She trained as a Lacanian analyst, but devised her own theory of feminist psychology, concerned with the repression of female sexuality and the difference between male and female experience. Ten years after her first work, *An Ethics of Sexual Difference* (1984) was published. Her work is generally considered to be post-structural, though some see her contribution as existential in nature.

irony

Much of the philosophy of **Kierkegaard** is written ironically. Indeed, his first publication was entitled *The Concept of Irony*. Borrowing from and further adapting the **Socratic method**, Kierkegaard writes first from one position, then another, sometimes pseudonymously attacking his own writing. His intention is partly to bring his opponents out into the open, so as to reveal their inconsistencies or hypocrisy. His other reason is one of fairness, to look at his own position objectively, and to use *empathy* to understand the subjectivity of his opponents' positions. This is similar to Socratic irony, where the philosopher affects ignorance in order to draw out knowledge and wisdom from the other. Kierkegaard speaks of mastered irony as an objective of life: to be able to be both at one with oneself and have sufficient distance, what he calls subjective objectivity.

irresoluteness

See **resoluteness**

I–Thou/I–You

This is a particular and profound kind of **relationship**, prefigured in a variety of writers, including the nineteenth-century German philosopher Ludwig Feuerbach, who writes of the incompleteness of the individual human being, which he believed was shown in sexual differentiation. As woman calls for man, and man calls for woman, so the I calls for a Thou. Later, Gabriel **Marcel** writes of how we may treat another as a He and so make him no more than an object. But, says Marcel, if we value another's **freedom**, then we should treat him as a Thou and help to free him.

But it is with Martin **Buber** that the idea is developed and promoted to the very foundation of a full **philosophy** and **theology**. Buber writes of the twofold nature of man. He argues that man dichotomises or splits; that he is inclined to treat his relationships with other mortal beings, and even with immortal God, in the same detached way that he treats inert things:

> In the It-world causality holds unlimited sway. Every event that is either perceivable by the senses and 'physical' or discovered or found in introspection and 'psychological' is considered to be of necessity caused and a cause ... [This] is of fundamental importance for the scientific ordering of nature, [and] is not felt to be oppressive by the man who is not confined to the It-world but free to step out of it again and again into the world of relation. Here I and You confront each other freely in a reciprocity that is not involved in or tainted by any causality; here man finds guaranteed the freedom of his being and of being. (Buber, 1923/1957: 100)

In an I–Thou (*Ich–Du*, sometimes translated as I–You) relationship, one does not study, measure or judge another according to his or her value for oneself, and one does not reduce the other to his or her constituent parts. Such an assessment detaches and reduces one, for only a part of one is in the I that relates to an It. Conversely, when one relates to another as a Thou, then one relates with one's whole being to the other's whole being:

> When I confront a human being as my You ... he is no thing among things ... He is no longer He or She, limited by other Hes and Shes, a dot in the world grid of space and time, nor a condition that can be experienced and described ... he is You and fills the firmament. Not as if there were nothing but he; but everything lives in his light. (Ibid.: 59)

Relation is reciprocity. The I and You of an I–You relation must change one another because each is open to the other, and each sees the **world** as it is for the other. This is a clue to the relevance of I–You relating to counselling and psychotherapy, a relevance of which in the *Afterword* to the 1957 edition of *I And Thou*, Buber writes directly:

> [A therapist may be] satisfied to 'analyze' his patient ... At best, he may help a diffuse soul that is poor in structure to achieve at least some concentration and order. But he cannot absolve his true task, which is the regeneration of a stunted personal center. That can be brought off only by a man who grasps with the profound eye of a physician the buried, latent unity of the suffering soul, which can be done only if he enters as a partner into a person-to-person relationship, but never through the observation and investigation of an object. (Ibid.: 179)

Other writers have adapted and extended these ideas. One of the authors (EvD) suggests a third level, beyond I–It and I–Thou, that of I–Me (van Deurzen, 2002). This is the merging of two beings, who in their self-forgetting transcend their separateness. Such a **transcendence** might occur in the communion of sexual union, a harmony of unity. And in this way, procreation – the creation of a third being – is just such a transcendence. This unifying experience is an aspect of the existential therapeutic relationship, when the client realises both she and her therapist *share* a concern for meaning. **Heidegger,** believing that I–Thou suggests an incomplete ego, and a single point of view, offers the idea of *Thou–Thou* to emphasise the mutuality of relationships.

Clearly, I–Thou relating is exceptional, and is unlikely to come easily. Some writers have accordingly reduced their ambitions. Harvey Cox, for instance, writes of I–You relating as distinct from I–Thou relating (Cox, 1965), suggesting that the former respects the other's humanity without being as intimate as the latter.

See also **client-centred psychotherapy; encounter; forgetting; interhuman, the; Other, the; technology**

I will!
See **Zarathustra** – spirit of the lion

James, William
See **pragmatism**

Jaspers
Karl Jaspers (1883–1969). German psychiatrist, psychologist and philosopher. Influenced by Spinoza, **Kant**, **Kierkegaard**, **Dilthey**, **Nietzsche**, **Husserl** and Weber. In turn, he influenced **Heidegger** and **Sartre**. His many publications include *General Psychopathology* (1913), *Philosophy* (1932), *Philosophy of Existence* (1938) and *The Way to Wisdom* (1950).

With very poor health throughout his life (at first it was thought his life would be short), he used his medical knowledge to treat himself and to adapt his style of living. When he married a Jewish woman, the response of the Nazis was to prevent him from teaching and publishing. After the war, he and his wife moved to Switzerland.

Jaspers was dissatisfied with the use of **science** to investigate humankind, because with its objectification it limits understanding of what human beings can *be*. Claiming that **philosophy** begins where reason has suffered shipwreck, he pursued a philosophical analysis of human being:

> I must *search for being* if I want to find my real self. But it is not till I fail in this search for intrinsic being that I begin to philosophize. (Jaspers, 1932: 1. 45)

Jaspers writes of the importance of *Weltanschauung*, or *worldview*. With its definite structures and categories, our worldview provides us with mental stability and comfort. Indeed, without worldviews we might **despair**. But worldviews also act as an impediment to considering new ideas and ways of seeing (see **sedimentation**). However, such dogmatism may be challenged by new and – especially – irrational experiences.

Jaspers describes four modes of being, of realising human potential (see **four worlds**), and of their accompanying modes of communication:

- *Naïve vitality*. Our emotions and self-interested behaviour. This is an unreflective mode, and its concomitant mode of communication is through instinct.
- *Consciousness*. This is rationality and reflection. Its mode of communication is intellectual, methodical and scientific.
- *Spirit*. This is the mode of ideals, and its mode of communication is communal.
- *Existenz*. Jaspers uses this term to denote the genuine, non-objective self, which is unfixed, comprising only possibilities, and which exists only in communication with others. Unlike the other three modes, *Existenz* cannot be communicated through

objective language. But it is revealed in limit situations (sometimes called boundary situations), which are situations of inescapable suffering, like **death**.

Jaspers writes of the *law of the day* (*Gesetz des Tages*), our rational desire for order, and its opposite, the *passion for the night* (*Leidenschaft zur Nacht*), our urge to ruin our imposed order. And it can be revealed in relationship with another person (see also **Buber**). Here is clearly an opportunity for the psychotherapist. And, preceding **Rogers**, Jaspers writes of empathy (*Einfühlung*), of participation in another person's experience:

> The love in this communication is not the blind love which fixes upon one object as readily as another. It is the struggling, clear-sighted love of possible Existenz tackling another possible Existenz, questioning it, challenging it, making demands on it. (Ibid.: 2. 59)

See also **cipher; comprehensive, the; interrogation**

joy
See *amor fati*; **laughter; yes-saying**

judgement
Heidegger links judgement with assertion, **logos** and **truth**. He disputes Kant's view that what is perceived by the senses is unreliable and that human understanding can only be gained through systematic theory-building. For Heidegger, 'perception is always true' (Heidegger, 1927b: 33), meaning that insofar as perception is subjective, if the thing being looked at is looked at properly, it can only be perceived in that way. However, like **Nietzsche**, Heidegger holds that we know the **world** not just through sense-perception but through experience of the world, through its resistance to our will (see **will to power**). Heidegger, like **Husserl** and **Aristotle** before him, also believed that some things are known before we ever hold a discourse about them, they are the things that are self-evident, *apophantic* (see **apophantic speech**), and which show themselves without our having to make a judgement about them.

Brentano believes there are three types of mental phenomena: 1. representations, 2. judgements, 3. emotions. This is not unlike Heidegger's three existentialia of: *Befindlichkeit* – or **disposition**; *Verstand* – or **understanding**; and *Rede* – or **discourse**. Each of these levels of our connection with **reality** involves a different quality of relatedness.

Rollo **May** cautions against the therapist making judgements in psychotherapy, for he regards such judgements to be anti-therapeutic.

See also **phenomenology**

jumping ahead and jumping in
See **leaping ahead** and **leaping in**

Jung

Carl Gustav Jung (1875–1961). Swiss founder of analytical psychology, a version of **psychoanalysis**. Collaborated with **Freud** 1907–13, when disputes between them culminated in their separation. Appropriately, a concept central to analytical psychology is **individuation**. Jung also originated the idea of the *collective unconscious*, a common and inherited layer of psychic materials.

Jung was one of Medard **Boss's** trainers and an influence on *Daseinsanalysis*.

See also **dreams; introversion**

Kafka, Franz
See **art and existential thought**

Kant
Immanuel Kant (1724–1804). German philosopher whose influence on existential philosophy is generally indirect. References to his ideas can be found under: **Dilthey; Heidegger; intuition; phenomenological method;** *praxis***; Schopenhauer; thing-in-itself.**

Kierkegaard
Søren Aabye Kierkegaard was born in København (Copenhagen), on 5 May 1813, and died in København on 11 November 1855.

Notable works: *The Concept of Irony* (1841); *Either/Or* (1843a); *Fear and Trembling* (1843b); *Repetition* (1843c); *Philosophical Fragments* (1844a); *The Concept of Anxiety* (also translated as *The Concept of Dread*, 1844b); *Concluding Unscientific Postscript* (1846a); *Purity of Heart* (1847a); *The Point of View* (1848); and *The Sickness Unto Death* (1849).

Influenced by: **Plato (Socrates)**, Christianity, G.E. Lessing, J.G. Hamann, **Hegel** (but in reaction against), and Schelling (to the extent that Schelling opposed Hegel).

Influence on: **Nietzsche**, Strindberg, **Tillich, Heidegger, Wittgenstein** and **Rogers.**

Life: Living through the Golden Age of Danish art and culture (1800–50), Kierkegaard's life was emotionally charged but externally uneventful, even reclusive, and he seldom left his home town. He was the youngest of seven children, five of whom died during his youth. His mother was illiterate, the former maid of his father's first wife, and she died when Søren was 21. She is rarely mentioned by him. He had a pious and oppressive upbringing due to his strict, and demanding, melancholy and guilt-ridden father, a man convinced he and his family were cursed (it is said he told his youngest son the reason for this was that as an unhappy young man he had once cursed God). This left Søren to conclude he himself would die by the age of 33, the age at which Jesus Christ had died.

When 17 years old, Kierkegaard entered Copenhagen University as a theology student, but chose to read philosophy and literature. It was to be a lengthy, dilettantish period of study. For a while he lived an outwardly hedonistic life (and an inwardly unhappy one), but abandoned it after his father's sudden death in 1838 – a death he saw as a kind of sacrifice on his behalf. In 1840 he proposed marriage to the highly eligible Regina Olsen, and was accepted but at once regretted it, and months later broke off the engagement. It is not clear, even from his journal, whether this was cruelty, lack of confidence in himself as a prospective husband, a desire for the intensity of life that sacrifice would bring, or if he wished to make a sacrifice for his own supposed sins. Regina spent a long time trying to win him back, but his show of indifference to her finally persuaded her to give up her quest. Kierkegaard continued to refer to her in his writings, however.

Kierkegaard was proud of his mother tongue, and wrote his undergraduate dissertation in Danish, a deviation from the usual scholarly Latin that required special permission from the King.

Always critical of the intellectual and academic establishment, he became increasingly hostile to the established Church. In 1845, offended by an article in *The Corsair*, a satirical weekly, he responded bitterly, and reaped weeks of mockery from the magazine, which he took as a public humiliation, and which left him deeply wounded. On his death, and against his wishes, he was given a funeral in Copenhagen Cathedral.

Major ideas: Kierkegaard's central tenet was that one should be able to live one's life by a philosophy. He made his own approach a subjective one, and objected (as later would Nietzsche) to the objectifying of human experience. He brought **existence** into his philosophy. And he rebutted Hegel's claim that absolute knowledge is possible on the grounds that God is beyond reason. He saw the highest form of self-actualisation as relating to God as the absolute Thou – not a merging with the cosmos, not a transcending of one's particularity, but relating with a particular being. And thus, Kierkegaard is opposed to being one of the **crowd**.

A writer with so many ideas, Kierkegaard's central philosophy is difficult to pinpoint. One way of entering his philosophy, however, is to begin with his mind–body dualism. Although a dualist (see **mind–body problem**), he believed duality could be overcome with development and will, for human beings are a synthesis of mind and **body**, a synthesis that results in spirit. According to Kierkegaard, there are three stages of self-actualisation (and these relate, in turn, to the dual states of humanity and their synthesis): the aesthetic, the ethical and the religious.

> The human being is spirit. But what is spirit? Spirit is the self. But what is the self? The self is a relation which relates to itself, or that in the relation which is its relating to itself. The self is not the relation but the relation's relating to itself. A human being is a synthesis of the infinite and the finite, of the temporal and the eternal, of freedom and necessity. In short, a synthesis. A synthesis is a relation between two terms. Looked at in this way a human being is not yet a self. (Kierkegaard, 1849: 43)

Kierkegaard's theory of the stages of life is important to understanding his overall philosophy. We all start out in an undifferentiated vegetative way and grow only gradually into our capacity to differentiate and to be ready for the first stage of development. The first stage is a state of mind in which the aesthetic, or sensual, or emotive is sought: this is the *aesthetic life*, and this is the foundation for everyday life and judgement, and thus can be likened to

Kierkegaard's own hedonistic phase. Contemporary European living tends to be like this. But this is the cellar of life – and a despairing stage, if one sees it for what it is. Only through commitment (a **choice** of **either/or**) can a person move to the next stage, the *ethical life* – a style of life exemplified by the figure of Plato's Socrates. This stage possesses a certain tragic heroism with preparedness for self-sacrifice. But like the aesthetic stage, it is also naïve, oblivious of the fact that rationality and will are insufficient to be virtuous. It is only when we come to a place of doubt about ourselves and about life and become capable of the acceptance of sin and **guilt** that we can take a **leap of faith** and learn to relate to God directly and in a personal way, living like the Knight of Faith. This marks the third stage, which is that of the *religious life*.

Humankind is a synthesis of the infinite and the finite, and is caught between the eternal and **nothingness**. Therein lies the dizziness of **freedom** experienced as **anxiety**. And Man is an egoist and must **despair** – must suffer angst. Kierkegaard insists that we realise ourselves through personal choice, through personal commitment.

Kierkegaard's writing and publishing style is ironic. He used a variety of pseudonyms in the publishing of his works (some of which are found throughout this book) in order to criticise his own ideas, and to demonstrate the subjectivity of human **interpretation**, obliging the reader to make a personal decision what to believe. (It also served to publicise the work under attack.)

Contribution to psychotherapy: this may be summed up by the axiom: 'We cannot be cured of despair, we can only learn from it'. A Kierkegaardian psychotherapy would seek to accommodate the patient to life, into facing difficulties rather than attempting to eliminate them. And it would view anxiety as a realistic response to life. Such a therapy would not set out to cure, or to make life easier, nor would it try to discover certainty. And it would not seek personality change, for according to Kierkegaard, we cannot in essence change. But it would try to reconcile the individual to the difficulties of living, to welcome and understand that tension and **paradox** pervade life. He offers specific guidance on helping others, advice that anticipates words later to be written by **Heidegger** and **Buber**:

> [I]f real success is to attend the effort to bring a man to a definite position, one must first of all take pains to find him where he is and begin there. This is the secret of the art of helping others ... I must understand more than he – yet first of all surely I must understand what he understands ... But all true effort to help begins with self-humiliation: the helper must first humble himself under him he would help ... be a servant ... be patient ... (Kierkegaard, 1848: 334)

See also **boredom; finitude and infinitude; friendship; immediacy; introversion; irony; repetition**

Kingsley Hall
See **anti-psychiatry**

Knight of Faith
See **leap of faith**; **Kierkegaard**

knowing and knowledge
Philosophical questions concerning knowledge are the province of epistemology, the theory of knowledge. Its areas of concern include the relationship of knowledge to **truth**, and the importance of belief, reason and experience. Knowledge is generally considered to be more than opinion, for it is founded in fact. But for **Husserl**, knowing cannot be divorced from experience, for living is prior to knowing, hence we should first understand the everyday world, the **lived world**. For **Heidegger** too, knowing depends on experience, on **being-in-the-world**:

> Knowledge means: to have seen something, to have something as something manifest ...
> To know means: Someone finds his way. (Heidegger, 1987: 145)

Knowledge derives from **consciousness**, for consciousness is always directed towards something (see **intentionality**). Thus, *Dasein* and consciousness imply a **world**, and a relationship with the world, and presuppose the means of knowing the contents of the world.

See also **absurd, the; meaning and meaninglessness**

Kristeva, Julia
Born in Bulgaria in 1941, but lived in France from the 1960s, a linguistic theorist, psychoanalyst and novelist, who brings together influences from Marxism, **structuralism** (see **Barthes**) and **psychoanalysis**. One of the prominent feminist writers who reacted to **Levinas's** assumption of the prominence and primacy of the **Other**.

Lacan

Jacques Marie Émile Lacan (1901–81). French psychoanalyst who reinterpreted psychoanalytical theory in structuralist terms. Thus he describes the unconscious as structured like a language, and believes that linguistic analysis is an aspect of **psychoanalysis**. His influences include **Hegel, Freud,** de Saussure and **Heidegger.** His own influence has been great in literary criticism and in establishing his own school of Lacanian psychoanalysis. There are many published collections of his notoriously difficult and obscure seminars, including *Écrits* (1966) and *The Four Fundamental Concepts of Psychoanalysis* (1973).

Lacan insists that psychoanalysis is not a division of biology, and he further diverges from Freudian orthodoxy in regarding environmental and pre-verbal experiences as insignificant to the development of the self. Instead he has a radical theory, based on the notion that the unconscious is structured like a language. This idea has far-reaching implications. Where classical analytical doctrine holds that the ego is a naturally strong aspect of the self, Lacan sees it as narcissistic. His own developmental model is that the child goes through a *mirror stage*, where the child's sense of his or her lacking leads to a wish for fulfilment, and a wish for omnipotence is psychically projected onto another, which may be a sibling or friend, thereby providing a mirror image. As this other person is then experienced as an omnipotent ideal, the child feels alienated and hostile towards them.

For Lacan then, the ego is the seat of neurosis, and the task of analysis is not to strengthen a damaged ego – this would be to bolster a pre-existing narcissism – but to show how alienated the ego, the self, the I is from reality. Reality constantly challenges the person, who needs to come to terms with its demands and move from a world of the imaginary to a world of the symbolic, where distinctions can be made between real and imaginary. To this end, Lacanian analysis has some singular techniques: the therapist will try to abstain from being the omnipotent ideal, and he or she will make use of the *short session*, where a session is abruptly truncated by the therapist in order to interrupt and thwart the process of the patient's projection onto the therapist. The aim of therapy, then, is for the patient to see the therapist as an **Other** and not as an ideal, not as a symbol.

In some respects Lacan's ideas broaden the approach of psychoanalysis in a way consistent with existential thought. For instance, his reformulation of the Oedipus Complex suggests it is not a desire for *sexual* intercourse, but for intercourse per se. And he argues that it is not libido but desire that motivates us. On the other hand, Lacan elaborates on Freud's emphasis on the importance of the phallus (that is, the erect penis as a symbol) by introducing the notion of the Law of the Father. The father holds the key to the child's entry into the symbolic world by prohibiting fusion with the mother and giving access to language. There have been many ripostes to this phallocentricity, for instance, in the work of Luce **Irigaray**.

See also **consciousness and unconsciousness; structuralism**

lack

For **Sartre**, human being is transcendent, that is, it cannot be defined by physical laws or by the contingencies of **psychology**. It is not a thing, but a nothing. The essence of human being is human **consciousness**, which projects **nothingness** into the **world**. Human consciousness is marked by negation, by what it lacks, for instance the being it intends to be in the future:

> It is through human reality that that *lack* comes to things in the form of 'potency,' of 'incompletion,' of 'suspension,' of 'potentiality.' (Sartre, 1943a: 196)

Thus there are voids in human being, holes that are the foundation of what psychologists have called *drives*:

> Thus the world is revealed as haunted by absences to be realized, and each *this* appears with a cortege of absences which point to it and determine it ... They are pure demands which rise as 'voids to be filled' in the middle of the circuit of selfness ... They are tasks, and this world is a world of tasks. (Ibid.: 199)

The lack manifests as desire when human beings focus on the world in a constructive way, but it may manifest as **nausea** when the lack is experienced as an absence and void.

See also **contingency; time and temporality; transcendence**

Laing

R.D. (Ronald David) Laing (1927–1989). Scottish psychiatrist. Born into a troubled and hostile family, and evidently an unwanted child. His theoretical influences were Marxist politics, **psychoanalysis** (especially Harry Stack Sullivan and D.W. Winnicott), the anthropologist Gregory Bateson, and existentialism (especially **Nietzsche** and **Sartre**). His published works include *The Divided Self* (1959), *Self and Others* (1961) and *The Politics of Experience* (1967). He co-wrote other books with Aaron Esterson and David **Cooper**. Laing was an important influence on the development of a British School of Existential Psychotherapy and was one of the founders of the Philadelphia Association, which established revolutionary therapeutic communities in London, starting with Kingsley Hall.

Laing is remembered for his bold initiatives in working with schizophrenic people in the therapeutic communities where hierarchies of power were abolished, health-care professionals and patients lived side-by-side, and patients were given great freedom to live out their madness. One of his most radical ideas is that mental breakdown or madness may be positive – an attempt by the sufferer to self-heal – and may lead to a breakthrough instead of a breakdown. He calls this process *metanoia* (from the Greek for *atonement*), and holds that mental health professionals should assist this natural cure, not block it or treat it with drugs or other intrusive therapies; such strategic interventions thwart the patient's **freedom**. Instead, mad people need a permissive freedom from which to choose their lives for themselves.

In practice, Laing's ideas were dominated by a psychoanalytic thinking which limited the extent of his existential thought, for his overall conceptualisation of his patients was deterministic. So he observed the oppressive role of the **Other**, but did not place it in the larger context of human **being**. He viewed families as having great potential for destruction, and believed schizophrenia was the result of the alienating power of the schizophregenic family. But he made an attempt at a greater holism with his *social phenomenology*, the observation of the individual in their social context. He worked with families at the Tavistock. His ideas of **psychopathology** somewhat resemble Sartre's, for they concern the toxic effect of others. However, Laing's observations and ideas are empirical, rather than philosophical. He did not always distinguish between the **ontic** and the **ontological** – the concrete particularities and the general conditions of human existence. And he did not conclude, as some have done, that schizophrenia is a more florid development of ordinary human living.

Laing developed a vocabulary for different forms of **anxiety** in people lacking ontological security and fearing the loss of their personal identity:

- *Engulfment* is a feeling or fear of being overwhelmed by another.
- *Implosion* is a feeling of emptiness, leading to the fear that one might explode inwardly with a total destruction of **identity**.
- *Petrification* is both a protective depersonalisation of **self** and a depersonalisation of the other. It is as it sounds, a turning oneself or the other to stone.

Laing tried to see the sense in the apparent nonsense of his patient's thoughts and emotions. In this way, his style of **interpretation** was hermeneutic. If a psychotic patient claimed people were trying to poison him, Laing would see this as being a demonstration of the patient's awareness and fear of the power of others to destroy. He also spoke of *co-presence* – actively being with another, being available for the other – as one of the most powerful therapeutic interventions.

See also **mystification**

language

According to **Heidegger**, language is an important aspect of the world into which we are **thrown**. It does not originate with the individual: it pre-exists, it already belongs to the **They**, and so the mere speaking of words may be an avoidance of **Being** (see **idle talk**). Language derives from talk, but properly it is more than the physical articulation of words, for it is a participation:

If one understands language as 'saying' in the sense of the letting-be-shown of something, receiving-perceiving is always language and jointly a saying of words. (Heidegger, 1987: 200)

For Heidegger, 'language is the house of Being' (Heidegger, 1947: 217):

We human beings, in order to be who we are, remain within the essence of language to which we have been granted entry. We can therefore never step outside it in order to look it over circumspectly from some alternative position. Because of this, we catch a glimpse of the essence of language only to the extent that we ourselves are envisaged by it, remanded to it. That we cannot know the essence of language [is the] advantage by which we advance to an exceptional realm, the realm in which we dwell as the *mortals*, those who are needed and used for the speaking of language. (Heidegger, 1959: 423)

Everyday language may be stale, but it is in language appropriated by the individual human being – especially in poetry (see **Hölderlin**) – that Being may be disclosed to itself. Heidegger's account of language can be compared with those of **Derrida**, **Gadamer** and others.

later Heidegger
See **turn/turning**

laughter
For **Nietzsche**, the gaining of wisdom should bring joy, lightness and laughter. The stoicism of Nietzsche's **Zarathustra** demonstrates an embracing of all that life is. We ought to ignore gloomy philosophies – those espoused by any Spirit of Gravity (like **Schopenhauer**), and we should be wholehearted about life:

He calls earth and life heavy: and so *will* the Spirit of Gravity have it! But he who wants to become light and a bird must love himself – thus do *I* teach. (Nietzsche, 1883: 211)

According to Nietzsche, we should fight our own opposition to hardship and face the imperfections of our lives without complaint:

I should believe only in a God who understood how to dance. And when I beheld my devil, I found him serious, thorough, profound, solemn: it was the Spirit of Gravity – through him all things are ruined. (Ibid.: 68)

We should relish the opportunity to test ourselves against ordeal – something Nietzsche practised. We should, in the manner of Zarathustra, laugh in the face of adversity.

See also *amor fati*; Stoics and stoicism; yes-saying; Zarathustra

law of the day
See **Jaspers**

leap of faith

For **Kierkegaard**, there can be no empirical proof or understanding of God. And in this sense, Christian belief is **absurd**, for a **relationship** with God cannot grow with reason and argument. Such a relationship cannot be developed in slow and certain stages, and to insist on rationality as a basis for belief is to exclude faith; it is to ruin the chance of a relationship with God. What is needed is the abandonment of reason and the personal commitment of a leap into eternity: '[T]he opposite of sin is not virtue but faith' (Kierkegaard, 1849: 115).

Faith is not easily got, since we have to risk ourselves and our rational understanding of the **world** to get there, though the risk is worthwhile.

> Without risk there is no faith. Faith is precisely the contradiction between the infinite passion of the individual's inwardness and the objective uncertainty. (Kierkegaard, 1846a: 182)

Kierkegaard believes the only worthwhile way to live is to take this leap of faith and live the spiritual life, as the Knight of Faith.

leaping ahead

(*Vorspringen*). A term from the philosophy of **Heidegger**. This is the authentic form of **care** for the **Other**, with an awareness of the Other as a person, as a *Dasein*. It consists of an attentive jumping ahead of the Other in order to give him back to care, that is, to himself:

> This concern which essentially pertains to authentic care; that is, the existence of the other, and not to a *what* which it takes care of, helps the other to become transparent to himself *in* his care and *free* for it. (Heidegger, 1927b: 122)

See also **authenticity; leaping in**

leaping in

(*Einspringen*). Offering so much solicitude that we take away the Other's **care** for himself. A notion from the philosophy of **Heidegger**, and directly applicable to the practice of psychotherapy, for out of **anxiety** or lack of belief in the Other we may jump in, take over their self-care, their **responsibility**. In some professions this may be required, but for the existential therapist, it is seen as unhelpful, as debilitating to the client, as disabling the growth of autonomy and selfhood:

> In this concern, the other can become one who is dependent and dominated even if this domination is a tacit one and remains hidden from him. (Heidegger, 1927b: 122)

See also **inauthenticity; leaping ahead**

Lebenswelt
See **lived world**

legacy

From *Erbe* or *Erbschaft,* literally, heritage or inheritance, used by **Heidegger** to refer to what is traditional or handed down (*überliefert*). Heidegger attaches particular importance to the traditions that we inherit. In *Being and Time*, he complains that too often we construe the past in terms of the present, and we do this quite deliberately, to conceal from ourselves the nature of our **freedom**. In this sense, the legacy of the past is a burden, and we fail to make use of it to remind ourselves of the possibilities of life:

> When, however, one's existence is inauthentically historical, it is loaded down with the legacy of a 'past' which has become unrecognizable, and it seeks the modern. But when historicality is authentic, it understands history as the 'recurrence' of the possible, and knows that a possibility will recur only if existence is open for it fatefully, in a moment of vision, in resolute repetition. (Heidegger, 1927a: 391–2)

The more authentically resolved we are, the more we are able to take over the heritage that has been handed down to us. Resoluteness is not just about grasping the possibilities of our future and anticipating **death**, it is also about resolutely grasping the legacy of the past.

See also **authenticity and inauthenticity; history; Moment, the; possibility; repetition; resoluteness; time and temporality**

letting be

See **releasement**

levelling down

Heideggerian term, from the German, *Einebnung* – meaning levelling or *evening out.* According to **Heidegger**, we humans find various ways of avoiding the **truth**. One way of shunning **authenticity** is **covering up**, another is levelling down, whereby a matter of great significance is reduced to insignificance. What was distinct is made similar, common. Human beings in inauthenticity wish to be ordinary. They try to be the same as others are, as they imagine they would and should be. Through **distantiality** (*Abstandigkeit*), we keep others at a safe distance, whilst fitting ourselves into their norm. He also speaks of **averageness** (*Durchschnittlichkeit*), where we try to not be more or less than the **They**. This process involves us in levelling ourselves down and eliminating any ways in which we stand out or are special. We make ourselves be part of the public way of being *(Offentlichkeit)* which keeps us safely in the middle of the road, not standing out.

Levinas

Emmanuel Levinas (1906–95). Lithuanian-born French philosopher. Influenced by **Hegel, Husserl** and **Heidegger**. Introduced **phenomenology** to France and so influenced **Sartre, Merleau-Ponty, Ricoeur** and **Derrida**. Works include *On Escape* (1935), *Totality and Infinity* (1961) and *Otherwise than Being* (1974). His poetical and mystical writing comprises assertion rather than argument, and is frequently baffling and contradictory; nonetheless it invites serious consideration.

Being, for Levinas, is a sacrifice and a gift from God. But God having withdrawn (into the gift of the world), we are now left alienated from ourselves. The only response to this is to give of ourselves with absolute gratuity, without expecting recompense.

As all beings are a part of this giving, we owe an obligation and a **responsibility** to the **Other**. Indeed, the Other has priority over the self, so there is an essential asymmetry in human **relationship**. Levinas refers to this as *alterity*. For Levinas then, ethical relationships have priority over **existence** and he is therefore critical of those philosophers who, like Heidegger, emphasise **ontology**. Levinas is also, like **Buber**, opposed to egoistic philosophies, those that emphasise the relationship of the **self** to the self. And he rejects the implication he detects in Husserl's account of **intentionality**, that through intentional thought the Other is possessed.

When two persons meet in physical proximity (when Levinas refers to the Other as the *face*), the self feels the ethical demand of the Other, the requirement for face-to-face conversation. However, when feeling this demand, and whether it is peaceful or warlike, the self may ignore it or meet it with love or violence. And in its answer the self is defined.

His characterisation of woman as the Other stirred Simone **de Beauvoir** and others to object to Levinas normalising the male outlook. His analysis of the face-to-face and the asymmetry of relationships has relevance for psychotherapy.

See also **alienation; death; I–Thou; nausea**

liberation

By *liberation*, **Heidegger** means a facing up to **truth**:

> He who is resolute knows no fear, but understands the possibility of *Angst* as *the* mood that does not hinder and confuse him. *Angst* frees him from 'null' possibilities and lets him become free *for* authentic ones. (Heidegger, 1927b: 344)

Heidegger emphasises that there is **freedom** *from* and freedom *for*: the first is from what restricts or obscures, and the second is the availability of **choice**. We cannot have freedom *for* unless we first liberate ourselves from things. The theme of the distinction between freedom for and freedom from resonates throughout existential therapy in authors like **May, Bugental** and **Yalom**. For **Sartre**, the idea of liberation is mainly connected with that of freeing ourselves from the chains of **bad faith**, since the human condition is founded in freedom and it is only society, **seriality** or bad faith that alienates us.

See also **anxiety; attunement; authenticity; possibility; resoluteness**

life

See **absurd, the; anxiety; authenticity; Being; consciousness; death; existence; meaning and meaninglessness; passion; relationship; repetition; world**

life space
See **hodological space**

light/lightening
See **clearing**

limit situations
See **Jaspers**

lion, the
See **Zarathustra**

literature
See **art and existential thought**

lived body
See **body**

lived world
Conventionally, **philosophy** attempts to clarify our understanding of the **world** by removing from consideration the facts and experiences of the everyday world. Thus, in an effort to be objective, its first principles are abstractions. In contrast, **Husserl** begins with the subjective everyday world, the lived world (*Lebenswelt*). The biologist von Uexkull had described the lived world of different animals and provided Husserl with the idea of tracing the experiences characteristic of an individual's stance towards the world. **Kierkegaard** and **Nietzsche** had already complained about the abstraction of philosophy and its impossible striving to objectify human life; existential philosophers after Husserl – especially **Heidegger**, **Sartre** and **Merleau-Ponty** – took inspiration from Husserl and founded their own philosophies with the starting-point of human beings in their lived worlds. They all held that human life cannot be abstracted from the world, and that any such attempts to do so lose valuable aspects of what it means to be a human being, and that what we take for granted – ourselves in our everyday worlds – should not be reduced, but given greater scrutiny.

See also **being-in-the-world**; *Merkwelt*

living by default
See **default**

living dangerously
An exhortation by **Nietzsche** to overcome oneself, to embrace one's fate (*amor fati*), to engage in the **revaluation of values** and to live as a **superman**.

See also **leap of faith**

locus

(*Ort, Platz,* or *Stelle*). When **Heidegger** writes of locus (or *place*, or *location*) he is eager to differentiate between the passive way in which inanimate objects take up space from the way a human being clears a **space** about itself. The human being, *Dasein*, is spiritual, and is never objectively present in space as is a mere thing. Instead, *Dasein* takes space in, makes room for itself. Heidegger's concept of *Spielraum* – playspace, often translated as elbowroom – refers to the way in which human beings need to clear a space in which they can move freely. Heidegger also uses the term *locus* in a figurative sense, in relation to the locus of **truth**. In his later work he refers to the way in which human beings reach out towards **Being** from the locus they find themselves in.

See also **being-in-the-world**

logos

Greek, with a variety of meanings, including word, order, **meaning** and **discourse**. The ancient **Stoics** believed (as had Heraclitus before them) in an underlying reason, or *logos*, to the functioning and order of the cosmos. So *logos* means reason or its application in words, ideas or principles. Thus in logotherapy (see **Frankl**), *logos* is taken as meaning therapy through the discovery of **meaning**.

See also **apophantic speech**

logotherapy
See **Frankl**

look, the

For **Sartre**, there is acknowledgement of one's existence in the gaze of another, although the result may be a loss of **freedom**:

> The Other looks at me and as such he holds the secret of my being, he knows what I am. Thus the profound meaning of my being is outside of me, imprisoned in an absence. The Other has the advantage over me. (Sartre, 1943a: 363)

There is, in the consciousness of the Other's gaze, great **meaning**, in realising that one has been made an object or a subject for the Other: 'It is shame or pride which reveals to me the Other's look and myself at the end of that look' (ibid.: 261). Thus, although it may seem that all others are objects to oneself as subject, this is not so. I may find myself an object to another as subject; and if I am an object, I am at the mercy of the Other as a subject to define me, to limit me, and I have no freedom in this, I have lost my freedom. Thus, we are rivals to other selves, whom we can delimit by seeing them as fixed objects. And so we try to dominate others or embrace their dominion over us, as in sexual desire, and more powerfully still, in **sadism** or **masochism**, or even murder.

However, these are relationships that to varying extents deny the other as a **being-for-itself**, reducing the other to a **being-in-itself**. We may instead, through **love** of the Other, permit the Other to be an other: a reciprocity such as this provides a foundation for the lover's freedom. But it is fraught too:

[P]recisely because I exist by means of the Other's freedom, I have no security; I am in danger in this freedom ... *If love were in fact a pure desire for physical possession, it* could in many cases be easily satisfied. Proust's hero, for example, who installs his mistress in his home, who can see her and possess her at any hour of the day ... ought to be free from worry. Yet we know that he is continually gnawed by anxiety. Through her consciousness Albertine escapes Marcel even when he is at her side, and that is why he knows relief only when he gazes on her while she sleeps. ... [T]he lover wishes to capture a 'consciousness.' He ... does not desire to possess the beloved as one possesses a thing ... He wants to possess a freedom as freedom. (Ibid.: 366–7)

See also **being-for-itself; Merleau-Ponty; shame; subject and object**

lostness

Heidegger describes how an individual may be lost in the crowd, listening only to **idle talk**. This lostness (*Verlorenheit*), this giving up one's **self** to the **They**, can only be reversed by a refusal to listen to the They, and this becomes possible when we let ourselves instead be summoned by our own **call of conscience** to find our ownmost potentiality for becoming our own self.

See also **authenticity; falling/fallenness; potentiality-for-being-oneself; publicness**

love

Religious existentialists are optimistic about God's love and the love of God. But both religious and atheist existentialists regard the love of one human being for another as at least problematic, perhaps impossible. Both draw their ideas on love from their theories of **relationship**.

Kierkegaard sees human love as naturally related to God's love, and he describes this in his analysis of **marriage**. He sees the love of one human for another as partiality, and therefore at odds with the equality of the Christian directive to love one's neighbour, as well as God's love of all humankind. For Kierkegaard, the wonder and the gift of Christianity is in the commandment, *Thou shalt love!* Only when love is thus enjoined, and is a duty, can it be eternal, and an assurance against disappointment and **despair**. One must love oneself too, and in the right way.

Nietzsche not only disagrees with Christian notions of love but is antagonistic to them. For him, love is located only in the physical **self**, and nothing further. He claims that the Christian love of God is a **no-saying** to life, a frightened attempt to flee the **world** and oneself. He derides the Christian injunction to love one's neighbour, and in the obligation sees proof that such love is otherwise unmerited, and that for the atheist it is unjustified.

In *Being and Time*, **Heidegger** does not directly address love, but he later denied complaints by **Binswanger** that his conception of *Dasein* was of a solipsistic being. He answered that *Dasein* is open to **Being** as shared in our essential being–with-others *(Mitsein)*, and that love is a part of **care**.

Like Nietzsche, **Sartre** locates love in the person, but he is even more pessimistic, with a philosophy markedly influenced by **Hegel**'s ideas of master–slave social relations, describing love in terms of desire, the wish to possess and to own the **freedom** of another, thus to assert one's own freedom. Sartre's notions of **masochism** and **sadism** derive from this. But the lover, as well as wanting possession of the Other, wants to be loved by the Other, and love can only come from a free agent. Love, then, is always doomed; it is an impossible **project**. Sartre's long-term romantic partner, Simone de **Beauvoir**, also sees the difficulty of love as one of enslavement, but she is more optimistic, seeing the problem of equality in love as a historically contingent one. Woman's body is being-for-man, she says, and love between man and woman generally fails because of women's subservience to men. But this need not be so, and one self might love another self without loss of freedom. **Jaspers** speaks of love as a commitment to solidarity for one another, to be responsible for each other and protect each other from the world.

See also **availability; constancy; despair; friendship; look, the; Other, the**

loyalty
See **constancy and loyalty**

madness
See **Foucault**; **Laing**; **Szasz**

Man, das
See **herd, the**; **They, the**

Marcel
Gabriel Marcel (1889–1973). French playwright, literary and music critic and philosopher. Influences upon him include F.H. Bradley and Josiah Royce, and his philosophy in turn influenced **Merleau-Ponty**. Notable publications include *Being and Having* (1935), *The Philosophy of Existence* (also translated as *The Philosophy of Existentialism* and which includes his 1945 paper 'Existence and Human Freedom') (1948) and *The Mystery of Being* (1951).

Marcel's father was an ex-Catholic, and an educated man; his mother, who was Jewish, died when Gabriel was four. He was brought up by his aunt, who, like his father, was agnostic. He considered his childhood to have been sorrowful. At the Sorbonne he studied **philosophy**. In 1929 he converted to Catholicism. He received the Grand Prix de Littérature from the Académie Française in 1948. In 1956 he was awarded the Goethe Prize, and in 1958 the Grand Prix National des Lettres. He was described by Jean-Paul **Sartre** as a Catholic existentialist, but rejected this, because he believed his philosophy could appeal to non-Catholics and because he did not like the term *existentialist*. Instead, borrowing a description made by one of his own students, he termed himself a neo-Socratic.

For Marcel, **Being** is not an object, and it cannot be directly understood but only by reference to relationships. Personal relationships are at the heart of a difficult and unsystematic philosophy in which he distinguishes between primary and secondary reflection. *Primary reflection* is an objective and rational approach to the **world**, one typified by **science**, for it deals with what should be believed through verification and proof. In this mode, the questioner is utterly distinct from what is in question. Whilst such an approach has its uses, it is inappropriate to more human concerns, and if used in this way, Marcel scorns it as the *spirit of abstraction*, an abstracting of human life, a *functionalised world* in which human beings are no more than the sum of their practical functions. It is a dehumanising attitude (see **technology and technological attitude**), one that at its extreme allowed the Nazis to regard Jews and Gypsies as subhuman.

Secondary reflection is concerned not with objective facts, but with faith. It has no aspiration to prove the accuracy of data or hypotheses but is instead concerned to reveal presences whether they be one's own, or another's, or God's. It is concerned with what Marcel calls *mystery* – not in the common theological sense, but with **ontological** mystery. It is thus that secondary reflection requires **love** and faith, and for **subject and object,** watcher and watched, to lose their distinction (see **I–Thou**). In secondary reflection, the I of the reflecting person is involved, for secondary reflection requires participation (and for the religious person, this particularly refers to participation in God). Participation in existence and with other people needs to be sustained by *fidelity.*

Marcel agrees with Sartre that **existence** is primary, but he agrees with little else in Sartre's philosophy, and he rails against the dogmatic negativity of the philosophies of both Sartre and **Jaspers.** For Marcel, life is always in jeopardy, but it is God-given, and to live requires faith in the afterlife. Marcel takes from his love of music a metaphor, and claims that in music there is an indication of the harmony for which human existence strives.

See also **availability; Buber; constancy and loyalty; Socratic method**

marriage

For **Kierkegaard**, marriage held personal and ethical difficulties. His philosophical response was to explore the meaning of marriage and **love,** which he did at length in his 1843 publication, *Either/Or.* In this volume is 'The Seducer's Diary', followed by a letter to the aesthete seducer, in which an ethical case is made for marriage. It is admitted that to marry is to lose the **freedom** to suit oneself, but argued that duty is not, as some imagine, the enemy of love. The essence of marriage is certainly being in love, for without it, marriage would be no more than an agreeable partnership with sexual satisfaction. But love promises eternity, and romantic love can only fail that expectation, for between mortals it cannot be eternal. There is a religious and ethical element to marriage missing in romantic love. Marriage thus should be about more than romantic love and should have a dimension of spiritual as well as of sensual love.

Kierkegaard's practical solution to the difficulties of marriage was to terminate his engagement to Regina Olsen and never to marry. Interestingly, Jean-Paul **Sartre** and Simone **de Beauvoir** also came to the conclusion that marriage is undesirable, but they considered that this is because it restricts human **freedom** and removes the need to remain open and alert to the choices one is constantly having to make in relation to love.

See also **constancy and loyalty; relationship**

masochism

According to **Sartre,** this is a response to the impossibility of **love.** He describes in *Being and Nothingness* how **being-for-itself** deals with the desire to dominate the **Other** and assimilate their **freedom.** Love is two persons trying to enslave each other and to escape enslavement at the same time. But since freedom cannot be captured, the lover needs to either pretend to be in control of the Other through dominance or **sadism,** or give up their own freedom to the Other through submission or masochism. The third solution is **indifference**, leading to withdrawal from relationships. In fact, all these solutions are of the order of **bad faith** and cannot in the end succeed:

> The Other *looks* at me and as such he holds the secret of my being, he knows what I *am*. Thus the profound meaning of my being is outside of me, imprisoned in an absence. The Other has the advantage over me. (Sartre, 1943a: 363)

Masochism is the attempt to overcome the tension between oneself and the Other by giving into the Other's power over oneself.

See also **look, the**

master morality and slave morality

Ideas from the philosophy of **Nietzsche**. Master morality is a morality derived from the outlook of the rulers of society, where *good* refers to the noble man, and *bad* to the ignoble or despicable. According to Nietzsche, master morality values are **values** such as courage, pride and power. Slave morality is exemplified by values such as kindness, pity and charity. It is noteworthy that in master morality it is the individual to which these terms are applied. But with slave morality, *good* and *evil* are applied to actions, namely those that benefit or harm the weak and powerless. Thus sympathy and kindness are considered good by the powerless, and the actions of the noble man thought evil, for he is strong and independent, so he is considered a menace to the weak.

This is the morality of the **herd**, which is a morality born of resentment (*ressentiment*) of the powerful, and a cowardly reason for stifling a noble life. It is a mentality which judges the noble man as evil, and which tries to claim superiority for the submissive mass. To be beyond good and evil is to rise above the moral mentality of the herd, which is a mentality that encourages mediocrity and discourages the **superman**. Belief in God is, of course, weak. Nietzsche believed that Jesus – an unresentful man – was misrepresented by Christianity, a religion forged from the resentment of his misunderstanding disciples.

Nietzsche does not simply reject what is customarily thought of as good, but argues that we should not be kind to others for reasons of an underlying resentment of the free and noble spirit.

See also **good and evil; master–slave dialectic; will to power**

master–slave dialectic

A philosophical and psychological theory from **Hegel**, which claims human beings seek conquest and public recognition as conquerors, and that the **self** desires to annihilate another self in order to assert its own **existence**. However, to physically destroy the loser would leave the victor without he who can acknowledge the victor's supremacy and selfhood, so regrettably the vanquished must be allowed to live, but in servitude, to continually acknowledge he who is master. Thus the master wins leisure, whilst the slave labours for his master. But in idleness and consumption, the master's life leaves no mark, and is merely destructive, whereas the slave, in working, in grappling with nature, is a creator. And in denying recognition of the slave's selfhood, the master denies himself a self as a captive, and so loses human recognition of his own humanity. The **dialectic** of the situation is that the master thus loses his mastery over the slave whilst the slave, through creative labour, objectifies himself and again becomes a human self. In Hegel's thinking, this then leads to the slave becoming master and the master enslaved.

Sartre used this idea in his thinking about human relationships, which he saw essentially as an extension of this principle, although he later developed the concept of **generosity**. One of the aspects of the dialectic is that master and slave define each other and are in this sense necessary to each other. There can be no master without a slave and no slave without a master.

See also **sadism; will to power**

materialism
See **idealism**

May
Rollo Reece May (1909–94). American psychotherapist. Influenced by **Kierkegaard, Nietzsche, Freud**, Adler, **Binswanger**, Rank, **Tillich, Boss** and **Camus**, amongst others. His own influence is widely felt, perhaps most notably upon **Yalom**. Publications include *The Meaning of Anxiety* (1950), *Man's Search for Himself* (1953), *Psychology and the Human Dilemma* (1967), *Love and Will* (1969b), *Existential Psychology* (1969a). And with Ellenberger and Angel, he co-edited *Existence: A New Dimension in Psychiatry and Psychology* (1958), thereby introducing Binswanger, Boss and others to the American public.

May had a difficult childhood in a strict household. As a young man, he took a degree in English, and went on to teach. During this time he attended Adler's seminars in Vienna, and took art lessons from the Viennese painter Joseph Binder. He then studied Divinity, and practised as a minister for two years before taking up **psychology**. He contracted tuberculosis and faced the possibility of death. Spending three years in a sanatorium he read widely, including Kierkegaard, and this profoundly affected his later theory and practice of psychotherapy. In 1962, along with Abraham Maslow, **Rogers** and others, he founded the Association for Humanistic Psychology.

May's notion of **anxiety** is central to his psychology, influenced by Kierkegaard and Freud. He sees *normal* anxiety, sometimes also referred to as existential anxiety, as the perceived threat to any value deemed essential to maintain the **self**; he views *neurotic* anxiety as stemming from conformity, and the accepting of conditional worth from others. He makes a similar distinction between normal and neurotic **guilt**.

Unusually for an existentialist, May elaborated a developmental theory, comprising four stages:

1 *Innocence* – the amorality of infancy.
2 *Rebellion* – the desire for freedom, with no corresponding wish for responsibility.

3 *Ordinary* – adult conformity.
4 *Creative* – authentic being, courage to face anxiety, self-actualisation.

But he explains that these are not directly linked to age. So whilst rebellion may typically occur in teenage years, this need not be so. Key issues for May include **freedom** and **responsibility**.

May is remembered especially for his ideas concerning the **daimonic**, an idea often misunderstood. Rogers, for instance, took it to mean *demonic*, and it may be the source of the belief that humanistic psychologists see human nature as essentially good while existential theorists see the potential for good and bad. The daimonic is a motivational collection of daimons, ranging from the wish for food and drink to the desire for **love**. If one daimon becomes so important that it takes over, the resulting imbalance is referred to as *daimonic possession*.

For May, a human being's ability to see him or herself as **subject and object** is a necessary aspect of being human. And **intentionality** is significant to May as the bridge between mind and **body**. It provides meaning and commitment, and is more than conscious intent. And it is in the free association of psychotherapy that the unconscious intentionality of the person as a whole is to be discovered.

Some find in May a simplification of existential thought, so that the richness of existential thinking is lost, but there is no doubt of his importance in introducing **existential psychotherapy** to America.

meaning and meaninglessness

The word *meaning* itself carries a number of different meanings. It can refer to the discovery or imposition of form, intention or importance. This is true at the most primitive level of **interpretation**, when through **perception** or reasoning, we give meaning to what would otherwise be a confusing barrage of colours and noises. At the highest level the search for the universal meaning of life or for a personal meaning of life is the search for an understanding of the human condition, or for a network of connections and **values** that makes sense of it. For when we ask for the meaning of a situation (and in the most general case, the situation we wonder about is our lives), we are asking for an account of how things come to be the way they are, what their present significance is, and what they imply for the **future**.

An explanation from the behavioural sciences may seem to be what is needed, a definite and unarguable scientific account, detailing cause and effect. In psychotherapy, symbolic interpretation (as distinct from **hermeneutics**) offers this kind of meaning. It is an attempt to place an event in a larger context, and to discover the deterministic rules that shaped it. It is the act of placing an experienced event into the perspective of an explanatory system. If we believe that such explanations can apply to human affairs, then this allows us to see that our lives are not frighteningly random. But such an explanation is seldom any consolation for grief or profound bewilderment. If someone cherished dies of cancer, an explanation of her illness offers no comfort. And when **love** is unrequited, no logical explanation can heal a broken heart. Then what is sought is the restoration of lost meaning, a remedy for shattered dreams.

Meaninglessness implies chaos, disorganisation and pointlessness. Thus it is often connected to the notion of **absurdity** or futility. **Sartre** and **Camus** consider the **world** and **existence** to be essentially absurd. They claim that it is up to human beings to engage with the world in such a way that meaning is engendered.

But even when meaning exists or is created, it can be positive or negative, constructive or destructive. A belief in Hell may induce fear, though it provides a meaning to life and direction to the believer's conduct.

A belief in the existence of God provides meaning because it places human life in the context of a grand design, and provides a set of **values** and an ultimate authority whose will should be obeyed. Yet atheists may find meaning in human values; and religious believers as well as atheists may believe that much in the world is not intrinsically purposeful, but needs to be carefully considered in order for meaning to be created.

Existential writers vary in their accounts of meaning. For **Kierkegaard**, there is meaning in God and in humankind's **relationship** to God. However, as God is beyond human **knowledge**, so for the committed Christian faith is as much as can be grasped, and there can be no cognitive understanding of the meaning of life. **Nietzsche**, on the other hand, urges the abandonment of religious meaning and acceptance of the human **will to power**. For **Heidegger**, the human world is in part one we are **thrown** into, and in part one in which we have **freedom** (in which we ourselves throw or project), so that meaning is in part made and in part given, that is, it resides in **Being**. Like Nietzsche, Sartre sees the world as meaningless, leaving humankind in authority, so that the individual should realise that all that remains is freedom and the exercise of personal **choice**.

Psychotherapy can be seen as partly or wholly consisting of a search for meaning. Indeed, **Frankl's** form of psychotherapy, **logotherapy** is mainly focused on the finding of meaning. He believes that meaning is to be found in experiential, creative and attitudinal values. For some, observing the apparent lack of justice in the world may lead to an acceptance of the lack of meaning. Such a meaninglessness may be experienced as powerlessness and may result in **despair**. **Tillich**, and after him, **Yalom**, considers meaninglessness to be one of the most profound challenges to personal being. To come to an understanding of life, to develop a theory of how things work, is to discover what stance to take towards life. An existential psychotherapist will help the examination of how the individual may create and find meaning in their lives.

See also absurd, the; alienation; ambiguity; Binswanger; Bugental; Camus; *Daseinsanalysis*; death; Derrida; determinism; Dostoevsky; Gadamer; nihilism; phenomenology; pragmatism; Ricoeur; will to meaning

meaning of the moment
See **will to meaning**

meditative thinking
See **thinking**

memory
See **time and temporality**

mental health and illness
See **Laing; Szasz**

Merkwelt
An idea from the work of the biologist Jakob von Uexkull (1864–1944), being the objective environment of an animal species in which certain objects represent signs that evoke a particular response from the animal. It is part of the *Umwelt*, which is the environment of the animal as it is experienced and it is contrasted with the *Aktionwelt*, or world of action of the animal. The *Merkwelt* varies according to the perceptual abilities of the animal. **Binswanger** was inspired by von Uexkull's observations and introduced these ideas into his work with psychiatric patients.

See also **lived world**

Merleau-Ponty
Maurice Merleau-Ponty was born in Rochefort-sur-Mer on 14 March 1908 and died in Paris on 4 May 1961.

Notable works: *The Structure of Behaviour* (1942), *Phenomenology of Perception* (1945), *Sense and Non-Sense* (1948), *The Primacy of Perception* (1961), *The Visible and the Invisible* (1964b), *Consciousness and the Acquisition of Language* (1964a) and *Texts and Dialogues* (1992).

Influenced by: **Hegel**, Marx, de Saussure, **Husserl, Gestalt psychology, Bergson, Marcel, Binswanger, Heidegger, Lacan, Levinas** and Lévi-Strauss.

Influence on: Diffuse.

Life: Merleau-Ponty had a happy childhood, despite the fact that his father had been killed in the First World War. He himself served as an infantry officer in the Second World War, and when the French forces were defeated he joined the Resistance, and with Albert **Camus** and Jean-Paul **Sartre** (a lifelong friend), he wrote propaganda. After the war he lectured at the University of Lyon, then in 1949 he was given a chair in Child Psychology at the Sorbonne, and in 1952 a chair in Philosophy at the Collège de France. With Sartre and Simone de **Beauvoir**, he founded *Les Temps Modernes*, a political and literary journal. His own very clear writing is marked by a preference for an aesthetic rather than a scientific attitude towards **existence**.

Major ideas: Merleau-Ponty was above all a phenomenologist, and he refined and extended the ideas of Husserl and Heidegger, particularly with his consideration of the **body**, an area which up until then had been somewhat neglected (it is attended to somewhat by **Nietzsche**, but not phenomenologically). Unlike Sartre, he was decidedly opposed to **dualism** and did not speak of object or subject. He refers to the person as the *body-subject*:

> Man taken as a concrete being is not a psyche joined to an organism, but the movement to and fro of existence which at one time allows itself to take corporeal form and at others moves towards personal acts … It is never a question of the incomprehensible meeting of two causalities, nor of a collision between the order of causes and that of ends. But by an imperceptible twist an organic process issues into human behaviour, an instinctive act changes direction and becomes a sentiment, or conversely a human act becomes torpid and is continued absent-mindedly in the form of a reflex. (Merleau-Ponty, 1945: 88)

But by the time he was working on *The Visible and the Invisible*, he believed that his earlier writing was not free of Cartesian thinking.

Merleau-Ponty differentiates between reflected and unreflected experience. And *radical reflection* (his term for analysis) can destroy the holistic unity of experience, by reducing it, by separating what cannot be separated:

> When I press my hands together, it is not a matter of two sensations felt together as one perceives two objects placed side by side, but of an ambiguous set-up in which both hands can alternate the rôles of 'touching' and being 'touched' … I can identify the hand touched as the same one which will in a moment be touching. (Merleau-Ponty, 1945: 93)

However, there is more to Merleau-Ponty's philosophy than an insistence on the Gestalt of experience. His concept of *flesh* is that the **body** precedes the dichotomy of self and other. If for Sartre, subject and object create tension, for Merleau-Ponty there is no such division:

> [T]he other's gaze transforms me into an object, and mine him, only if both of us withdraw into the core of our thinking nature, if we both make ourselves into an inhuman gaze, if each of us feels his actions to be not taken up and understood, but observed as if they were an insect's. This is what happens, for instance, when I fall under the gaze of a stranger. But even then, the objectification of each by the other's gaze is felt as unbearable only because it takes the place of possible communication. A dog's gaze directed towards me causes me no embarrassment. (Ibid.: 361)

And his idea of embodiment says we are profoundly a part of the world, we are indeed intertwined with it, to the extent that as we live our experiences, we are so absorbed that we cannot make sense of it: 'The world is not what I think, but what I live through' (ibid.: xvi–xvii). There is a recurring theme in Merleau-Ponty's writing of the **ambiguity** of existence.

Merleau-Ponty is often considered as a mere companion to Sartre – even his younger inferior, but this is far from true, and his ideas are often developed in radically different directions. For Sartre, **freedom** is mental, and the body is mere **facticity**, an unhelpful given. But for Merleau–Ponty, freedom is in physical action, and the possibility of action:

> The rationalist's dilemma: either the free act is possible, or it is not – either the event originates in me or is imposed on me from outside, does not apply to our relations with the world and with our past. Our freedom does not destroy our situation, but gears itself to it: as long as we are alive, our situation is open … (Ibid.: 442)

For Sartre, there is **being-in-itself** and **being-for-itself**, but for Merleau-Ponty it is an error to dichotomise in this way. Likewise, Merleau-Ponty disagrees with Sartre that we alternate between being a **self** and an **Other**. Merleau-Ponty insists that we are always both, intertwined.

Contribution to psychotherapy: one of the most useful ideas for therapists is Merleau-Ponty's notion of *sedimentation*: the notion that we sometimes believe or act as if **truth** were fixed, and our lives and identities fixed. Like Heidegger and Sartre, Merleau-Ponty argues that **time** is an important dimension to being, that we live in time, and that action changes our lives. Merleau-Ponty takes the idea of *sedimentation* from Husserl's later work and juxtaposes it with the idea of **projection**, to argue that we can always project new ideas into the future and so loosen the sediment of the past.

A psychotherapist influenced by Merleau-Ponty will stress the entwining or intertwining of ourselves with others, and the ambiguity of life (rather than the ambivalence of Sartre or **Kierkegaard**).

See also **either/or; mineralisation; probability; subject and object**

metamorphoses of the spirit, the three
See **Zarathustra**

metanoia
See **Laing**

metaphysics
Literally, what is *beyond-physics* or *after-physics*. Used by a cataloguer of **Aristotle's** works to name the books after *Physics*, it possesses an unintended significance, being the study of what lies beyond the physical **world**. Metaphysics is the **philosophy** of **Being**, of **existence**, of **reality**, the **onto-logical** status of the world. Notable metaphysicians include Parmenides, **Plato**, Aristotle, Aquinas, **Descartes**, **Spinoza**, Leibniz and **Hegel**. British philosophers, preferring empiricism, have often been suspicious of metaphysics, and the subject has had many opponents, the most colourful of whom was Hume, who declared that a book lacking abstract reasoning on quantity or number or experimental reasoning on matters of fact and existence is no more than sophistry and illusion and should be committed to the flames. Certainly, metaphysics has special difficulties due to the intangible nature of its concerns. And the problems of wrestling with acutely abstract language has led some to accuse metaphysics of being logically incoherent.

Existential philosophers have in various ways attempted to refresh metaphysics, and they have in common the belief that existence itself is not debatable. Instead, they begin with subjective experience, and in this sense lean towards empiricism. Sometimes the existential approach to metaphysics has led to a single, unifying and explanatory principle, such as **Nietzsche** and his notion of the **will to power**. Sometimes it has led to highly meticulous analysis, as with **Heidegger** (for whom philosophy is metaphysics), and his poetical examination of Being.

See also **totality**

mind–body problem

An area of great philosophical controversy, often inspiring high passion, concerning the relationship between the mind and the **body**. It is an area of thought that impinges on psychotherapy theory and practice. Probably the greatest issue within this area is how thought, which seems immaterial, influences physical outcomes. I imagine how pleasant a cup of tea would be and I get to my feet and walk to the kitchen. How is this possible? How did my mind interact with my body to cause my body to move?

Dualism is the idea that mind and body are two different kinds of things. *Monism* is the counter view, that there is only one thing. This can either be mind, as in **idealism** which claims there is only mental substance, or body, as in *materialism* or *physicalism*, which claims that there is only material substance. A third view is that of *dual aspect theory*, which considers that what goes on in the brain and what one experiences are two aspects of the same thing.

Epiphenomenalism, which began as a form of dualism, asserts that without causal connection, features in one situation arise by virtue of those in another.

Husserl tried to solve the mind–body problem. At times he believed that the mind (the 'pure ego') transcends the physical entirely and can survive apart from it, that the mind is or can be disembodied. His view is similar to **Plato's** idealism. **Nietzsche** asserts that the body is all there is, propounding a firm kind of materialism, or physicalism; and **Marcel** and others follow his lead. On the other hand, **Sartre** appears to be a dualist, very similar to **Descartes**.

For existentialists the mental life is embedded in physical being, and even the thoughts of human beings are about physical life. This is not reductionism, it is a unifying of the mental and the physical so tightly that there is no separation. For most existentialists, they are not two substances, mind and body. How else can one learn about the **world** and speculate on it profitably but with the experience of living? Thus for **Merleau-Ponty**, our **knowledge** is a 'knowledge in the hands' (1945: 143). This does not mean that 'mind' and 'brain' are identical. If it did, sadness and meningitis would be the same kind of phenomenon.

For the existential philosopher and psychotherapist, how the mind and body co-exist is of immense importance, for upon it depends one's view of one of the most important givens of life. The existential therapist will usually not separate the client's physical and mental experiences. However, the rejection of dualism carries the risk that psychotherapy might be seen as a branch of physical medicine.

See also **freedom and free will**

mineness
See **identity**

mineralisation
A Sartrean concept that the individual's created world, or *totalisation*, is ever-changing – or if it is not, it petrifies. According to **Sartre**, when we possess something we do so by crystallising it for ourselves so that it represents the **world** to us, and becomes more solid until it seems set in stone. The individual's

movement and thought is then greatly hampered. However, it is possible to reverse this mineralisation by a conscious effort, as described by Sartre in relation to his decision to quit smoking: 'In order to maintain my decision not to smoke, I had to realize a sort of decrystallization' (Sartre, 1943a: 597).

Compare with *sedimentation* (see **Merleau-Ponty**)

Minkowski
Eugene Minkowski (1885–1972). French psychiatrist of Polish origin. Influenced by Bleuler, **Bergson** and **Husserl**, he himself influenced **May**, Ellenberger and **Laing**. He also had a considerable effect on French psychiatry, drawing attention to, amongst other things, the dimension of **time** in a patient's experience. Main publications are: *Schizophrénie* (1927), *Lived Time* (1933) and *Traité de Psychopathologie* (1966). The latter proposes a phenomenological investigation of the experience of mental illness, in a tradition similar to that of **Jaspers** and **Binswanger**.

mirror stage
See Lacan

Mitsein
See **being-with**

Mitwelt
See **four worlds**

Moment, the
The Moment (*Augenblick*, also translated as *moment of vision* – literally meaning the blink of an eye) as **Heidegger** describes it, is a moment of truthfulness, a transcendent moment of awareness of one's plight and one's possibilities. It is in the moment of vision that *Da-sein* makes its resolute decision and is authentically present:

> We call the *present* that is held in authentic temporality, and is thus *authentic*, the *Moment*. This term must be understood in the active sense as an ecstasy. It means the resolute raptness of Da-sein, which is yet *held* in resoluteness, in what is encountered as possibilities and circumstances to be taken care of in the situation ... 'In the Moment' nothing can happen, but as an authentic present it lets us *encounter for the first time* what can be 'in a time' as something at hand or objectively present. (Heidegger, 1927b: 338)

When *Da-sein* is in the moment, it comes into what Heidegger calls the **situation**.

See also **authenticity and inauthenticity; ecstasy; encounter; possibility; present-at-hand; resoluteness; time and temporality; transcendence; truth**

monads
See **other minds**

mood
See **attunement**

mortality
See **death**

motive
In behavioural **psychology**, in **psychoanalysis**, and often in everyday discourse, the term *motivation* is used to mean impetus, that which in itself creates
or causes behaviour. **Sartre** similarly uses *motive* (*mobile*) to mean the desires,
passions and **emotions** that urge one to act, but he insists that these are
chosen, not given. From an existential perspective then, motivation is often
seen in a teleological rather than in a causal sense: what provides the motive is
that which we aim for rather than that which pushes us from the past.

See also **causality; choice; freedom and free will; project**

music
See **art and existential thought**

mystification
Laing uses this idea to indicate the process of **alienation** that can occur in
human communication, especially when one person deliberately confuses
the other so as to retain dominance over them. Laing's thinking in this area
was based on Bateson's use of the term *double-bind*. Especially applied to the
schizophrenic person, it refers to an intensely uncomfortable **paradox**, a
practically untenable predicament whereby another person's words or judgements give contradictory messages that make it impossible to win, no matter
what one does. One is condemned if one does what the other demands, but
also condemned if one does not.

If a person is subject to contradictory or conflicting emotional demands or
prohibitions, he or she will be unable to satisfy whoever is making those
demands. If this situation is the everyday, the double-bound or mystified person lives with very great mental stress. If these impossible demands are made
by a parent (usually, mother) on their child, then that child, needing **love** and
approval, cannot escape the situation, and may become mystified, behaving
and communicating in confused, paradoxical and contradictory ways. Laing
warns psychotherapists to beware lest they mystify their own patients.

narrative
See **generosity**

natural attitude
See **Husserl**

nausea
(*La nausée*). A term used by **Sartre**, and fundamental to Sartre's existential position, although first used by **Levinas**. In the essay 'On Evasion' Levinas writes of *la nausée* and the need to escape oneself, and how in conversation one may move out of oneself. For Sartre, it is a disgust at confronting the **contingency** of the **world**, discovering that nothing need be as it is, and that there is no real shape to the world except that which we ascribe to it. This metaphysical doubt assails Roquentin, the central character of Sartre's 1938 novel, *Nausea*. And Roquentin's experience of nausea extends to **time**, as he realises that there are no real narratives, no true stories, and that narrative is a device to explain events in hindsight. Nausea is brought on by the insight that there is no inherent **meaning**, and the realisation that to give meaning to **nothingness** is false. Roquentin's panic is at the sudden loss of certainty, of predictability. Without meaning, there is no justification, no value in life. And Roquentin reflects, 'Existence everywhere, to infinity, superfluous always and everywhere' (Sartre, 1938: 190). Of objects, that now seem so strange to him, he thinks, 'Things have broken free from their names' (ibid.: 180). And he is ashamed at his own incapacity to create meaning: 'But is it my fault if the beer at the bottom of my glass is warm, if there are brown stains on my mirror, if I am superfluous' (ibid.: 247). Nausea is therefore the experience of the inexorable substantiality of a world in which one is doomed to be nothing.

necessity
Literally, a state of affairs that cannot be otherwise than it is. Philosophers have long debated what is necessary and what is not. They distinguish between (1) *logical necessity*: things that must be the case in order to avoid contradiction (2) *physical necessity*, as imposed on us by the laws of nature, and (3) *moral necessity*, the things required of us as moral beings.

Kierkegaard based his **philosophy** of **paradox** on the conflict and complementarity of the principles of **possibility** and necessity. Human beings strive for **freedom** and for the realisation of their potential, but the limits of what is physically necessary must be taken into account:

> The self is freedom. But freedom is the dialectical aspect of the categories of possibility and necessity. ...
>
> Possibility and necessity belong to the self just as do infinitude and finitude. A self that has no possibility is in despair, and likewise a self that has no necessity. (Kierkegaard, 1849: 29, 35)

Most existential philosophers accept that some things are human or **onto-logical** givens and are therefore necessary. This is often related to the concept of **facticity**. For **Nietzsche** the necessary is based on our biological reality, while for **Jaspers** the necessary is linked to the reality of our **limit situations**. And **Sartre** speaks of **being-in-itself** as having a certain necessary **facticity**.

In *Being and Time*, **Heidegger** refers to actuality as the opposite of possibility, using it almost in the sense of 'necessary'. Unlike Kierkegaard, he assumes a hierarchy rather than a tension between the two: 'Higher than actuality stands *possibility*' (Heidegger, 1927b: 38). In his later work, he sometimes refers to *Notwendigkeit* (necessity), a derivation of *Not* (need, or want or distress). According to Heidegger, philosophy is necessary because of humankind's abandonment of **Being**, of our distress at this abandonment, and our need for Being.

neurotic anxiety
See **Bugental**; **May**; **Tillich**

neurotic guilt
See **guilt**; **May**

Nietzsche
Friedrich Wilhelm Nietzsche was born in Rocken, Prussia 15 October 1844, and died in Weimar on 25 August 1900.

Notable works: *The Birth of Tragedy* (1872); *Human, All Too Human* (1878–9); *Joyful Wisdom* or *The Gay Science* (1882); *Thus Spoke Zarathustra* (1883); *Beyond Good and Evil* (1886); and *On the Genealogy of Morals* (1887).

Influenced by: Christianity; **Kant**; F.A. Lange; **Schopenhauer**; Classical Greek philosophy; literature and culture, and Wagner. The influence of Schopenhauer was fundamental, but left Nietzsche wishing to find a positive, more affirming view of life. It is uncertain whether Wagner truly influenced Nietzsche or whether instead Wagner's art for a while epitomised Nietzsche's own ideals.

Influence on: Nietzsche became very influential after his death, inspiring psychoanalysts **Freud**, Adler and **Jung**, writers Thomas Mann, Hermann Hesse, Gide, Shaw, Yeats and **Camus**, as well as Martin **Buber**, Paul **Tillich**, **Sartre**, **Derrida** and **Foucault**. Some of Nietzsche's writings were employed by the Nazis to justify their own politics, using his expressions out of context, based on interpretations of his work by his sister, Elizabeth Forster-Nietzsche. It is unlikely that Hitler read or understood any of Nietzsche's philosophy. Nietzsche's anti-nationalism, his criticism of Germany, his anti-anti-Semitism, his disdain for political parties and mobs were in fact the antithesis of Nazism.

Life: the son of a Lutheran minister, his father died when Friedrich was four, and he was brought up in the feminine household of his mother, sister, grandmother and two aunts. As a youth, he was extremely religious, but then rejected religion, and became attracted to Schopenhauer's atheism. At the age of 24 he was granted a chair in Classical Philology at Basel, and became a Swiss subject. A year later he took leave to serve as a medical orderly in the Franco-Prussian war, where, tending to sick soldiers, it is possible he was infected with syphilis. Very poor health encouraged him to retire on a small pension at 34. He was a disciple and friend of Richard Wagner, but broke with him in 1876, partly to find his own voice, partly from principled disagreement, and partly in reaction to his own frustrated attraction to Wagner's wife, Cosima. Up to this time he claimed that the only justification for the existence of society lies in its producing great artists. In January 1889 Nietzsche collapsed in the street, embracing a horse flogged by a coachman. He soon fell into a madness that lasted to his death.

Nietzsche was a reclusive man, a misogynist with little or no sexual experience. He hated the sacrosanct, was morally courageous and determined in his honesty. He had a great enthusiasm for the work of the poet **Hölderlin** and believed in the value of **laughter** and of dance. If Arthur Schopenhauer said no to life, then Nietzsche affirmed life, perhaps not in a light-hearted way, but in something like the manner of the **Stoics**. Most of his writing is rhetorical, with little care for argument. This is both his strength and his weakness, freeing him from the banality and constraint of modern **philosophy**, but making it difficult for others to argue with him.

Major ideas: As much a psychologist as a philosopher and never a philosopher in the modern academic and analytic sense, Nietzsche chose to write in a poetical and epigrammatic way. He had no system, and indeed opposed systems of thought, claiming that his views at any one time served his own purposes in his psychological and moral development. Early on, he studied the classical world and related it to his own **existence**, finding contemporary ideas wanting, especially in relation to life. He reacted to this, and perhaps against his own upbringing, in becoming the supreme iconoclast and critic of the modern world.

Finding insufficient cause to accept Christian values and beliefs, he nonetheless refused to embrace **nihilism**, wishing instead to develop a positive answer to what he saw as the collapse of Christianity. Nietzsche's thought is essentially one of **relativism**, the notion that morality derives from the contingencies of the human world. He therefore takes a multi-perspectival stance to **truth** and **knowledge**, insisting that our views come only from our **interpretation** of our circumstances. In this he echoes one of the Sophists, Protagoras, who wrote: 'Of all things, man is the measure'. For Nietzsche, all truth is fiction, that is, interpretation and perspective. It is a useful fiction, it offers stability; but there is no stable truth, **reality** is flux. He rejects **idealism**, but is never amoral, and his philosophy is always restlessly spiritual and questing. Nietzsche portrays himself as no mere heretic, but a prophet of new **values**.

Nietzsche believes human beings are somewhere between animal and God: 'Man is a rope, fastened between animal and superman – a rope across an abyss' (Nietzsche, 1883: Prologue, sect. 4), and he considers the positive use of **sublimation,** saying that people should sublimate their **will to power** in order to become a new and ultimate form of human life, the **superman** *(Übermensch)*. By loving our destiny (see *amor fati*) we can overcome what constrains us. And taking up the spirit of what he refers to as the *Dionysian mentality* (see **Dionysian and Apollonian mentalities**), and living in a joyful, passionate manner, we may discover the inevitability of an **eternal return** of all that is.

Contribution to psychotherapy: Some see in Nietzsche's ideas the prototype for the **humanistic psychology** movement, with its rejection of mechanistic causality and its emphasis on the positive potential of the individual rather than the analysis of **psychopathology**. Other critics accept this only in part, arguing that humanism is too optimistic compared with Nietzsche's insistence on the animal nature of human beings, and our capacity for destruction. For Nietzsche there is a need to educate this nature to cope with the demands of everyday social life, accepting pain and unhappiness as a natural part of life, and not as flaws. For Nietzsche, pain is the accompaniment to the will to power's striving, and a useful stimulus with which to overcome obstacles.

A Nietzschean psychotherapy might aim to challenge assumptions of what is good and what is bad, and to further confront the *Spirit of Gravity*, to find a way of laughing at it. It would aim not to cure a sickness, but to develop health and fitness, to discover how to labour towards joy. Such a psychotherapy would view idealism as an enemy of life, reflecting Nietzsche's belief that the life worth living is one strong enough to withstand the trials of existence without retreating to imaginary worlds.

In Nietzsche's psychological philosophy there is much of potential use to a psychotherapist, or someone seeking to examine life. Its main points might be:

1 *The multi-perspectival nature of life.* It may be true for one person that warfare is both a noble, attractive opportunity to demonstrate courage and that it is senseless waste of human life; it may be true for another person that they can both love and hate their mother; for a third person, sexual adventuring and sexual loyalty are both ambitions. Contradiction may be real or apparent, and in either case worth examining (see **revaluation of values**). But some paradoxes are irresolvable, are part of the human condition, the result of an ambivalence that is the stuff of human life: to want admiration, to be ashamed; to want peace, to want war. But we should affirm both what is glorious and what is shameful about us. We ought to affirm uncertainty, ambivalence and **ambiguity**.

2 *The affirmation of suffering,* a kind of stoicism.

3 *Questioning* personal certainties, systems and theories, as well as other people's suppositions, axioms, principles, icons and authority.

4 *Taking control of one's power.*

Other Nietzschean entries: **dragon, the great; ethical life; good and evil; herd, the; master morality and slave morality; Noontide, the Great; no-saying; paradox; resentment; yes-saying; Zarathustra**

nihilism

A term originating in Russia and popularised by Turgenev in his 1862 novel *Fathers and Sons*. Then it meant the rejection of traditional **values** and a belief in the necessity of social destruction in order to start anew. And thus it is closely akin to anarchism, as described by writers like Proudhon and Bakunin. Since then the term has been used with a variety of meanings, but always to express belief in the non-existence of something, whether knowledge or social, political or moral values. And it is commonly used pejoratively to disparage an opponent. For instance, some nineteenth-century Christian writers were wont to class all atheists as nihilists, implying that in them lay a dangerous want of values.

This last claim is inevitably and intensely denied by many existential writers. **Nietzsche**, for instance, pronounced a profound moral and religious scepticism. His nihilism was a response to what he described as the death of God and the death of illusion. But just as Bakunin had already claimed that the passion for destruction is also a creative passion, so Nietzsche strove for a creative response to the death of established beliefs. **Camus**, who claimed that he believed in nothing, that everything is **absurd**, nonetheless affirms **responsibility** as **Sartre** affirms **choice**. Existential theorists are often characterised as nihilists, but for the existential thinker, nihilism can only be a transition, something to be overcome, a position from which new values must be generated.

In so far as psychotherapy is a search for personal **meaning**, the existential therapist will be interested in signs of a lack of meaning, whether it betrays itself as a passive and defeated acceptance of the absurd, or an angry rejection of meaning imposed from without.

See also **Dostoevsky; nothingness**

Nobody, the
See **They, the**

noema
See **phenomenological method**

noesis
See **phenomenological method**

non-being
See **Being; Tillich**

non-thetic consciousness
See **pre-reflexive consciousness**

Noontide, the Great

In *Thus Spoke Zarathustra*, Nietzsche writes poetically of the crisis to come, of the transformation, the judgement, the Great Noontide of earth and man, the point at which man realises he stands between animal and **superman**:

> And this is the great noontide: it is when man stands at the middle of his course between animal and Superman and celebrates his journey to the evening as his highest hope: for it is the journey to a new morning. (Nietzsche, 1883: 104)

At the noontide human beings realise and accept that all gods are dead and they must rely on their own knowledge and effort.

See also **crowd, the; herd, the; They, the**

no-saying

No-saying is a denial of life, according to **Nietzsche**. It represents a discontent with life as it is, with the **world** as it is. Nietzsche associates it with **Schopenhauer** and his pessimistic philosophy. It is in opposition to **yes-saying**.

not knowing

Drawn from the **phenomenological method**, this is the suspension of certainty, the openness to lived experience. **Husserl** refers to such suspension of one's prejudice as *epoché*. In **existential psychotherapy** it is the stance the therapist takes towards his or her experience of the patient. A similar attitude has been adopted in some other therapeutic schools, including George Kelly's *personal construct* therapy, and Wilfred Bion's form of **psychoanalysis**. It is not unlike Keats's *negative capability*.

Nothing, the

In the philosophy of **Heidegger**, not only is **Being** significant, but so too is nothing. The Nothing (*das Nichts*) is whatever has not come to be, whatever has no Being. For instance, unicorns are possibilities, ideas, but lack Being. Heidegger considers that beings are between Being (for they are in existence, so participate in Being) and the Nothing (for the life of a being is finite). Awareness of the Nothing is hard to bear, and often human beings avoid directly facing it, so **falling** into **inauthenticity**.

Critics accuse Heidegger of mistaking linguistic analysis for analysis of the world, but in discussing nothing, Heidegger is making a point about what it means to be. **Sartre** too believes it is important to take nothing into account and he considers nothing to be the centre of a human being's existence.

See also **nothingness**

nothingness

That there is such a thing as negation is of paramount importance to **Sartre**. He wants to know how human beings can make negative judgements. He sees it as deriving from contingent facts like **death**:

Now the characteristic of Heidegger's philosophy is to describe Dasein by using positive terms which hide the implicit negations. Dasein is 'outside of itself, in the world'; it is 'a being of distances'; it is care; it is 'its own possibilities', etc. All this amounts to saying that Dasein 'is not' in itself, that it 'is not' in immediate proximity to itself, and that it surpasses the world inasmuch as it posits itself as *not being in itself* and as *not being the world.* (Sartre, 1943a: 18)

For Sartre, nothingness (*le néant*) is an essential aspect of human **Being**, for human beings introduce it into the **world**. We contrast ourselves with non-conscious things, and beyond these things we project a background of non-being, or nothingness. Nothingness is thus a kind of general concept or category, and from this, human **consciousness** derives an unwelcome but inescapable **freedom**.

See also **being-for-itself; being-in-itself; care; contingency;** *Dasein*; **Heidegger; Nothing, the**

numbing

Benommen is also translated as *fascination*, or simply, *benumbing.* It actually means to be taken over, to be taken away, or to be captivated, to be dazed and it is an unavoidable state for *Da-sein* to be in as a starting point. Animals are always like this.

Being-in-the-world, as concern, is *fascinated by* the world with which it is concerned. (Heidegger, 1927a: 61)

Heidegger uses it to describe the difficulty of seeing the **world** as it is:

Taking care of things always already occurs on the basis of a familiarity with the world. In this familiarity Da-sein can lose itself in what it encounters within the world and be numbed by it. (Heidegger, 1927b: 76)

We are benumbed by **idle talk**, fascinated by **everydayness**.

On the other hand, angst results in a kind of numbing, yet through it we can develop **authenticity**, because in **anxiety** we get numbed in relation to the world with which we were fascinated and thus regain the freedom to become taken over by our original *homelessness.*

See also **care; rapture; uncanniness**

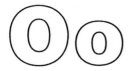

object
See **subject and object**

objective spirit
See **spirit**

objectness
See **subject and object**

One, the
See **They, the**

ontic
Heidegger sharply distinguishes between the ontic and the **ontological** dimensions of human **Being**. Ontic refers to the concrete **world**, to existing beings or things, whereas ontological refers to those conditions that are the essential conditions of human **existence**. Thus, ontic investigation is concerned with particular beings or things (*existents*), as they are actually manifest in the world, beings whose existence is taken for granted.

> Da-sein is a being that does not simply occur among other beings. Rather it is ontically distinguished by the fact that in its being this being is concerned *about* its very being. (Heidegger, 1927b: 12)

Heidegger does not set out to analyse ontic conditions. His primary concern is with the ontological.

See also *Da-sein*

ontological/ontology
In general **philosophy** ontology is the **metaphysics** of **Being**. For **Aristotle**, ontology was the First Philosophy, the study of the **essence** of things. It is in this sense that **Heidegger** is sometimes considered a metaphysician, for he is an ontologist, whose concern is with Being. Unusually for an ontologist, but typical of existentialists, Heidegger's starting point is the assumption that Being exists. His interest is not as a traditional metaphysician, in doubting the

world, but with understanding Being. Being is a general given, but manifests in an exemplary way through *Da-sein*. Heidegger therefore gives priority to the examination of *Da-sein*, since this must reveal the nature of Being, for *Da-sein*, as a **being-in-the-world**, itself discloses Being. Thus Heidegger writes, 'Da-sein has proven to be what, before all other beings, is ontologically the primary being to be interrogated' (Heidegger, 1927b: 13). He argues that *Da-sein*'s ontic being is first and foremost concerned with the ontological. In other words: 'The ontic distinction of Da-sein lies in the fact that it *is* ontological' (ibid.: 12). Heidegger's point is that an essential aspect of human being is a concern with Being. Nonetheless, we often neglect Being and lose ourselves in our everyday – or ontic – concerns.

All existential thinkers are concerned with the nature or essence of human Being. **Kierkegaard** emphasises the subjective experience of Being. **Nietzsche** has as his starting-point a complaint that philosophy since **Plato** has limited itself blindly to what *is*, neglecting the possibility of **becoming**. And **Sartre** echoes this in his distinction between **being-in-itself** and **being-for-itself**, between the fixed nature of things and the **freedom** of being human.

ontological insecurity/security
See **Laing**

ontonomy
Literally, *lawfulness of being*. Used by van Deurzen (1998) to describe the possibility of a science of living based on the lawfulness of **existence** and on the givens of the human condition. It is described as a middle way between self-government (autonomy) and subjection to external control (heteronomy), being ruled by life itself.

See also *eudaimonia*

orientation
See **disposition**; **attunement**

Ortega y Gasset
José Ortega y Gasset (1883–1955). Spanish philosopher, politician and essayist. Despite a prosperous background and a proclivity to intellectual elitism, he became first a socialist, and then an active republican, choosing to leave Spain at the outbreak of the Civil War in 1936, and returning in 1948. He was not influenced by any particular thinkers, but was himself responsible for introducing modern ideas to Spain, where foreign **philosophy** had for centuries been held in suspicion. His publications include *Meditations on Quixote* (1914), *The Revolt of the Masses* (1931) and *Man and Crisis* (1933).

Ortega saw **idealism** as an **ontological** prioritising of the **self**, and realism as giving priority to things. Rejecting both, together with absolute and objective **truth**, he argued that **reality** is the interaction between the self and the world of things, each impacting on and constituting the other. He described his philosophy as a 'metaphysics of vital reason' because it is founded in vitality, that is, the lived life of the individual. He disapproved of existential philosophers who wrote of human **existence**, for he held that *things* exist whereas human beings *live*.

Ortega saw life as a mission. He argued that we are the authors of our lives, that we cannot have choices made for us, and that our own **choice** should be for **authenticity**. However, this does not require a particular commitment, for living itself is a commitment, and to live is to find oneself. His *perspectivism* is the belief that the **world** can only be known from a single, living perspective. Ortega disdained French existentialism as sentimental. Many ideas in the philosophy of **Heidegger** he admired but claimed to have conceived first, though he complained that Heidegger had not explained the significance of **Being**. According to Ortega, a being is a point of view of the world, a unique perspective.

Other, the

Another human being cannot be the same as ourselves to ourselves, for we have only our own **consciousness** and perceptual equipment, somehow located within our **self**. *The Other* – as philosophers often call it, is therefore usually or perhaps always foreign, distant and unknown.

Because of the existentialist concern with **Being**, questions concerning the Other are of considerable poignancy, both to philosophers and to psychotherapists. At its broadest, the Other is everything human but alien from our experience, including other persons, **death**, and whatever is not conscious. **Sartre** argued that the presence of the Other is a threat to the individual's survival, since the Other apprehends us from outside as an object. Simone de **Beauvoir** thought that woman essentially plays the role of being the Other for man. **Heidegger** considered the **existence** of others in the **world** as an essential aspect of our ontological **fallenness**. We relate to ourselves in the first instance as if we were the Other, the anonymous **They**. However, **Levinas** turned the issue upside down by positing the importance of the Other as the **essence** of our being. To be concerned for the Other brings us into true Being. This is reflected in the psychoanalytic theories of **Lacan**, who considers that the acceptance of the existence of the Other is fundamental to the individual's emotional development.

See also **look, the**

other minds

A problem in the **philosophy** of knowledge is how we can know that there are minds other than our own. It is less a thorough scepticism of the **existence** of other minds, than a concern with *how* we know. Further to this is the question: How can we know how much other minds are like our own? This question is of great significance to the psychologist and the psychotherapist. One answer is to argue from analogy, that if other beings behave in a way that resembles our own behaviour, or if their verbal expressions resemble our own, then we can assume that they have a like state of mind.

The existential stance goes beyond this rather weak reasoning and contends that human beings (whose physical existence is not doubted) share the same plight and the same concerns, and that analysis of our human plight and human concerns reveals the **essence** of **Being**. **Husserl,** when accused of a solipsistic stance in relation to the **transcendental ego**, argued that the transcendental ego includes the experience of others in itself and in this sense is rather like a community of *monads* (independent and immaterial mental entities: an idea from the philosophy of Leibniz). The phenomenological approach to selfhood is therefore that it is not separate and that human consciousness is fundamentally shared and bound together. In this way existential philosophy has begun the process of understanding other minds. Still, very little attention has been given to differences between men and women. And as for the question of whether animals (or other entities, such as plants or machines) have minds, and if so of what sort, the anthropocentric basis of existential theory is revealed in its complete neglect.

See also **Beauvoir, de; being-in-the-world; body; Descartes; solipsism**

pact of generosity
See **generosity**

paradox
This refers to a seemingly absurd or contradictory proposition or an argument from acceptable premises to an incredible conclusion. A paradox thus excites astonishment and invites investigation of its supposed facts and its reasoning. It is therefore a powerful device in teaching philosophical ideas. The existential practitioner is likely to hold that human **existence** is often paradoxical, so that we need to learn for instance that we have to face up to the reality of death, if we are to truly come to life. Paradox also means that which goes against Church dogma, although it is seldom used in this sense. In the area of existential philosophy, **Kierkegaard** and **Nietzsche** made liberal use of paradox:

> The supreme paradox of all thought is the attempt to discover something that thought cannot think. (Kierkegaard, 1844a: 46)

> [I]t is an infinite merit to be able to despair. (Kierkegaard, 1849: 45)

> You crowd together with your neighbours and have beautiful words for it. But I tell you: Your love of your neighbour is your bad love of yourselves. (Nietzsche, 1883: 86)

For the existential psychotherapist, contradictions and paradoxes abound in human living. But the aim of therapy is not to eliminate them, but to confront them and live constructively with their tension.

See also **absurd, the; dialectic; irony**

paradoxical intention
See **Frankl**

participation
See **Jaspers; Marcel; Tillich**

passion
Originally, from the Latin *patio*, this means suffering, but it has come to mean barely contained or extreme emotion. Yet it may also be used to mean

a lust for life, a wholehearted commitment to living, and a determination to be undaunted by failure and humiliation – in short, a will to live to the full. Indeed, for **Nietzsche**, one is wise to test one's **will to power** against resistance. But Nietzsche thought passion destructive if unalloyed with wisdom. His **superman** would undoubtedly be passionate, but not reckless or wanton.

Like Nietzsche, **Kierkegaard** encourages a **sublimation** of passion. And for Kierkegaard, religious faith is a passion, for it is beyond the power of reason. **Jaspers** speaks of the *passion for the night*, the experience of letting intense emotions break through the veneer of normality, putting the individual in touch with the things that really matter. He opposes this to the notion of the *law of the day*, which requires us to take into account the realities of a more ordered existence. **Heidegger** distinguishes between feelings that are occasional affects (*Affekt*), such as anger, and those that are more permanent and intensely clear passions (*Leidenschaft*), such as hatred.

See also **emotions; leap of faith**

passion for the night
See **Jaspers; passion**

past
See **time and temporality**

perception
In everyday conversation, this often means speculation, judgement or **point of view** (see also **intuition** and **interpretation**), but in **philosophy** and **psychology** it is usually limited to sense perception. Such a theory of perception tries to address the issue of how we apprehend the **world** and the objects in it, and is essential to understanding **consciousness** and **knowledge**.

Amongst the many problems concerning perception is whether the perceived **phenomenon** is active or passive, and whether it reliably refers to anything external. Perception may seem passive, for light enters the eye, and sound excites the eardrum. However, most contemporary theorists hold that we actively interpret such sensory stimulation as perception. But many writers hold that we only perceive sense stimuli, and that we do not directly apprehend the world, and that seeing is not worth believing. They point to the existence of illusions and hallucinations as evidence of the unreliability of sense perception. For others, including existential, phenomenological, and **Gestalt** theorists, a phenomenon is a whole and is directly perceived, therefore the idea that perception is like a private cinema show in one's head, removed from the real world, is rejected. Thus **phenomenological method** is a means to uncover the distortions of higher-order interpretation (for instance, emotional bias and prejudice), and to return to unspoiled perception: 'To the things themselves!', as **Husserl** insisted. **Merleau-Ponty** typifies this attitude, as he takes a forthright position, placing perception at the heart of his philosophy:

> The world is not what I think, but what I live through. I am open to the world, I have no doubt that I am in communication with it. (Merleau-Ponty, 1945: xvi–xvii)

He goes on to explain how perception arises through **intentionality**, an innate, bodily anticipation towards the world. For Merleau-Ponty, as for other existential philosophers, the person is never a mere observer in the world, but always integral to it. Everything we do and are is related to the intentional arc through which we connect with the world:

> [T]he life of consciousness – cognitive life, the life of desire or perceptual life – is subtended by an 'intentional arc' which projects round about us our past, our future, our human setting, our physical, ideological and moral situation. (Ibid.: 136)

person

A significant issue in **metaphysics** is what it means to be a person. Most philosophers have reduced the question to a quality of human being, such as self-consciousness, rationality, free will or conscience. But questions abound: Is God a person? Might some animals other than *homo sapiens* be persons? Are there degrees of personhood? And is it a technical attribution, or are we merely giving or refusing membership of a group with particular rights – the human race and its dominion over the Earth?

Descartes defines a person as one possessing a **body** and soul. But critics object that soul is impossible to define and identify. Existential philosophers have not dealt with the issue directly but have dealt directly with what it is to be human. **Kierkegaard** prefers to speak of an **individual** and believes it to be important for each of us to become an individual. When **Rogers** writes of *becoming a person* (see **becoming**) he is writing of the person's potential to be free. And this is typical of the existential approach, that *person* is not to be narrowly defined. **Sartre** writes of **freedom** and possibilities. Paradoxically, this is the closest we can get to an existential description of personhood, in that it cannot be defined and limited.

person-centred approach
See **client-centred psychotherapy**

personal dimension/world
See **four worlds**

personal identity
See **identity**

personality
See **becoming; change; choice; client-centred psychotherapy; existence precedes essence; freedom and free will; hodological space; identity; person; project; self; thrown and thrownness**

perspective
See **profiles**

perspectivism
See **Ortega**

petrification
See **Laing**

phenomenon
That which is manifest, or that which is revealed in experience. From the Greek verb *phainestai*, to show itself. It is used in different ways by different philosophers, sometimes as simply meaning what is experienced of the **world**. **Husserl** significantly established **phenomenology** upon the belief that we should return to the close observation and description of things (or phenomena) themselves. **Heidegger** characteristically discovered a greater complexity, differentiating between phenomenon and appearance:

> *Phenomenon* – the self-showing in itself – means a distinctive way something can be encountered. On the other hand, *appearance* means a referential relation in beings themselves such that what does the *referring* (the making known) can fulfil its possible function only if it shows itself in itself – only if it is a 'phenomenon'. (Heidegger, 1927b: 31)

Heidegger further separates out *semblance*, which is where experience implies the sign of something hidden when it is not so, for instance, when someone under red light has the semblance of a red skin, itself the appearance of a fever.

See also **phenomenological method; thing-in-itself**

phenomenological method
In *Cartesian Meditations*, **Husserl** asserts that we must start 'in absolute poverty, with an absolute lack of knowledge' [1928 (1, 2): I44]. **Kant** had earlier distinguished between three kinds of statement: (1) *empirical* – of fact; (2) *analytic* – true by definition; and (3) *synthetic a priori* – knowable without recourse to facts or analysis but through direct apprehension. In a similar way, Husserl distinguishes between the *contingent* – what happens to be, and the *necessary* – what is essential to a thing's identity. He maintains that *Wissenschaft* (science, philosophy, history) should concern itself with the latter. Like Kant, Husserl distinguishes between the empirical and the a priori (practical evidence, which is fallible, versus what can be seen at once – which, because it is only descriptive, cannot be false). We can detect certain facts with our physical senses, and through reason we can deduce others. But **essence** can only be understood directly, through a kind of **intuition**. Husserl's chant *'Zu den*

Sachen selbst!' (To the things themselves!) means a rejection of theoretical judgement. Instead, the phenomenologist must investigate through *Anschauung* (which means *seeing* or view, but is usually translated as intuition within context). Husserl suggests different reductions: epistemological, transcendental, phenomenological, psychological, etc., but he does not clearly explicate the differences between them or their required techniques. He employs the terms *noema* and *noesis* to mean, respectively, the objects of our attention and the experience as it is experienced, and the act of **consciousness** itself – an act that is intentional, inherently laden with meaning, and not objective.

Epoché is one aspect of reduction, a bracketing of assumptions for the sake of gaining sight of the transcendental **truth**. It is not simply an open-mindedness, it is a spirit of **not knowing**, of not-at-all-knowing, a new theoretical scrutiny of lived experience. The phenomenological *epoché*, or *reduction*, is the bracketing of **existence** – that is, the suspension of belief in the naturalistic attitude where we make constant interpretations of the world, but it is not the doubting of existence itself. Bracketing is necessary because the phenomenological inquiry is not mere fact-finding, it is the apprehension of intentional acts. The intuition of essences is *eidetic*, so *eidetic reduction* is not a here-and-now experience, but a contemplation of essences ultimately leading to the uncovering of the **transcendental ego**. However, existentialists have generally denied the possibility and the appeal of phenomenological reduction to the extent Husserl envisaged.

phenomenology

Phenomenologists reject the assumption, common in psychotherapy, that what is visible or apparent is shallow and uninformative. They take the opposite view, that what is apparent should be looked at more closely, though not with a mind to discover what is beneath it. Simply put, this is the setting aside of preconceptions, theories, bias and prejudice, and letting oneself experience the **world**.

There are two kinds of phenomenology: transcendental phenomenology and existential phenomenology. The originator of the first, **Husserl**, held that the best kind of scientific or philosophical investigation would not form opinions before the facts, as he thought modern **science** and **philosophy** did. For Husserl, the objects of phenomenology are absolute data grasped in pure and imminent **intuition**. Phenomenology is thus description rather than explanation. For example, one of Husserl's methods is *equalisation* (or *horizontalisation*), by which no judgements are made as to importance and everything described is given equal value.

Heidegger, although inspired by Husserl, used the **phenomenological method** to describe the most fundamental aspects of being human: the ontological givens of existence, and the facts of our **being-in-the-world**. **Sartre** has a different existential phenomenology (or **existentialism**): he emphasises that we are living, thinking creatures who actively engage as we experience; we are not passive receptors for data, we are not like the photographic emulsion or the radio receiver. Unlike these, we are actors in the world, inseparable from it.

Some critics see phenomenology as endorsing a purposeless and naïve reliance on intuition, but it is a particular kind of intuition that is called for. For the Marxist or collectivist, it may seem a bourgeois or unsociable individualism. The existentialist would retort that what is explored is not just personal meaning, but that of the individual in the context of their being-in-the-world.

Importance to psychotherapy: Phenomenological ideas have great implications for the practice of psychotherapy. Unlike the psychoanalytical belief that **meaning** is buried beneath a symbolic and often distorted surface, a phenomenological approach to psychotherapy holds that what is apparent is rich with unquestioned significance.

Freud, though no existentialist, often writes of being phenomenological, and if this was not frequently put into practice, it is there in principle, for instance in his advice on analysing dreams, to consider all the elements of the dream. It is also present in the fundamental rules of free-floating attention and free association. The phenomenological psychotherapist or counsellor, whether existential or not, will assist his or her client to examine their own experiences in as raw a state as possible, as free from existing, self-imposed theories and judgements, allowing a fresh look at their life.

See also **Brentano**; **essence**; **facticity**; **hermeneutics**; **intentionality**; **interpretation**; **judgement**; *Lebenswelt*; **Merleau-Ponty**; **psychology**; **reality**; **thrownness**

philosophical counselling and consultancy

Recent movements in **philosophy** have been to reinstate the philosopher's position as a practical searcher for wisdom and a consultant to those who seek to live a better life. Until the twentieth century, not all philosophers were academic and bound to universities. Often their teaching and writing was not solely for other scholars, but for the interested public. Before **Plato's** time, for instance, there were philosophers (the Sophists) who were itinerant teachers and consultants. There is thus a long history for the practice of philosophical counselling and consultancy. But in the 1980s there commenced a revival of this movement, credited to Gerd Achenbach and Ad Hoogendijk of Germany and Holland respectively. It is a practice which has since spread to many other countries.

Philosophical counselling or consultancy is explicitly not psychological, but instead is an intense discussion in which the philosopher searches to assist his client (or 'visitor', as they are often termed) in gaining a greater understanding of life, and who enters into an examination of whatever problem in living the client brings. It is a discussion intended to be free from particular philosophical bias, and which moves between the abstract and the concrete, often looking at what the client means by the words he or she uses, with the object of gaining insight into the themes of the client's life. Most philosophical counsellors make use of the **Socratic method**.

Several psychological therapists and some psychological therapies have the character of philosophical enquiry in their practice. This is most evident in **existential psychotherapy**. It is present to an extent in some other therapies, and **Rogers** viewed **client-centred psychotherapy** as philosophical. Cognitive (or cognitive behaviour therapy) employs logical method, although this should perhaps be cautiously distinguished from the spirit of open enquiry that is philosophy.

philosophical faith
See **comprehensive, the**

philosophical thinking
See **thinking**

philosophy
With a literal meaning of 'love of wisdom', the formal study of philosophy is notoriously difficult to define, and is itself a philosophical question. It might roughly be characterised as the conceptual questioning and analysis of fundamental suppositions of **existence**, human **knowledge** and essential issues of morals, ethics, aesthetics and politics. The approach to living that is sometimes called 'philosophical' is related to this, but somewhat easier to explain, being an individual's interest in looking beyond the surface of his or her beliefs, and perhaps finding the determination and courage to face the possibility of potentially uncomfortable answers. Philosophy, then, whilst the most abstract of disciplines, can also be the most personal, for the search for understanding or the dispelling of confusion can yield findings that demonstrate one was inconsistent or in error, or that indicate **paradox**, contradiction or dilemma, and imply a need for change in one's way of living. It is in this spirit that existentialists consider philosophy, and in this manner that it is applicable to **existential psychotherapy**.

See also **metaphysics**

philosophy of ambiguity
See **ambiguity**

physical dimension/world
See **four worlds**

place
See **locus; space**

Plato

(*c.* 429–347 BC). Greek philosopher, influenced by **Socrates**, whose own influence is felt throughout Western philosophy. References to Platonic ideas can be found under: **Being; emotions;** *eudaimonia***; Husserl; intuition; mind–body problem; rationalism**

plural mode of relating

See **Binswanger**

poetry

See **language**

point of view

In *The Point of View*, **Kierkegaard** argues that to help another person, one must know more than they, and one must understand their point of view:

> [T]he helper must first humble himself under him he would help, and therewith must understand that to help does not mean to be a sovereign but to be a servant, that to help does not mean to be ambitious but to be patient, that to help means to endure for the time being the imputation that one is in the wrong and does not understand what the other understands. (Kierkegaard, 1848: 334)

The implication of Kierkegaard's words for psychotherapy is that objectivity cannot truly help, but that the search for **truth** begins with subjectivity.

possibility

A term used with special meaning in the philosophy of **Heidegger** (and used by **Sartre** in a similar way). It does not merely refer to what might happen, but is a reference to the future, for it refers (with one exception, that of **death**) to the essential **freedom** of humankind. Understood simply, it means potential, or capacity, for it is the capacity of the human being (*Da-sein*) to choose its actions, and to make use of things. Human beings are possibility rather than **actuality**. And **understanding** the **world** reveals this:

> Da-sein is not something objectively present which then has as an addition the ability to do something, but is rather primarily being-possible. Da-sein is always what it can be and how it is its possibility ... The being-possible, which Da-sein always is existentially, is also distinguished from empty, logical possibility and from the contingency of something objectively present, where this or that can 'happen' to it ... Da-sein is a being-possible entrusted to itself ... (Heidegger, 1927b: 143–4)

Heidegger points out that not only is our mortality our greatest and most extreme possibility (for it brings the end of future possibilities), but that it is a

thrown possibility, not one created by *Da-sein*. But whilst it is a given and unavoidable fact, it is ultimately personal. Any other task might be given to another to perform, but not one's personal death. With death as with all possibility, we can face it in an authentic or an inauthentic way.

See also **authenticity and inauthenticity; existence precedes essence; sight**

post-modernism
See **deconstruction**

potentiality-for-being-oneself
Heidegger is constantly concerned with **authenticity and inauthenticity**, the latter according to him always the starting point of our being through *Dasein's* loss of him or herself in the **They**. Authentic being is possible: 'But because *Da-sein* is lost in the "They", it must first *find* itself' (Heidegger, 1927b: 268). It is the **call of conscience** that summons the *They-self*, upon which the They collapses, leaving the self of the They-self:

> However, this is not the self that can become an 'object' for itself on which to pass judgement, not the self that unrestrainedly dissects its 'inner life' with excited curiosity, and not the self that stares 'analytically' at states of the soul and their backgrounds. (Heidegger, 1927a: 273)

There is nothing one can say of the **self** as an actuality. *Da-sein* is always potentiality, that is, **becoming** rather than actuality.

> Dasein is not something present-at-hand which possesses its ability to be something as an extra; it is primarily being-possible. Dasein is always what it can be, and in the way in which it is its possibility. (Ibid.: 143)

It is not a core, a psychological **essence**. It is not even the potential for action. And this potentiality for being oneself can only be realised through an awareness of one's being in **time**, and it begins to emerge through resolute **anticipation** of the possibility of one's end. This is what Heidegger calls **being-towards-death**, and it is this that brings *Da-sein* into relation with itself and its ownmost possibility of being a self. To maintain this requires *constancy*.

See also **anxiety; resoluteness**

potentiality-to-be-evil
See **projection**

power, will to
See **will to power**

practico-inert

In the political philosophy of Jean-Paul **Sartre**, and his revision of Marxist theory, the practico-inert is the product of work. The production of the workers is the result of chosen action (*praxis*), but itself is fixed, or *inert*. This differentiation between the product and the process is similar to Sartre's earlier distinction between **being-in-itself** and **being-for-itself**. But where Marx argues that workers are alienated from their means of production, Sartre argues that the workers are alienated from the own products because of their fixedness, because they serve to constrain **freedom**. The result is that work itself transforms people into inert objects. The practico-inert leads to relations of **seriality**, where individuals relate to themselves and others as objects. We define ourselves by our *praxis*, but we can always transcend the practico-inert by re-engaging with our **project**.

pragmatism

Like the **existential** approach, this is a **philosophy** of **meaning** and **truth**. It was fully formulated by C.S. Peirce, then revised by William James, and then others still, but its roots go back at least as far as the works of **Plato** and **Aristotle**. A related philosophy (especially to Peirce's ideas) is *logical positivism*, an extreme form of *empiricism* in which meaning and truth are granted only to claims that are physically or logically verifiable. Behavioural psychology and behavioural psychotherapy constrain themselves in similar fashion by their search for measurable causes and effects. In ethics the nearest relative to pragmatism is *utilitarianism*, in which human actions are judged moral according to their overall utility in providing pleasure or alleviating pain.

Peirce's pragmatism was emphatically objective, an attempt to resolve the meaning of statements through clarification and translation of what is obscure, but William James (to Peirce's disappointment) emphasised the subjective. James's pragmatism, which he termed *radical empiricism*, is one that sees no possibility of verifying abstract assertions or theories and therefore settles for an examination of the practical consequences of holding particular beliefs. If belief in God is of emotional benefit, then it is true. His pragmatism is thus a philosophy of utility, and he is concerned only with the 'cash value' of ideas.

Existential philosophy and **psychology** differ from pragmatism, even in the theories of writers like **Sartre**, who emphasise the significance of action, and even though existential theorists in general base their systems on lived experience. For existential thinking is not concerned with mere practical reasoning, but with the examination of human **existence**. Moreover, it is neither purely subjective nor objective in approach, for existential philosophy sees an intertwining of the two.

See also **lived world**; *praxis*; **subject and object**

praxis

Greek, meaning *action*. For existentialists, this term is associated with **Sartre**, as well as **Cooper** and **Laing**. But its use goes back to **Aristotle**, for whom it meant voluntary action, especially *doing* as distinct from *making*. **Kant** used it to indicate practical reasoning, and Marx used it to describe the subordination of theory to action. Sartre's usage derives from Marx in arguing that **history** rests upon individual *praxis*. For Sartre, *praxis* is the exercise of **freedom**, and so is transcendent. In his later work Sartre develops the idea that individual *praxis* eventually has to give way to common *praxis* if societies are to progress and change.

Cooper and Laing use *praxis* to mean the authorship of action that is the individual's in a group such as a family. They distinguish this from the *process* of the group, which they hold to be without authorship, lacking accountability and responsibility.

See also **practico-inert; pragmatism; transcendence**

pre-reflexive consciousness

Pre-reflexive (or *pre-reflective*, or *non-positional* or *non-thetic*) **consciousness** is the simple awareness of objects. It is, according to **Sartre**, what we are aware of before we are aware of ourselves, before we are conscious of the **self** as an object. As reflective beings, we have the capacity of self-awareness, of subjectivity, of consciousness of consciousness, that is, reflexive (or *thetic*) consciousness, in which the ego is present to awareness. But pre-reflexive consciousness is pure **intentionality**, where we simply focus on the object of our attention without self-awareness and without awareness of the process of consciousness itself: 'The consciousness of man in action is non-reflexive consciousness – it is consciousness of something' (Sartre, 1943a: 36).

Descartes and those he influenced (for instance, **Freud**) take the fundamental basis of consciousness to be self-awareness or reflexive consciousness. But holding this notion results in a difficulty with certainty of belief in an exterior **world**. Sartre, on the other hand, holds basic awareness to be of the world and its objects. For Sartre, then, not all consciousness is self-aware. But there is a great range of consciousness, and much of what we are aware we are not self-consciously aware. And this is Sartre's answer to the psychoanalytic notion of a buried repository of forbidden thought, *the unconscious*. Much of human awareness, for Sartre, is unconscious, or rather pre-reflective, but it is all in principle available for reflection, not repressed into a mythical place.

See also **hodological**

presence

Philosophically, this term signifies the momentary but actual existence of a thing or being. It implies physical existence in the present. But the term is full of uncertainties. Does the memory of a deceased loved one mean she has presence? Or is this merely a **representation**? **Heidegger** sees **Being** as more than the traditional synonym for presence. But he is also concerned with absence (see **Nothing, the**), and berates traditional metaphysicians, and their *metaphysics* *of presence*, for neglecting absence and how it illuminates Being. For Heidegger, this traditional view is of humankind apart from nature. It is a **technological attitude**, which sees the **world** only as a source of usefulness to our own everyday purposes. But Being is more than the present: we are located in **time**, and have a past and a future.

Psychologically, *presence* is used by many psychotherapists to mean the therapist's psychological availability to the client. **Rogers**, a year before his death, spoke of it in spiritual terms, saying that when he was in touch with the unknown in himself, his transcendent core, then his presence itself seemed healing. **Laing** speaks of *co-presence*.

See also **encounter; existence; relationship**

present
See **time and temporality**

present-at-hand/presence-at-hand
See **world**

priority
(*Vorrang*). **Heidegger** speaks of the priority of **Being**, or the priority of **care**, meaning these factors are fundamental and form the basis of other factors. In Heidegger's writing there is a hierarchy of elements, and of these the most basic is **time**, which in turn gives rise to Being. This in turn gives rise to human being, and therefore to the concept of care. Consideration of all other matters can only be addressed when the fundamental questions have been successfully dealt with.

See also *Dasein*; **project; time and temporality**

probability
In his discussion of **freedom**, the French existential philosopher **Merleau-Ponty** criticises rationalist attitudes to the concepts of **possibility** and probability. He considers that the rationalist might say of statistical thought that it is not thought at all, since it deals with no actual entities, no actual events, and no moment of **time**. His answer to this is that probability is not an abstraction but a **phenomenon**. As always, Merleau-Ponty insists on examining what is concrete, and in doing so he escapes the dilemmas induced by idealist thought, by objective thinking. Like Martin **Buber**, he voices a complaint against dichotomous thought:

The rationalist's dilemma: either the free act is possible, or it is not – either the event originates in me or is imposed on me from outside, does not apply to our relations with the world and with our past. (Merleau-Ponty, 1945: 442)

We are always physically in the **world**, and living in time. Our **situation** affects us, but our freedom is still available to us. Whatever limits and restrictions, whether physical or through force of our own habitual thinking, our situation is always open.

Heidegger put a similar emphasis on the freedom of thinking that **phenomenology** has brought to **science**:

> Our comments on the preliminary conception of phenomenology have shown that what is essential in it does not lie in its actuality as a philosophical movement. Higher than actuality stands possibility. We can understand phenomenology only by seizing upon it as a possibility. (Heidegger, 1927a: 38)

Indeed, it was **Husserl's** intention that scientific discourse would move away from probability to possibility and that the freedom of the recognition of different shadings of meaning in everything would come to be recognised.

See also **profiles; rationalism; sedimentation**

profiles
Abschattungen, also translated as *adumbrations*, is a concept Edmund Husserl used to describe the different shadings and refractions that we perceive in objects. As we grasp objects through our **intuition**, we unify the different profiles that we are able to perceive. A **phenomenon** is presented to us in constantly varying shadings and from different perspectives, which makes for the shift in phenomena whilst the actual object remains the same. We can only ever consider objects from a particular perspective, through a particular profile or adumbration that shows itself to us. In his later thought, Husserl began to see the ego as presented in temporal profiles, so that just as we exist in **time**, mere aspects of ourselves are presented at any given time.

See also **consciousness; intentionality**

project
From the philosophy of **Sartre**, and sometimes referred to as *fundamental project, original project* or *initial choice*, it refers to the chosen way of being of the **being-for-itself**. It explains how our current choices, often seemingly inexplicable, are derived from earlier, more profound choices. Sartre's notion of the project came from **Heidegger's** descriptions of *Dasein* as being always projected or **thrown** into the **world** and therefore always having a direction, or a fundamental project. While many subscribe to the idea of personality, or hold that biology forms our **identity**, Sartre claims that it is with our projects that we define ourselves, for instance, whether to be authentic or inauthentic. He also claims that situations are not merely contingent, but are of our own making, for our projects actively shape each **situation**. For example, war may offer only the threat of destruction to one person, but to one who has chosen fame through valour it is a wonderful opportunity to prove himself.

Although Sartre's account of **freedom** is for many the quintessential existential position, most existential theorists have rejected Sartre's stance, as he himself did in later years, when he took to a more Marxist philosophy. Many instead emulate Simone de **Beauvoir** in considering that while one's original **choice** is one's own, it is the result of **contingency**, and we own it only in the way we own our own bodies, ours to **care** for, to be responsible for, but not originated by us.

Ortega y Gasset, on the other hand, goes further than Sartre in claiming a human being is *causa sui*, the cause of itself. This is problematic: how can a thing create itself? To create myself, I must already exist. How can an I create an I? Nevertheless, Ortega urges us to see ourselves as the authors of our own lives, whether we are entirely original or whether we choose to plagiarise.

It is important to note that projects are not irreversible. For instance, the person who realises she has chosen inauthenticity can elect to choose **authenticity** or choose to remain inauthentic.

See also **intentionality; responsibility; totalisation**

projection

Literal meaning, *throwing forward*. Because **Dasein** is **thrown** into the **world**, its **existence** is always projection, or project. This idea is used by various existential writers, but especially **Heidegger** and **Sartre**. Human beings project themselves ahead to their possibilities. Human Being is always **being-ahead-of-itself**, and projection is thus the future in the present. Heidegger uses the term *Entwurf,* which also means design, outline or draft. Projection thus refers to the way in which the future is designed by *Dasein*, a design that can change at different times. **Binswanger** and **Boss** take the idea of a *world design* from this notion.

The existential concept of projection is very different to the psychoanalytic one. In **psychoanalysis**, projection is the unconscious denial of one's personally unacceptable wishes or feelings and the claim that they are present in another when they are not. It is a kind of scapegoating. Heidegger contends that Freudian theory unrealistically claims an objectivity to the psychoanalytic process that is not present. Human beings, with their **freedom**, have the potential to be evil. Thus the evil perceived in another is his or her *potentiality-to-be-evil*, and is not a misreading or projection. It is a diversionary manoeuvre, an avoidance of one's own essential qualities.

In Sartre's **philosophy**, the idea of **project** is the individual's pursuit of their possibilities. He speaks of the 'original project' that each person conceives for themselves out of the possibilities offered. It is this project that accords value to the world.

See also **design; possibility**

psychoanalysis

Sigmund **Freud** must be credited with assembling and formulating the ideas and practice of professional psychotherapy, even if many of the elements of its practice had long existed. The brilliance of Freud's thinking is evident, yet he later overthrew many of his early notions, and his successors discarded and replaced still more. However, if the theoretical underpinnings have changed, what remains relatively unaltered is the practice of psychoanalysis, in which a distressed person meets with a person who is in a quiet state of mind and who provides an accepting and neutral environment for the distressed person to focus on their troubling experiences and become aware of the motivations and latent meanings that have thus far escaped them.

Some existential psychotherapists, notably **Boss**, consider Freud's practice as a therapist to be generally correct, but take great issue with his theories. This is why he coined the term *Daseinsanalysis* to replace the term *psychoanalysis*. Existential practitioners are dissatisfied with the simple *determinism* (see **freedom and free will**) of psychoanalysis, and its acceptance of a medically based model of **psychopathology**, which promotes the idea that there must be something especially wrong with a psychologically distressed person rather than that they are suffering through the very nature of their humanity. Other complaints against psychoanalysis are the objectification of the patient that comes from the distance that the analyst maintains, and the psychoanalytic model of the mind (see **consciousness and unconsciousness**).

Some existential-phenomenological ideas have filtered down into psychoanalytic thinking, e.g. the idea of **not knowing**, and many psychoanalytic therapists practise in a way comfortably familiar to existentialists. However, analysis by an existential analyst does not focus on the isolated psyche, but on the person's relation to **Being**.

See also **interpretation; phenomenological method; phenomenology; slime**

psychological defences
See **defences, psychological**

psychology
Psychology is literally the science of the *psyche*, or soul. It investigates all matters related to human experience in a scientific manner. And since existential thinkers are concerned with understanding the human condition, they often address psychological issues. So they have often contributed to the understanding of and the debate on human psychology, even though **philosophy** tends to be their field of reference. **Nietzsche**, for example, wrote:

> A genuine physio-psychology has to struggle with unconscious resistances in the heart of the investigator ... Supposing, however, that someone goes so far as to regard the emotions of hatred, envy, covetousness, and lust for domination ... [as] essentially present in the total economy of life ... (Nietzsche, 1886: 138)

These words, published at a time when **Freud's** concern was still with neurology, speak of self-deceit and the suppression of unacceptable impulses. More recently, **Sartre** outlined a theory of human **emotions**:

[T]here are two forms of emotion, according to whether it is we who constitute the magic of the world to replace a deterministic activity which cannot be realized, or whether the world itself is unrealizable and reveals itself suddenly as a magical environment. (Sartre, 1939: 86)

At the same time as contributing to the literature of and on psychology, existential authors have shown the same dissatisfaction with the conceptual and experimental bases of psychology as they have with **science and scientific method**.

Psychology and **psychoanalysis** in their original forms depend on the applicability of Newtonian laws of causality to human behaviour. This entails the search for causes (whether in the psychology laboratory or the psychotherapy consulting-room), and leads to research based on empirical observation and measurement. If human life obeys physical laws in every respect, then psychology is capable of being a science in this way, and psychotherapy might be a technology, at least by way of providing theoretical accounts of a person's life. However, if the causal laws that govern the movement of billiard balls and planets and the known and limited factors that dictate the processes of digestion and decay do not also apply to human thought and behaviour, then the status of psychology as a behavioural science is radically compromised.

Husserl and his followers, with their **phenomenology**, produced an alternative to the attempts by psychologists to measure human behaviour objectively. Existential writers, with their model of the human being as essentially involved with the **world** and inseparable from it, offered an alternative to the atomism of early psychology.

Wittgenstein, whose philosophy combines a phenomenological with an analytical approach, writes:

The confusion and barrenness of psychology is not to be explained by calling it a 'young science' ... For in psychology there are experimental methods and *conceptual confusion* ... The existence of the experimental method makes us think we have the means of solving the problems which trouble us, though problem and method pass one another by. (Wittgenstein, 1953: 232)

The existential therapist sees psychology, even when it attempts to be holistic and subjectivist, as insufficiently philosophical. It is argued that psychology avoids fundamental issues, assuming too much, and taking as axiomatic what is culturally normative. In short, existentialists believe that psychology does not enquire deeply enough.

psychology of ambiguity
See **ambiguity**

psychopathology and diagnosis
The object of the **science** of psychopathology is to systematise **knowledge** of mental illness, deriving from that system the means to examine symptoms

thence to elicit diagnoses from which the best form of treatment can be decided. In this way it is exactly analogous to physical pathologising. However, existential psychotherapists question the suitability of the mind to be treated in the same way as the **body**.

Existential therapists, along with authors such as **Szasz**, tend to see psychological distress as problems with living, problems that need not indicate a fault or an illness in the sufferer, nor prove they have distorted perceptions. Conventionally, once a patient has been diagnosed with a psychopathology – say, an anxiety disorder – then the psychologist, psychiatrist, psychotherapist or counsellor, knowing in what way the patient is different from the norm, takes on the task of alleviating the patient's distress by removing the cause of their problem. There are a number of possible objections to this, which include that it is culturally normative and encourages conformity. Further still, it is a model of disease rather than health, and does not allow that what may seem a deficiency could also be or could become a strength.

Another disadvantage of diagnosis and pathologising is that it is an objectification and **alienation** of the patient, and this is not only dehumanising and disrespectful, but encourages the patient to yield personal **responsibility**.

Existential therapists prefer a phenomenological descriptiveness, considering the person in an open and unprejudiced manner, in a way that invites the patient's involvement and responsibility as a person.

Jaspers wrote a treatise on psychopathology, in which he shows how to discover the patient's hidden subjective experience. However, unlike later existential theorists and practitioners, he did not see subjective and objective in a holistic way, but as distinct. He also argued that certain objective aspects, for instance, body-posture, are open to direct and simple **interpretation** by the therapist.

Existential mental heath practitioners seldom use medico-pathological diagnoses. However, they will pay attention to moods (e.g. **anxiety**) and to manner (e.g. signs of inauthenticity). They will also carefully observe how a person is in their world relations at different levels, but will not attach these to personality traits or to categories of psychopathology.

See also **anti-psychiatry; authenticity and inauthenticity; bad faith; defences, psychological; Laing; phenomenology**

psychotherapy
See **existential psychotherapy**

public, the
See **crowd, the**

publicness
(*Öffentlichkeit*). According to **Heidegger**, a mixture of **averageness, distantiality** and **levelling down**, the insistent and intolerant attitudes of the **crowd**, an inauthentic characteristic of the **They**. The **Being** of human beings

(**Dasein**) tends to be lazy, to surrender itself to the undifferentiated mass, with the result that 'Everyone is the other, and no one is himself' (Heidegger, 1927b: 128). The public world exists pre-formed, available and tempting, needing no thought, no effort. When *Dasein* gives in to this, then *Dasein* as an **individual** vanishes, and becomes a *nobody*, as do individual others. Heidegger rails against this unthinking mass behaviour because it makes **authenticity** impossible, so that human possibilities cannot be realised.

See also **everydayness; Other, the; possibility; undifferentiation**

purity of heart

In *Purity of Heart* (1847), **Kierkegaard** bemoans the endless waste that results from choosing an aesthetic life. To wish for earthly satisfaction, even **love**, is to search in **despair**, whether one's goals are obtained or not, for they are all empty. Instead, to will one thing, the Good, is to discover eternity. In the light of Kierkegaard's personal life this may be a self-serving philosophy, but it carries with it a prescription for holism and wholeheartedness.

radical reflection
See **Merleau–Ponty**

rapture
Entrückung, or rapture, is a state in which *Dasein* is being transported beyond itself. It is often used by **Heidegger** as a synonym for *Ekstase*, or **ecstasy**. Rapture is a state in which we are carried away towards our possibilities and concerns. In some of his writing (e.g. 1927a and b), Heidegger distinguishes ecstasies from raptures by showing that ecstasies take *Dasein* in a particular direction, whereas rapture does not transport *Dasein* in the way ecstasy does. Rapture can be negative, passive and inauthentic as well as positive, active and authentic. In a positive sense, rapture is crucial to the **Moment** when rapture is combined with loyalty (see **constancy and loyalty**) and an attitude of **resoluteness**: 'The resolute rapture which carries us away in the moment of vision is what makes an authentic future possible' (Heidegger, 1927a: 338).

rationalism
Any philosophical stance emphasising the significance of reason, especially deductive reasoning. It thus gives less or no significance to sensory experience, or to mystical notions. Many of the early Greek philosophers gave rationality primacy in their philosophies, considering the evidence of the senses to be unreliable. But Western philosophy as a whole has since then allowed greater trust to the senses, and to some extent is indeed empirical, that is, it claims that knowledge may derive from physical evidence.

In its most general form, a rationalist **philosophy** is one that holds that at least some knowledge derives from rational thought alone. This may be, but is not necessarily, an elevation of logical thought, for some rationalists, like **Plato**, believe that some ideas are innate, as some contend that our notions are a priori (meaning, prior to experience), for instance that our moral judgement is understood a priori. Rationalists like **Husserl** may also consider **intuition** as a form of rational apprehension of the **world**.

The various existential philosophies cover a range of attitudes towards the significance of rationality. Existential thinkers are not extreme empiricists, neither are they wholehearted rationalists. The former implies that **truth** resides in the external world, and the latter that it resides in the mind of the person, but each is a kind of dualism (see **Descartes**), proposing separation of thought and experience. Existential philosophy insists that the human being is not merely located in the world, but that **Being** and the world cannot be separated. Therefore neither empiricism nor rationalism contain sufficient truth, for each is incomplete. The existential philosopher makes use of lived experience (see **lived world**) and of reason, and is usually opposed to the exclusive use of either, but especially the latter.

For the psychologist or psychotherapist, an important consideration must be the source of our knowledge, judgements and **values**. Common-sense views on this are so confused and unhelpful that it is well for the clinician to consider in what way his or her client can re-evaluate their knowledge and attitudes towards life.

See also **idealism; judgement; knowing and knowledge**

ready-to-hand/readiness-to-hand
See **world**

realism
See **Husserl; reality**

reality
What is real? Is it the physical **world**? Is it **time**? Is it other people? Numbers? Right and wrong? The realist believes that these and other aspects of the world exist independently of the mind, while the anti-realist denies it. However, few philosophers are extreme realists or anti-realists, or indeed are realists or anti-realists on every question. The existential stance towards **existence** is largely one of realism, accepting that there is an external world, to which we are closely connected and that exists whether we think of it or not. But existential philosophers insist that the world can only be interpreted, and cannot be known objectively.

Reality and actuality can be easily synonymous, and **Heidegger** often refers to things that are actualised or to human beings who are actualised or not actualised. In this context the term *Eigentlichkeit*, though usually translated as **authenticity,** could be translated as actuality or even reality. Human beings then have a choice between making their lives real and actual or letting them remain unactualised and unreal.

See also **actualisation; interpretation; phenomenology; time and temporality**

reciprocity
Important concept in the later **philosophy** of **Sartre**. When people are capable of liberating themselves from relationships of seriality, in which they are competitive and take no responsibility for their own impact on the **world**, they become open to the principles of co-operation and mutuality. Then they can enter into reciprocal relationships in which each takes **responsibility** for their own actions and effects on others and **generosity** becomes a **possibility**.

See also **intersubjectivity; look, the; relationship**

recollection
See **time and temporality**

reduction
See **Being; client-centred psychotherapy; phenomenological method; transcendental ego**

reductionism
In general **science**, this is the practice of reducing what is complex to what is simple. According to its adherents, it offers greater understanding and clarity. But the great debate on reductionism is whether it can be carried out without loss. Water is made of the elements hydrogen and oxygen, so in understanding water a reduction might be made to these separate elements, and consideration given to their qualities. But however thoroughly done, the qualities of water – for instance, its wetness, are not explicable through considering the elements of hydrogen and oxygen. Yet a study of oceans might be made by studying the behaviour of brine in a glass tank. The legitimacy of reductionism is thus a debate of holism versus atomism.

The point of reductionism rests on the notion of *supervenience*, that there are levels of complexity and of explanation, and that one layer supervenes upon another, for example, chemistry upon physics. In **psychology**, various schools of thought have their assumptions of supervenience, that mental acts supervene upon biological facts; that behaviour is reducible to the causal connections of stimulus and response; and – borrowed from ethics – that acts of kindness or affection are reducible to egoistic advantage.

Existential philosophy is more-or-less holistic, with an insistence on **Being** and **world** as inseparable. So if an existential philosopher or psychotherapist practises reductionism, it will not be by eliminating either, but by concentrating on a small and concrete unit of study, for example, a person in a **situation**.

There are existential philosophies which investigate what is fundamental, what constitutes an **essence**, but they are not reductionist, and the search by **Heidegger** for the nature of Being is not an attempt to reject complex explanations of human living. On the other hand, in the works of **Nietzsche**, the notion of **will to power** is a reduction, for it seeks to explain the complex by means of what is simple. As with all reduction, the question stands whether it has sufficient explanatory power.

Generally, existential psychotherapists object to reductionist explanations of human behaviour such as are found in cognitive or behavioural approaches to psychology. For instance, R.D. **Laing** fought against the kind of reductionist explanations generated by the medical model, which he complained attempted to explain rather than understand human experience and motivation.

reflexive consciousness
See **pre-reflexive consciousness**

relationship

Without a sense of **self** and of the **Other** there can be no awareness of relationship. For **Kierkegaard**, the self is a metaphysical synthesis of opposites, or polarities, including infinitude and finitude. The self is a relation, one that relates to its own polar aspects. The most important external relationship for a human being is with God, and close relationships with other human beings make relations with God difficult. The fiercely atheistic philosopher **Nietzsche** holds in one respect a surprisingly similar belief that human beings are at odds with themselves and their seemingly ambivalent natures: 'Man is a rope, fastened between animal and Superman – a rope over an abyss' (Nietzsche, 1883: 43).

Marcel writes of *participation*, of being at the disposal of others, of reaching out and offering oneself. And **Buber** goes further, putting relationship at the very heart of his philosophy. Indeed, for Buber we only exist as a relationship to the Other. Like **Sartre**, Buber sees that one can treat and see the Other as an object. But for Buber the consequence is that we become objectified ourselves in the process. Unlike Sartre, Buber believes it is within our power to experience the Other (and ourselves) as a subject. Like Kierkegaard and Marcel and many other religious existential theorists, Buber describes a special relationship between the person and God, and argues that a relationship with God is an inherent aspect of our **Being**. In proposing the primacy of the Other, **Levinas** puts relationship at the centre of his philosophy.

Heidegger believes we have lost touch with Being. Our relationship with Being, and therefore with ourselves, is therefore inadequate. It is necessary that we become capable of authentic being-for-ourselves before we can come to our relationships with others in an open and authentic manner.

Binswanger describes the different forms of relationship that people are capable of, and speaks of anonymous, singular, dual and plural ways of relating.

For the psychotherapist, the relationship between therapist and client is always of considerable importance; for some, it is all-important. The practitioner who subscribes to Buber's ideals of the **I–Thou** relationship will see the relationship or the **encounter** itself as healing. Those more influenced by Heidegger will probably encourage a more equal partnership in discussing and investigating the issues and difficulties of living.

See also **authenticity and inauthenticity; finite and infinite; generosity; interhuman, the**

releasement

The Heideggerian notion of releasement or letting be (*Gelassenheit*) is a counterweight to his earlier notion of **resoluteness**. *Gelassenheit* literally means having been left or let, whilst it also means calm or cool composure. Whereas resoluteness is about *Dasein*'s determined attitude towards life and **death**, releasement is on the contrary about *Dasein*'s receptiveness to **Being**.

The notion of releasement is a response by **Heidegger** to the threat of **technology**, or the tendency to regard the **world** merely in terms of what is useful. It counteracts the assumption that **science** can understand humanity. Releasement, or detachment, instead allows things simply to be, and Heidegger argues that if we are to use technology, we should also know when to let go of it. This letting-go is neither a passive nor an active matter, but beyond such categorisation. And it is only when we let go of technology that the mystery of Being can reveal itself. Conventional **science** and logic, with their presumptions of simple **causality** and their intolerance of contradiction, miss the **freedom** of humanity to live in ways beyond the limits of ordinary physical objects. Through releasement we release things back into the open space in which Being can come to light. This is not unlike the Stoic notion of *apatheia*, or **indifference**, which is the attitude required to let things be as they are.

See also **phenomenology; stoics and stoicism**

religious life
See **Kierkegaard**

remembering
See **forgetting**

repetition
The fact of repetition has profound significance, though it is seldom discussed. According to the author of *Ecclesiastes*, there is no new thing under the sun, and human life is the unwitting repetition of previous experiences. **Heidegger** takes a similar but Romantic stance towards repetition (*Wiederholung*), arguing that authentic living involves an active conversation with past figures and the positive retrieval of past ideas. For Heidegger, repetition is an authentic attitude towards the past, and stands in stark opposition to **forgetting**, an inauthentic mode of relating to the past: 'If being as having-been is authentic, we call it "repetition"' (Heidegger, 1927a: 339). Thus we choose from the possibilities of our *heritage* (see *Erbe*) and reinterpret it for ourselves. There is a similarity between Heidegger's argument that repetition is the correct stance to adopt towards the past and **Nietzsche's** notion of **eternal recurrence**.

Heidegger, like **Plato's Socrates**, has a **philosophy** of just a few powerful but difficult ideas, and his philosophical style (see **Zollikon Seminars**) is intentionally repetitious. This is generally true of existential writers.

Rhyme and rhythm in poetry and song show the universal appeal of deliberate repetition. **Kierkegaard**, in a work first published in 1843, *Repetition*, considers the dialectic between **change** and repetition. He also portrays a search for a second chance, for psychological and spiritual redemption. He shows how self-conscious efforts may fail but that a chance glance backwards may provide a fresh appraisal of the past and an opportunity to choose it afresh.

See also **authenticity and inauthenticity; choice; possibility**

representation
Representation (*Vorstellung*) features in the philosophies of **Brentano, Husserl** and **Heidegger,** and is used in a variety of ways. For Brentano, the representation

of something is the first stage of thought prior to **judgement** and emotional concern. Heidegger disagrees, believing instead that we see, hear and touch things themselves, not mere representations of them. In the same way he believes that we have worlds (*Welten*) rather than just a *worldview* (*Weltanschauung*). He claims it is only possible for us to have a representation of our **world** because we are only now properly present in the world.

resentment
See **master morality and slave morality**

resoluteness
Heidegger uses *Entschlossenheit*, literally meaning openness, to describe an authentic openness or **disclosedness** to the **world**, to present, past and future:

> As *authentic being a self*, resoluteness does not detach Da-sein from its world, nor does it isolate it as free floating ego. How could it, if resoluteness as authentic disclosedness is, after all, nothing other than *authentically being-in-the-world*? Resoluteness brings the self right into its being together with things at hand, actually taking care of them, and pushes it towards concerned being-with with the others. (Heidegger, 1927b: 298)

Resoluteness consists of **Da-sein** running ahead to its own **death** whilst retrieving its own past all at once. This results in an intersection between past and present which *Da-sein* holds in an attitude of determined and decisive openness.

However, the dominant position of the unthinking **They** is *irresoluteness*, a denial of what is. Because *Da-sein* is influenced by the They, *Da-sein* is always ready in irresoluteness.

See also **anticipation; anxiety; authenticity and inauthenticity; being-in-the-world; being-with; care; constancy and loyalty; *Erbe*; liberation**

resonance
R.D. **Laing** encouraged the psychotherapist to be touched by his or her client's material, to identify with the patient's plight. Without resonance, the **relationship** of the therapist to his or her client is an objectified, inhuman and unhelpful one. Resonance is said to be distinct from *empathy*, in that it does not involve putting oneself in the other's place, but rather consists of letting oneself experience the reverberations of the human condition, which is just as relevant to one person as to another. It is achieved by tuning to the same wavelength as the client and allowing oneself to receive the messages that arrive. This **attunement** is also called *atonement*, or rather at-one-ment, being at one with the **Other**. It is a consequence of a therapeutic stance of *co-presence*.

responsibility
This is one of the great themes of existential philosophy, yet while responsibility is frequently referred to, comparatively little has been written explicitly

concerning it. Broadly speaking, an existentialist speaking of responsibility is referring to the acknowledgement of personal accountability, to holding oneself accountable. But it is not only accountability for that over which one has direct power: it is more that one's own life is one's own concern. For instance, **Sartre** writes:

> [Responsibility is consciousness of] being the incontestable author of an event or of an object ... Thus there are no accidents in a life ... To make myself passive in the world, to refuse to act upon things and upon Others is still to choose myself. (Sartre, 1943a: 553–6)

Heidegger also writes of responsibility, since **authenticity** is based on an awareness of one's choices, one's potential and one's limitations. He also speaks of existential **guilt** in relation to responsibility.

Responsibility is also a constant theme in both the theory and practice of **existential psychotherapy**. Theoretically, its significance lies in its direct connections with autonomy and authenticity. Rollo **May** proposes that responsibility be understood as *response-ability*, the capacity to be answerable. In practice, the existential therapist or counsellor will aim to provide and promote an ethos of personal responsibility, of examining personal roles. For some, responsibility will seem purely a moral matter, perhaps the very discussion will seem a preparation for moral condemnation, but in existential therapy this is not the intention. Just as no message is conveyed to the client or patient that they have utter control over their lives, so moral questions are raised in a philosophical spirit, without either approval or disapproval from the therapist.

See also **bad faith; choice; freedom; identity**

reticence
According to **Heidegger**, a reticence to speak has **meaning**, for in such a chosen silence, the reticent person is not dumb, and their silence may be understood better than if they had chosen energetic chatter. Moreover, the reticent person is able to truly listen, and so enter into **being-with** another. Unlike resistance, reticence is a positive quality, allowing opportunity to reflect.

See also **discourse; idle talk**

revaluation of values
Sometimes translated as *transvaluation of values*. **Nietzsche**, having considered **good and evil**, and contemporary and ancient moral codes (see **master morality and slave morality**), and having rejected all ideas of absolute moral right and wrong, contended that socially acceptable moral codes exist primarily to preserve society, and possess no greater **truth**. He decided that a new moral outlook was needed:

> 'You shall not steal! You shall not kill!' – such words were once called holy ... But I ask you: Where have there ever been better thieves and killers in the world than such holy

words have been? Is there not in all life itself – stealing and killing? And when such words were called holy was not *truth* itself – killed? (Nietzsche, 1883: 219)

The replacement for such wrong-headed thinking should not be a codified moral system, for that would be to commit anew the fallacy of considering good and bad to be absolute and objective. Instead, Nietzsche urges **freedom** from the cowardly tyranny of mob-rule (see the **herd**), and a new and noble free-thinking in which the individual constructs his or her own judgements and devises their own virtues. The individual thus overcomes the desire to follow society's rules, rules that serve to hamper the development of humankind towards the **superman**. The revaluation of values leads to clear thinking which requires individuals to live in the **Moment** and consider things anew from day to day, and to live by the standards of *amor fati* and **eternal recurrence**.

See also **values**

Ricoeur
Paul Ricoeur (b. 1913). French philosopher, Professor at Strasbourg, Sorbonne, Nanterre and Chicago Universities. Influenced by **Husserl, Freud**, Marx, **Nietzsche, Heidegger, Jaspers, Marcel** and **Gadamer**. Influence felt in theology, literary theory and **psychoanalysis**. Publications include *Freedom and Nature* (1950), *Freud and Philosophy* (1965), *Conflicts of Interpretation* (1969) and *Time and Narrative* (3 vols, 1983–5).

If **phenomenology** investigates only what is apparent, Ricoeur argues that it should go further, towards a **hermeneutics** that considers the meanings beneath **meaning**. He argues that **consciousness** is not transparent, and he accepts the psychoanalytic notion of the unconscious. For Ricoeur, people can be read as texts can be read – an approach that has passed into contemporary **psychoanalysis** – but we should also be aware of subtext and context. Thus he is interested in all sorts of texts, including myths and symbols, Marxist readings and Nietzsche's **will to power** in order to mine their underlying meaning. He holds **interpretation** never to be exhaustive. Like **Gadamer**, he emphasises that an interpreter cannot be neutral, for interpretation uses language, and the language an individual uses is not his own but has pre-existing meanings. The interpreter is thus never free, and the historical and cultural context of the language of interpretation must be taken into account. Ricoeur believes that metaphor can grasp and draw together themes from various sources, revealing a **reality** that cannot be analysed or appropriated but only interpreted in multiple ways. With its critical openness, and suspension of certainty, Ricoeur's *hermeneutics of suspicion* thus seeks to unmask and demystify. Ricoeur claims this is a way for **truth** to be explored in all its diversity.

Rogers
Carl Ransom Rogers was born in Oak Park, a Chicago suburb, on 8 January 1902, and died in La Jolla, California on 4 February 1987.

Notable works: *Client-Centered Therapy* (1951), *On Becoming a Person* (1961a) and *A Way of Being* (1980).

Influenced by: **Kierkegaard, Buber,** Otto Rank, Karen Horney, Jessie Taft, Frederick Allen, Eugene Gendlin, Kurt Goldstein and Abraham Maslow.

Influence on: After **Freud,** the most influential single writer in counselling and psychotherapy.

Life: With a scientific father – a civil engineer – and a deeply religious mother, he was a dreamy, independent boy, bookish and scientifically minded. When he was 12 his family moved to a farm. At first heading towards an agricultural career, and then a religious one, he finally rejected both in favour of training in clinical and educational psychology, gaining a PhD in 1931. He first worked with children and families, becoming Director of the Rochester Guidance Center. From 1945–57 he ran the University of Chicago Counselling Center. From 1946–47 he served as President of The American Psychological Association, and in 1964 became co-founder of the Center for the Study of the Person at La Jolla, where he was active until his last years. As a writer he was prolific, with a dozen books and over 200 papers to his name.

Major ideas: Rogers's legacy includes a theory of personality and behaviour, and a theory of the conditions of the therapeutic process (for these, see **client-centred psychotherapy**). Rogers also pioneered the use of research evidence in psychotherapy. With his Q-sort measurements and factor analyses, not just of whole therapy sessions but of entire therapies, he demonstrated a courage and openness unmatched in process-led therapy in putting his ideas and his practice to the test. Rogers's grasp of existential concepts is not as thorough, but certain elements of existential thinking are in clear evidence in his writing:

> Man has long felt himself to be but a puppet in life – molded by economic forces, by unconscious forces, by environmental forces ... [and] enslaved by persons, by institutions and by theories of psychological science. But he is firmly setting forth a new declaration of independence. He is discarding the alibis of unfreedom. He's choosing himself, endeavoring, in a most difficult and often tragic world to become himself – not a puppet, not a slave, not a machine, but his own unique individual self. (Rogers, 1964: 130)

Contribution to psychotherapy: pervasive but often misunderstood and diluted. His theory of psychotherapy is also a metatheory, describing the necessary conditions for therapy which, he argued, are in themselves sufficient. His detractors claim they have tried his conditions and found them useful but not sufficient. Rogerians in turn argue that in such cases, the provision of these conditions has not been met, and that these therapeutic conditions are not easy to provide, especially from untrained therapists. The debate continues, yet there is no sure evidence to prove Rogers's six conditions are insufficient. Most existential therapists believe these conditions to be compatible with existential work when conjoined with a philosophical exploration of the client's issues.

See also **May**

sadism

The philosophy of **Sartre** emphasises that the **self** lacks definition and solidity (see **being-for-itself**), and so tends to be restless and striving. It constantly desires to become something it is not. It is also always in danger of being captured by the **Other**. In the matter of **relationship** with others, especially in desire and **love**, the self may strive to make the Other an object, so as to appropriate the Other and overcome the threat of being possessed and reduced by the Other:

> In order to make myself recognized by the Other, I must risk my own life ... but at the same time I pursue the *death* of the Other. (Sartre, 1943a: 237)

However, we soon discover that we can never fully possess or control another:

> I can grasp the Other, grab hold of him ... compel him to perform this or that act ... But everything happens as if I wished to get hold of a man who runs away and leaves only his coat in my hands. It is the coat, it is the outer shell which I possess. I shall never get hold of more than a body. (Ibid.: 393)

> The sadist discovers his error when his victim *looks at* him; that is, when the sadist experiences the absolute alienation of his being in the Other's freedom. (Ibid.: 405)

The seed of sadism is in desire itself. The sadist seeks to appropriate the Other's flesh. Sartre insists this is not in order to dominate, not to have power over the other person. But like the lover, the sadist wants to own the Other's **freedom**. However, the sadist mistakenly takes the **body** to be the incarnation of that freedom:

> The sadist has reapprehended his body as a synthetic totality and center of action ... His goal, like that of desire, is to seize and to make use of the Other not only as the Other-as-object but as a pure incarnated transcendence ... Thus sadism is a refusal to be incarnated and a flight from all facticity and at the same time an effort to get hold of the Other's facticity. (Ibid.: 399)

See also **facticity; look, the; masochism; master–slave dialectic**

Sartre

Jean-Paul-Charles-Aymard Sartre was born in Paris on 21 June 1905, and died in Paris on 15 April 1980.

Notable works: (Philosophy) *Being and Nothingness* (1943a), *Existentialism and Humanism* (1946); (Psychology) *Imagination* (1936b); *Sketch for a Theory of the Emotions* (1939); *The Family Idiot* (1971); (Politics) *Critique of Dialectical Reason* (1960); *Notebooks for an Ethics* (1983); (Novels) *Nausea* (1938); *The Age of Reason* (1945a), *The Reprieve* (1945b) and *Iron in the Soul* (1949) (the first three of an incomplete series: *The Roads to Freedom*); (Plays) *The Flies* (1943); *No Exit* (1944); (Literary Criticism) *What Is Literature?* (1948); (Autobiography) *The Words* (1964).

Influenced by: **Descartes**, **Hegel**, Marx, **Dostoevsky**, **Kierkegaard**, **Freud**, **Husserl**, **Bergson**, Proust, **Heidegger** and **Levinas**.

Influence: Widespread, but diffuse.

Life: Sartre's father was a naval officer who died from a fever when his son was just one. Jean-Paul and his mother, Anne-Marie, then went to live with her family (who were related to Albert Schweitzer). Her father was a strict disciplinarian and hard to please, but he owned a library of books that the young boy soon learned to make use of, becoming a voracious reader, especially of fiction. When Jean-Paul was 12, his mother remarried and her son experienced this as a betrayal. He was an unhappy, lonely child, and sickly. Worse still, he came to realise his appearance was odd and unattractive to others, and he was taunted by other children. In reaction to this, he made himself the centre of attention wherever possible by playing the fool. And he developed a great pride in his intellect at the expense of his physical self, so that as an adult he neglected his physical health quite recklessly.

Sartre studied **philosophy** in France, Switzerland and Germany. At the Sorbonne, he was initially failed, coming fiftieth out of fifty students; but on his second attempt he came first. He taught philosophy at Le Havre, but hated the experience, and wrote *Nausea*, a novel about the futility of the human condition. Conscripted into the Army, he was captured in 1940, and released the following year. He then taught in occupied Paris, wrote *Being and Nothingness* in 1943 and joined the Resistance. When the war ended, he quit teaching and, with Simone de **Beauvoir** (his lifelong companion and lover, though they declined ever to live together) and Maurice **Merleau-Ponty**, he founded the political and literary magazine *Les Temps Modernes* (named after the Chaplin film). His increasing preoccupation with politics led him in 1951 to try to form his own party. In 1964 he was offered but rejected the Nobel Prize for literature (as he had earlier refused the Legion of Honour), saying acceptance of it would compromise his integrity as a writer.

As a person, Sartre passionately desired social and political change. As an author, he was a propagandist, writing mainly to sway his reader's opinions. Many critics find his writing disorderly and unclear, and at times deliberately inaccurate. However, his popularity and iconic stature are indisputable. At his funeral, fifty thousand Parisians lined the route. And today, for the general public, he is still the quintessential existentialist.

Major ideas: Sartre's existentialism is the simplest of the major theorists, characterised by his much popularised assertion that **existence precedes essence**. For Sartre, there is no logical necessity to how things are, for the **world** is an absurdity, and there is no fixed and objective meaning to life. Sartre recognises the unpalatability of such a view, and believes people generally try to ignore the **truth** of the matter (see **bad faith**). Nevertheless, for conscious beings like ourselves, there is no given **meaning** to life, there is only personal meaning or there is nothing. Human beings are unique in having no defined **essence**: if we have an essence, it is **nothingness**, so the essential nature of human existence consists of **choice**, to *make* ourselves something. This theoretical model of human beings defining themselves (see **freedom and free will**) is at odds with the psychoanalytic idea of innate drives, where the existence of unconscious instincts provides a ready-made identity:

> Consciousness has nothing substantial, it is pure 'appearance' in the sense that it exists only to the degree to which it appears. But it is precisely because consciousness is pure appearance, because it is total emptiness (since the entire world is outside it) – it … can be considered as the absolute. (Sartre, 1943a: xxxii)

Instead, humans define themselves through their actions. Even then, the individual is not fully defined, for future choices will remain until **death**, when at last that person's life can be described and is fixed. His ethics, unsurprisingly, is a manifesto for action, asserting that there is no abstract morality, and moral choices exist only in situations, so a moral life must be reactive and spontaneous rather than prejudged through simple principles.

Contribution to psychotherapy: It is in his direct commentary on **psychology** and **psychoanalysis** that Sartre is so valuable to the contemporary psychotherapist. He insists that psychology as a **science** of facts cannot be the starting-point for the investigation of human nature. Instead, **phenomenology** is the way, making use of our own human awareness: 'What must differentiate all research into man from other types of strict investigation is precisely this privileged circumstance, that the human-reality is *ourselves*' (Sartre, 1943b: 23). His psychological analysis begins with the idea of **prereflexive consciousness**, the idea (echoing Husserl) that consciousness has no content, but is always directed *towards* objects, so that it is *transcendent*. Thus, the existence of **subject and object**, the **self** and the world of things are not in doubt, and for the human being there can only be the relationship of subject and object, of self and others, and the potential **alienation** of the self from the world.

His theory of **consciousness** means Sartre rejects the psychoanalytic belief in a removed and unknowable unconscious. A Sartrean psychotherapist would instead assert the infinite richness of what is in awareness.

He holds the notion of an *ideal self*, that our behaviour is always in the direction of realising that idea: this is our **project**, our original intention. Our **emotions** reveal this direction:

> [Emotion] is a transformation of the world. When the paths before us become too difficult, or when we cannot see our way, we can no longer put up with such an exacting and difficult world. All ways are barred and nevertheless we must act. So then we try to change the world; that is, to live as though … [it was governed] by magic. (Sartre, 1939: 63)

The task of the existential psychoanalyst is to help the client realise how they have chosen:

Existential psychoanalysis seeks to determine the original choice. This original choice operating in the face of the world and being a choice of position in the world is total like the complex; it is prior to logic like the complex. It is this which decides the attitude of the person when confronted with logic and principles; therefore there can be no possibility of questioning it in conformance to logic. (Sartre, 1943a: 570)

Like **Nietzsche**, Sartre asserts the importance of power, and our unwillingness to accept that fact. And echoing **Kierkegaard**, he asserts that we must live our lives forwards, not backwards.

Sartre warns that existential psychoanalysis has 'not yet found its Freud' (ibid.: 575). For Sartre, then, existential psychoanalysis is now possible. However, there is much work yet to do.

See also **absurd, the; being-for-itself; being-for-others; being-in-the-world; facticity; generosity; intentionality; look, the; nausea; nothingness; situation; slime; transcendence**

saying
See **language**

schizophrenia
See **Laing**

Scheler
Max Scheler (1874–1928). German philosopher, from Lutheran and Jewish background, who mixed humanism, Catholic philosophy and **phenomenology**. Though he disagreed with many of **Husserl**'s ideas, he applied the **phenomenological method** to religious questions and to problems in **metaphysics** and philosophy of mind, including the questions of how we come to **knowledge** of others, and what we cannot know. He also wrote on the role of **love** in the disclosure of **Being**, and held that human beings are fundamentally loving beings. One of his best-known books is *Nature of Sympathy*, comprising an exploration of feelings as **values**, and a contention that love is at their centre and the relational aspects of being human are paramount.

Scheler influenced many existential philosophers, though his work is relatively little known. In his later work he argued for the importance of the Eternal in human beings and the absolute as a crucial sphere of **existence**.

Schleiermacher, Friedrich
See **hermeneutics; theology**

Schopenhauer
Arthur Schopenhauer (1788–1860). German philosopher, inspired by **Plato**, **Kant**, and Indian metaphysics. He was not an existentialist, but he influenced the young **Nietzsche**, as well as Wagner, **Freud** and **Wittgenstein**. His greatest

work is *The World as Will and Representation* (sometimes translated as *The World as Will and Idea*, 1818).

Born into a wealthy merchant family, his father died when Arthur was 15, and he endured an extremely difficult relationship with his mother. He was a man of independent means, who could please himself, and did so, although he seldom pleased others, being vain and sarcastic. He once shoved a servant down a flight of stairs, crippling her. His view of human nature is that human beings are egotistical and cruel.

From Kant, his **philosophy** takes the notion of **thing-in-itself**, but goes further than Kant, in naming it as the **will to live**. According to Schopenhauer, we know ourselves in two ways. First, we know ourselves as we know external things, by looking. Second, we know ourselves from within. He claims that if we attend to our inward experience we can detect the will to live, for this lies in the very actions of our bodies. The **body** is in fact objectified will. This will to live permeates the very universe, but is not conscious, and is not the result of a mind, but is blind impulse, eternal **becoming**. And thus human beings are doomed, for our lives can have no rest, no completion, no lasting satisfaction:

> All satisfaction, or what is commonly called happiness, is really and essentially always negative only, and never positive ... For desire, that is to say, want, is the precedent condition of every pleasure; but with the satisfaction, the desire and therefore the pleasure cease; and so the satisfaction or gratification can never be more than deliverance from a pain, from a want. (Schopenhauer, 1818: 319)

Will, for Schopenhauer, does not mean **free will**. This philosophy is one of hard determinism, and there are just two escapes from its tension. The first is temporary, through aesthetic contemplation; the other is permanent, through personal extinction. Schopenhauer famously made use of the first, but despite his pessimism, declined the second.

The influence of these ideas upon Freud's theories is evident. **Nietzsche** grew disenchanted with Schopenhauer's negativity, and transformed the **no-saying** of the will to live into the **yes-saying** of the **will to power**.

science and scientific method

It is popularly believed that scientific **knowledge** is in principle, if not in practice, objective and reliable. In other words, we suppose science to be capable of discovering ultimate **truth**, and assume that its principles, if not its research methods, are beyond question. Not all scientists are as confident, and perhaps fewer philosophers. Strident advocates of modern science may claim that philosophical questions are either meaningless or reducible to scientific questions, but existential philosophers have for many years been critical of claims that science is superior to **philosophy** and to the arts for the purpose of investigating and **understanding** the **world**. The ability of scientists to collect data cannot be in doubt, but it is not beyond dispute that we should subscribe unquestionably to the proofs, laws and theories of science.

One issue that critics of science have is that scientific research derives from common-sense hypotheses which the researcher then tests using common-sense logical principles. This reveals a deeper difficulty, namely, that science is at base the methodical application of common-sense thinking. And anthropological studies show that common-sense – what is seen as beyond question – varies according to culture and sub-culture, so cannot be objective. And unlike philosophy, science does not investigate its own foundations for thinking. Yet science rests ultimately on axioms – unproved assumptions about what is. Edmund **Husserl**, himself a mathematician, challenged the principles of the exact sciences and contended that we needed to find new principles for observing and understanding the world based on phenomenological description.

Existential thinkers and practitioners invariably challenge the validity of scientific axioms. Medard **Boss**, for instance said:

> During the Middle Ages everything was conceived of as being fundamentally a creation caused and produced by God out of nothing. Today's science rests on an equally prescientific presupposition, the belief that all things are of the nature of calculable objects. (Boss, 1957b: 28)

Many existentialists, though not all, allow science its place in examining the material world, yet do not consider it appropriate for the non-material aspects of the human world. (Indeed, many non-existentialists doubt that **psychology** qualifies as a behavioural science.) One of the greatest controversies here is that science relies on mechanical causality, but it is not certain that human beings live causally determined lives (see **freedom**). Instead, the preferred method for most existential philosophers and psychologists is **phenomenology**, a particular scientific approach. According to Boss:

> There are good reasons to suppose that Martin Heidegger's 'analysis of Dasein' is more appropriate to an understanding of man than the concepts which natural science has introduced into medicine and psychotherapy … [A]nalysis of Dasein may well deserve to be called more 'objective' as well as more 'scientific' than the behavioral sciences, which use the methods of natural science. (Ibid.: 29)

What constitutes a sound method for investigating and understanding the world, and whether there may be more than one such method, is still debated. And what constitutes sound theory and sound evidence, equally so.

sedimentation
See **Merleau-Ponty**

self
Is there such a thing, or such a **phenomenon** as the self? The answer is not as clear as common-sense suggests.

In general, existential authors hold the self to be more of a process than a thing. Therefore the self is seen as being in flux, always **becoming**. They take the view that there is no such thing as a substantial or solid self. But this fluidity, and the self-determination it implies, holds a ready terror for the self. All existential writers agree that it is difficult to accept **responsibility** for oneself, and all concern themselves with a certain kind of self-deceit: the denial of self-determination, of responsibility.

Other questions about the self concern the **relationship** a person has with him or herself. How can we be self-referential? Does it make sense to say we can understand ourselves? How can we misunderstand ourselves? Can we love or loathe ourselves?

Sartre claims that we start out with **pre-reflective consciousness**, at which point we are mere **project**, we have not yet reflected on our own being to become aware of self. Later on we become aware of ourselves as subjects and objects in the world. It is thus that I become conscious *of* my I:

> In fact the consciousness which I have of the 'I' never exhausts it, and consciousness is not what causes it to come into existence; the 'I' is always given as having been there before consciousness ... (Sartre, 1943a: 103)

Other people's descriptions of us make us imagine we have an ego. But for Sartre the adoption of such a sense of self is a form of **bad faith**. Essentially self is nothing, is pure **consciousness**, or **being-for-itself**. It cannot truly become a **being-in-itself**, although we constantly strive to pretend that we can. Sartre says we human beings are uncomfortable with our status as free beings and would prefer to be objects. In becoming aware of our self as a project in progress, which is nevertheless also fully embodied, we may achieve the possibility of creating a self that is of value.

Kierkegaard is more metaphysical and more modest, but like Sartre he sees relating to oneself as one of the greatest strains in living:

> The human being is spirit ... Spirit is the self ... The self is a relation which relates to itself ... The self is not the relation but the relation's relating to itself. A human being is a synthesis ... A synthesis is a relation between two terms. Looked at in this way a human being is not yet a self. (Kierkegaard, 1849: 43)

Buber says the self is always in relation: 'There is no I as such but only the I of the basic word I–You and the I of the basic word I–It' (Buber, 1923: 54). **Heidegger** also stresses the essential fact of relationship to the **world**, in that he does not write of 'I' or of *ego*. Instead he speaks of *Da-sein*, emphasising the holistic nature of the human self. *Da-sein* finds itself always in relation to others, drawn into others at first in an inauthentic mode of being and has to first of all extract itself out of this fallen way of being before it can begin to be aware of its ownmost potentiality for being itself.

Nietzsche takes a typically forceful and paradoxical attitude, seeing the self as something to be asserted and overcome by the will: '*will* a self and thou shalt *become* a self' (Nietzsche, 1879: 232).

In psychotherapy, the question of what the self is, is of enormous significance. In the everyday practice of psychotherapy it is played-out in the way the therapist understands the client or patient and construes their differentness. The tension between finding **freedom** or a sense of **identity** which gives confidence in self is one of the creative polarities with which existential therapists work.

Laing, following Winnicott, contrasts false self and true self – most existential therapists would be sceptical of such a distinction.

See also **authenticity and inauthenticity; body; emotions; individuation; introversion; master–slave dialectic; nothingness; Other, the; paradox; potentiality-for-being-oneself; solipsism; substance; will to power**

self-deception
See **authenticity and inauthenticity; defences, psychological; good faith; projection**

self-forgetfulness
See **forgetting**

semblance
See **phenomenon**

seriality
Sartrean concept from *Critique of Dialectical Reason* (1960). In a social and political world based on the **practico-inert**, human beings are alienated and related to each other through the roles they play and the functions they hold. They are therefore dominant or submissive towards each other. **Sartre** opposes this concept to that of reciprocity (see **look, the**, and **intersubjectivity**), which is the kind of **relationship** people become capable of when they accept their **freedom** as a **project** and therefore the necessity of creating a fair social exchange between each other where each contributes something to the other in a co-operative way.

See also **alienation; indifference; masochism; *praxis*; sadism**

sexuality
The quality of being sexual. This is to be distinguished from gender, which is the fact of being male or female. However, to acknowledge gender, to describe a person as a man or a woman is to acknowledge their sexuality. Unlike **psychoanalysis**, with its theory of pan-sexualism, writers on **existential psychotherapy** tend to ignore sexuality (e.g. **Heidegger**) or to consider it as another aspect of **choice** or *embodiment* (e.g. **Sartre** and **Merleau-Ponty**).

Sartre addresses one aspect of sexuality, namely desire, but does not consider that desire and **love** might be commingled. For Sartre, desire is, like love, a mutual effort to enslave the **Other** and to escape enslavement. Nor does Sartre consider nature to have any part in desire:

> [D]esire can be called the desire of one body for another body ... The being which desires is consciousness *making itself body* ... in order to appropriate the Other's body ...

> [...] Desire is a lived project which does not suppose any preliminary deliberation but which includes within itself its meaning and its interpretation. As soon as I throw myself towards the Other's facticity, as soon as I wish to push aside his acts and his functions so as to touch him in his flesh, I incarnate myself, for I can neither wish nor even conceive of the incarnation of the Other except in and by means of my own incarnation. (Sartre, 1943a: 389, 395)

Simone de **Beauvoir** analyses the relationship between men and women, but her interest is not in the realm of sexuality, but rather autonomy and **freedom**.

Merleau-Ponty writes more fully on sexuality than any other existential theorist. He complains that psychoanalysis treats sexuality as so great in scope that all of human existence is contained in it, making it impossibly ambiguous. We should not, he says, reduce sexuality to **existence**; sexuality has existential significance, but that does not mean it is only a symbol of some existential drama. And neither should we reduce existence to the **body**:

> [W]e must recognize in modesty, desire and love in general a metaphysical significance, which means that they are incomprehensible if man is treated as a machine governed by natural laws, or even as 'a bundle of instincts', and that they are relevant to man as a consciousness and as a freedom. (Merleau-Ponty, 1945: 166)

All aspects of human being have meaning, and this includes sexual behaviour no less:

> The intensity of sexual pleasure would not be sufficient to explain the place occupied by sexuality in human life ... if sexual experience were not, as it were, an opportunity ... of acquainting oneself with the human lot in its most general aspects of autonomy and dependence. (Ibid.: 167)

There is much in the area of sexuality that existential theorists have yet to consider. For instance, to be sexual is to be differentiated from the other sex, and to be sexual is to be incomplete (men and women are each half of the reproductive process). There is an opportunity to analyse what it means to be a man, what it means to be a woman, to examine maternity and paternity, childbearing and the experience of childbirth, and men's presence and absence in procreation, of relationships with the same-sex parent and opposite-sex parents, of homosexuality, bi-sexuality, masturbation, of rape (violence is always a **possibility** in human relationships), and of the relationship between sex and love.

See **masochism; project; relationship; sadism**

shame

The feeling of having gained the contempt of others. Psychologically, shame results in a feeling of inferiority even though the feeling of shame is no proof of one's inferiority. **Sartre** explains it as resulting from the **look** of the **Other**. And he further explains that he who objectifies another with such a look will himself feel **guilt**. Thus there is no escape from shame and guilt.

Nietzsche considered shame to be one of the negative ways of human interaction and he is intensely scornful about it:

> Whom do you call bad? Him who always wants to make ashamed. What is to you the most humane thing? To spare anyone shame. What is the seal of freedom attained? No longer to be ashamed of oneself. (Nietzsche, 1882: 268–75)

The existential psychotherapist, as well as attending directly to the discomfort of shame, tries to bring attention to what that discomfort reveals, for instance, the sufferer's **values**.

sickness unto death

A theme in the **philosophy** of Kierkegaard, and the translated title of his 1849 work, *Sygdommen til Døden*, it refers to a profound **despair**, resulting from denial of the **relationship** of the self to God, and a conviction that there is nothing beyond physical **death**. We all have at least a little of this *malaise*, from which we may try to escape, and from which if we do, we feel only greater despair at our **guilt**. Yet the more conscious we are, the more intense is our despair.

Kierkegaard is not only describing the psychology of the atheist but of those Christians (and churches) who pay lip-service to Christianity, who lack faith, **passion** and imagination. In the individual, this sickness is the consequence of an imbalance, for the true self, the fully conscious self, is a balance of the finite and the infinite, the temporal and the eternal, necessity and **freedom**. Lacking such balance, the sick soul is not grounded in relationship to God, and is in a state of sin. A person with this sickness is not fully a person:

> Personhood is a synthesis of possibility and necessity ... The determinist's self cannot breathe because it is impossible to breathe necessity alone ... The fatalist is in despair, he has lost God and thereby his self; for a person who has no God has no self either ... The petty bourgeois lacks any spiritual characteristic and is absorbed in the probable. (Kierkegaard, 1849: 70–1)

This sickness of the spirit is obviously a defect. But it is also a merit: 'The possibility of this sickness is man's advantage over the beast ... the Christian's advantage over natural man' (ibid.: 44–5). Thus the sickness to death is potentially a means of redemption, of recovery into faith. Everything is possible with God. Accepting this, one can pray: 'To pray is also to breathe, and possibility is for the self what oxygen is for breathing' (ibid.: 70). To reject the mundane as all there is, to accept the possible, is to escape despair. But it requires great effort: 'For to be aware of his self and of God, a man's imagination must whirl him up higher than the dank air of the probable' (ibid.: 71). Kierkegaard in this way opposes despair to angst, or *existential anxiety*, since to open oneself to **possibility** introduces the experience of **anxiety**. It might therefore be concluded that at all times human beings are balancing their lives between the opposites of despair and anxiety.

See also **bad faith; finite and infinite; relationship**

sight

Heidegger makes use of a number of terms to do with sight (*Sicht*), by which he means gaining a grasp of one's possibilities through the disclosure of what is there. *Dasein* is deeply preoccupied with sight. Heidegger often uses terms that relate *Dasein*'s ability to see Being's fundamental character of shining forth or illuminating things. This relates to his use of the notion of a **clearing** in which things get disclosed. *Umsicht*, which literally means looking around, Heidegger uses to indicate circumspection towards the *ready-to-hand* (see **world**). It is a kind of **pragmatism**, a looking out for what physical things might be of practical use. (See also **technology**.)

Vorsicht literally means foresight or caution, and is used by Heidegger to mean having insight into what needs to be interpreted. It is a kind of preconception or a priori **understanding**:

> The interpretation of something as something is essentially grounded in fore-having, fore-sight, and fore-conception. Interpretation is never a presuppositionless grasping of something previously given ... [W]hat is initially 'there' is nothing else than the self-evident, undisputed prejudice of the interpreter. (Heidegger, 1927b: 150)

Rücksicht is literally looking back, but is used to mean respect or considerateness in relation to others. It refers to the concerned view we have of others, deriving from a regard for others we have whether we admit it to ourselves or not. As **being-with**, human **Being** is always for the sake of others.

Durchsichtigkeit, or through-sight, is used to mean transparency, the sight related to grasping one's **being-in-the-world**. It is thus a kind of self-knowledge, but since *Dasein* does not have a **self**, this is based on **knowledge** of the world rather than on the knowledge of oneself.

See also **interpretation; Moment, the; possibility**

silence
See **reticence**

Silentio, Johannes de
Pseudonym used by **Kierkegaard** for *Fear and Trembling* (1843).

sin
See **guilt; Kierkegaard; leap of faith**

singular mode of relating
See **Binswanger**

situation and situation ethics
Human beings, according to the **philosophy** of **Sartre**, are essentially engaged in the **world** and therefore always in a situation. Judgement of an individual's plight is an individual matter, because the individual has his or her own projects, **values** and intentions. An individual's situation includes his given circumstances, his past, and his fellow human beings. Situations are thus made up of environment and personal attitudes. Sartre emphasises that the former matters only as judged by the latter. A person's circumstances affect them only as they contribute to or oppose their pre-existing desires and intentions. Two prisoners in a cell share the same immediate environment, but if one has a **project** of personal liberty and the other of philosophical speculation, then their situation is radically different.

Moral philosophy usually looks to discover general principles of right and wrong conduct. However, in judging particular instances of right and wrong, the circumstances of the situation will usually be taken into account. A principle of truthfulness may be agreed, but a lie told in order to save someone's life will probably be applauded. Sartre places the situational factors in the foreground, so that fixed principles matter little and are seen as no guide to the right ethical **choice**.

Heidegger's definition of situation is entirely different, since he uses the term specifically to indicate that **time** when the **moment of vision** enables *Dasein* to have an overview of past, present and future and an authentic awareness of its situation and context.

See also **authenticity and inauthenticity; coefficient of adversity; engagement; facticity**

slave
See **master–slave dialectic**

slave morality
See **master morality and slave morality**

slime/stickiness
Sartre's lengthy discussion of the slimy illustrates how he believes existential analysis differs from **psychoanalysis**. Where the psychoanalyst believes in the primary importance of the psychic, the existential analyst considers psychological concerns only as evidence of something greater, the relationship with **Being**:

> What ontology can teach psychoanalysis is first of all the *true* origin of the meaning of things and their *true* relation to human reality ... [A] feeling is not an inner disposition but an objective, transcending relation which has as its object to learn what it is. (Sartre, 1943a: 603–4)

Sartre points out that an experience, like a handshake or a smile or thought can be slimy (*le visqueux*, sometimes translated as the *sticky*). It reveals a mode of being which is repulsive and disgusting and similar to liquidity:

> The slimy is *docile*. Only at the very moment when I believe that I possess it, behold by a curious reversal, *it* possesses me. Here appears its essential character: its softness is leech-like ... Slime is the revenge of the In-itself ... the absorption of the For-itself by the In-itself ... (Ibid.: 608–10)

This is not a practical possibility, it is an *antivalue*, a negative ideal, the opposite of **consciousness**, which itself is a **project** of appropriation. It is the nightmare of the hunter being hunted. It is what we experience in the face of the imposing actuality of the material **world** and it leads to the experience of **nausea**. But beyond being a psychic attitude, it reveals something about the world, a possible **meaning** of Being.

See also **being-for-itself; being-in-itself; existential psychotherapy; psychoanalysis**

social dimension/world
See **four worlds**

social phenomenology
See **Laing**

Socrates
(*c.* 470–399 BC). Greek philosopher who influenced **Plato**. He left no writings, but is known entirely through the works of Xenophon, Aristophanes and (especially) Plato. References to Socratic ideas can be found under: **dialectic; emotions; irony; repetition; Socratic method; Zollikon Seminars.**

Socratic method
Attributed by **Plato** and Xenophon to **Socrates**. Sometimes referred to as Socratic questioning or Socratic dialogue. The Socratic method is a dialectical technique used for teaching or debating. It proceeds through a series of questions and answers, and has a paradoxical character, for it is a way of eliciting what a person is unaware that he knows or of demonstrating that he does not know what he thinks he knows:

> *Agathon:* Eros is beautiful.
> *Socrates:* And is Eros love of something, or of nothing?
> *Agathon:* Of something, naturally.
> *Socrates:* And does Eros desire what he loves?
> *Agathon:* Of course.
> *Socrates:* And does Eros desire what he already has or what he does not have?
> *Agathon:* What he doesn't have, I suppose.
> *Socrates:* Isn't it certain that anything that desires something must lack it?
> *Agathon:* Yes, I agree.
> *Socrates:* Then you agree that Eros loves what he lacks?
> *Agathon:* Yes.
> *Socrates:* So Eros has no beauty, but lacks it?
> *Agathon:* Yes, that must follow.
> *Socrates:* And can you still say that Eros is beautiful?
> *Agathon:* Socrates, I begin to think I did not know what I was saying.
>
> (Edited from Plato's dialogue, *Symposium*)

The Socratic method is, with some adaptation, well suited to **existential psychotherapy**. As Socrates seems to have practised it, it often angered those who thought themselves wise, for not only were they revealed to be unwise, but Socrates would throughout his conversation maintain an irritating posture of utter lack of expertise and **knowledge**. Such *Socratic irony* would be unhelpful in any therapeutic application of Socratic method; the therapist must be frank that his or her own views are irrelevant and are being withheld in order to focus on the client. Nor should it be used to persuade, as it often is in Plato's works. There should be no rhetoric, but genuine and open enquiry. Socratic dialogue is fundamental to the contemporary practice of **philosophical counselling and consultancy**.

See also **dialectic; paradox**

solicitude
See **being-for-another; being-with; care; leaping in**

solipsism
From the Latin, *solus ipse*, meaning the **self** alone. Solipsism is the philosophical position of isolation, when the self is cut off from others or the outside **world**. Knowledge derives from subjective experience, according to **phenomenology**. This makes it difficult to be certain of the **existence** of anything external to the self. Phenomenology is thus open to the criticism of being solipsistic, that is, of only believing in the self and seeing external **reality** as the product of the self. Probably no critic means this literally, but it does indicate a systematic difficulty in the **philosophy**, namely, how subjective **knowledge** can result in objective knowledge, or at least in the knowledge of external existents. This may be true of transcendental phenomenology, even though **Husserl** vigorously defends his position by arguing that the transcendental ego includes the existence of others. However, existential phenomenology, or existential philosophy, begins from a different premise, not one of extreme scepticism, but one of accepting existence, the world and other beings. This is illustrated vividly in the thinking of **Sartre**, where some **emotions** presuppose the existence of others (for instance, **shame**), and where a **being-for-itself** experiences the **Other** (through the **look**) as another **being-for-itself**.

See also **other minds**

soul
See **body; Descartes; idealism; identity; person; psychology; self; sickness unto death**

space
It is not at all obvious what space is. Is it something or nothing? According to Newton it is an objective fact, a region. And in this manner, **Descartes** believed that if space can be measured, then it cannot be a vacuum. On this account it is something. But Leibniz claimed it is only the spatial relations between

things. On his account space is nothing, as it is for **Sartre**, for whom space is a **nothingness** in which human beings are revealed.

Existential philosophers are more concerned with the experience of space than its empirical nature. One evident feature of space as it presents itself to human perception is that it distinguishes a person's **body** from the **world**; thus **Merleau-Ponty** describes the body as a *frontier*, and shows that space has **meaning** for human beings in relationship to their physical orientation.

Heidegger follows **Aristotle** in describing space in terms of *place*, that things have places, but he also describes space as room for living. He accords great importance to the region and range of things. Things merely occupy space, but a human being clears a space about itself, makes room for itself, allows space to be. Thus space is an essential aspect of human being, of **being-in-the-world**. Human beings have a direction in space and the capacity for *Entfernung*, or deseverance, **de-distancing**: they can make things come closer or nearer to themselves: '[Dasein's] spatiality shows the characters of deseverance and directionality' (Heidegger, 1927a: 105). For Heidegger, space and **time** are intimately related, or even a unity. Like Sartre, he holds that space derives from time. And he rails against the use of **technology** to make the world smaller, claiming that to bring things nearer is to flee from time.

See also **clearing; locus**

speech
See **Derrida; discourse**

Spinoza
Baruch or Benedictus de Spinoza (1632–1677). Dutch rationalist philosopher of Portuguese Jewish origin who made important contributions to a wide range of philosophical ideas. His magnum opus is his posthumously published *Ethics* (1677), a vision of a **world** where God, nature and human beings are interconnected and united. His pantheism results in a search for happiness through understanding the necessary **freedom** that is typically human. For this reason Spinoza's philosophy may be considered a precursor to existential thinking.

See also **rationalism**

spirit
Being comes into **existence** in the human spirit, according to **Hegel**. The *subjective* spirit exists in the human mind: it is aware of its finiteness. Hegel also refers to *objective* spirit, which manifests itself in human institutions such as the state. Both of these are *finite* spirits. But *absolute* spirit is that which rises above its finitude, and knows itself as Being.

Søren **Kierkegaard** considers spirit to be one of the most important factors of being human:

> Man is a synthesis of the psychical and the physical; however, a synthesis is unthinkable if the two are not united in a third. This third is spirit. (Kierkegaard, 1844b: 43)

For human beings to begin to live in a spiritual way demands a **leap of faith**, according to Kierkegaard.

See also **spiritual dimension**

spirit of abstraction
See Marcel

Spirit of Gravity
See **laughter**

spirit of seriousness
(*L'esprit de sérieux*). A term used by **Sartre** for the attitude of believing that human beings live in a world of absolute and objective **values** and are therefore like solid objects. Sometimes Sartre refers to this as **good faith**, which would seem to be in opposition to his concept of **bad faith**. However, he contends that the spirit of seriousness, or being in good faith, is tantamount to being in bad faith:

> It is indifferent whether one is in good or in bad faith, because bad faith reapprehends good faith and slides to the very origin of the project of good faith. (Sartre, 1943a: 70)

Sartre also refers to the *champion of sincerity*, who asks people to be true to themselves and who takes sincerity very seriously. For Sartre, such sincerity is actually another form of bad faith, since it involves a denial of **freedom** and an attempt to constitute the **self** as a thing:

> Thus the essential structure of sincerity does not differ from that of bad faith since the sincere man constitutes himself as what he is *in order not to be it.* (Ibid.: 65)

spiritual dimension/world
See **four worlds**

stages of life
See **Kierkegaard**

state of mind
See *Befindlichkeit*

statistics
See **probability**

stickiness
See **slime/stickiness**

Stimmung
See **attunement**; *Befindlichkeit*

Stoics and stoicism
Philosophical school founded in Athens in about 300 BC, by Zeno of Citium, and famous for the use of **paradox** in its teaching. Stoicism was a comprehensive **philosophy** in which a way of life followed from an ideological system. God is the creative fire of the universe, a spirit that makes itself into all things and constructs a universe bound by rational order. This pantheistic view means that human beings are seen as sharing a little of this rational and creative fire and should live in accordance with the laws of nature. Divine providence, or the law of nature, or *logos*, subordinates all, and rules for the best. From this it follows that what seems to be misfortune is really for the best and people should practise indifference to their problems. The wise person therefore accepts hardship with uncomplaining fortitude, and aspires to the virtues of intelligence, bravery, justice and self-control. For a Stoic, virtue is the sole good. Emotions are regarded as the result of judgement and therefore within control. Kindness is approved of, but not **fear** or pity, for they are misjudgements of providence. Stoicism was further developed by the Athenians Cleanthes and Chrysippus, and was later turned into a popular doctrine by Roman writers such as Marcus Aurelius, Seneca and Epictetus.

See also *amor fati*; emotions; *eudaimonia*

structuralism
An approach that emerged in response to existentialism and its claims of personal **freedom**, structuralism describes the individual as inserted into a structured **world**, one that influences behaviour and understanding. Structuralists analyse language, culture and society to reveal their underlying structures. Originating with Ferdinand de Saussure's *Course in General Linguistics* (1916), it was also championed by the anthropologist and ethnographer Claude Lévi-Strauss, whose concern is the kinship structures of human society. **Foucault**, Piaget and **Lacan** are also part of the movements of structuralism and post-structuralism (see, for instance, **Kristeva**). The movement was followed by deconstructionism (**Derrida** and others).

See also **Barthes**

Stumpf
(1848–1936). Philosopher and psychologist, inspired by **Brentano**, later a tutor of **Husserl** as well as of the Gestalt psychologists Köhler and Koffka. He wrote on the psychology of music and sound perception, but probably his greatest achievement was to nurse **psychology** from its dependent position as a branch of **philosophy** to becoming an independent scientific discipline.

subject and object
René **Descartes**, in a profound thought experiment which consisted of doubting everything, now referred to as the *cogito* (see **Descartes**), derived the conclusion,

'I think, therefore I am' (*Discourse on the Method*, 1637). This set the tone for subsequent Western philosophical thinking, and seeped into those everyday philosophical beliefs we call *common-sense*, so that it now seems evident to the man or woman in the street that the subject *I* is separate from the objects of the **world**.

Existential philosophers (amongst others) have been unhappy with Descartes's reasoning even though, following **Husserl's** lead, they often recognise Cartesian doubt to be a good starting point for phenomenology. **Heidegger**, for instance, objects to the notion of an absolutely distinct *I*, **a self** isolated from the world. This is more than an objection that the self is not set in context, that human beings and the world have a symbiotic relationship, for he argues that self and object are inseparable: ***Dasein*** is neither simply subject nor object. For if the self as a subject of experience is not an integral part of the world, then the experiencing subject, the self, must be alienated from the world. The existential view is that self and object are integrated, that they overlap. We are not disembodied minds viewing the world as if it were a show. **Merleau-Ponty** argues that a person is a *body-subject*, that is, has a **body** and relates physically to the world.

Sartre writes of *objectité* (*objectness* or *object-state*), referring to being objectified by another person, being an object to another's subject (see **look, the**). Sartre does not allow that a person might view another as both subject and object. Simone de **Beauvoir** gives an account of how women feel themselves to be both subjects and (for men) objects. It is left unclear how much this is a fact of **existence** and how much a matter of culture. Other existential philosophers are more optimistic. **Berdyaev** argues that we are wrong to split object from subject, whilst Martin **Buber**, writing of the I–Thou relationship, allows that although we usually fall into experiencing other beings as mere phenomena, in an *I–It* relationship, we can sometimes realise we are in contact with a like being. And **Marcel** adds that **Being** is not an object, and cannot be understood objectively. Yet other existential writers permit a subject–object split. Karl **Jaspers** is quite content to distinguish between subject and object, while Rollo **May** claims human beings are necessarily both subject and object.

All this is of great account to the psychotherapist, for it addresses the issue of how people experience themselves, and how they understand themselves to be in **relationship** to the world, especially the world of the **Other**.

See also **alienation; encounter; intentionality; intersubjectivity;** *Mitwelt*; **other minds; solipsism**

subjective and objective
See **ambiguity; consciousness and unconsciousness; existential psychotherapy; hermeneutics; Husserl; idealism; Kierkegaard; psychopathology and diagnosis; solipsism; subject and object; time and temporality**

sublimation
Utilitarian philosophers like Bentham hold that we are subject in all our behaviour to the pursuance of pleasure and the avoidance of pain. **Nietzsche**

opposes this idea. He does not believe that a profit and loss account is sufficiently subtle to explain human behaviour. For instance, how is it that people sometimes deliberately endure pain? Just as **Freud** would later develop a view of human behaviour with sex as its basis, so Nietzsche's view has a single underlying motive, the **will to power**. Sublimation is the transformation of the will to power. According to Nietzsche, one ought not to suppress or submit to **passion**, but to reveal it without **shame**. This does not mean laying waste to the world or exercising unbridled sexuality; instead, it implies the discovery of one's inner resources of strength and energy. For instance, cruelty – itself an expression of the will to power – might be turned into asceticism:

> The *artistic* view of the world: to sit down to contemplate life. But any analysis of the aesthetic outlook is lacking: its reduction to cruelty, a feeling of security, playing the judge and standing outside, etc. One must examine the artist himself, and his psychology (critique of the drive to play as a release of force, a pleasure in change, in impressing one's soul on something foreign, the absolute egoism of the artist, etc.), what drives he sublimates. (Nietzsche, 1901: 677)

As well as an artistic view, Nietzsche writes of a scientific view, a religious view and a moral view.

The idea of sublimation was taken up by Freud, although Freud adapted it to suggest repression of the instincts, a process by which unacceptable sexual or aggressive drives are diverted into non-instinctual behaviour, usually creative, religious or intellectual pursuits. It thus allowed Freud to fit artistic, mental and spiritual activities into his pan-sexual meta-theory.

See also **Kierkegaard** (on the stages of life)

substance

In general **philosophy**, this usually means the enduring matter or form of a thing. Thus, aspects of a substance may change, but its **essence** will persist. Similarly for **Heidegger**, *substanz* is objective **presence**. **Being** is not a physical entity. The essence of *Da-sein* is existence, so the essence of selfhood is existential, but it is not substantiality, and the Being of human beings cannot be investigated in the way that a substance can, with the tools of **science**.

Sartre similarly claims that human beings exist first and only later define themselves, but his distinction between **being-for-itself** and **being-in-itself** suggests that the substance of objects is highly desirable to human beings who aspire to make themselves feel substantial.

See also **existence precedes essence**

suicide

See **Camus**; **choice**; **Szasz**

suffering

See **Frankl**; **Nietzsche**; **passion**

superman

Nietzsche's concept of *Übermensch*, literally overman. This idea is popularly misunderstood, and by the Nazis, wilfully misrepresented. Nietzsche generally describes the *Übermensch* not as a superior person or race, but rather, as an ideal to which all may aspire. Nietzsche possessed an ambition for humankind to go beyond what humankind is now, for 'Man is a bridge, not a goal' (1883: prologue, sect. 4). He says little about the nature of the superman beyond this, maintaining that it cannot be known how such striving will turn out.

Nevertheless, at times Nietzsche implies that a superman would possess superior strength, intelligence, **passion** and culture. He adds that the superman would be tolerant of others, and reject both virtue and vice. This idea of the superman is linked with the notion that we need to reassess all **values** and pass from a slave morality to a **master morality**.

See also **revaluation of values**

Szasz

Thomas Stephen Szasz (b. 1920). Hungarian-born American psychiatrist and psychoanalyst. His many writings include *The Myth of Mental Illness* (1961), *The Ethics of Psychoanalysis* (1965), *The Myth of Psychotherapy* (1978) and *Fatal Freedom* (1999). His analyses of the harm that psychiatry and psychotherapy can cause have prompted much discussion in the mental heath professions.

In speaking of the 'myth of mental illness', Szasz means to firmly reject the idea that emotional torment is analogous to physical disease. True, there are illnesses of the brain or other physical organs that have consequences for mental functioning, but these are physiological illnesses, not mental ones. Otherwise, the term 'mental illness' is at best a metaphor for mental distress.

His arguments are at once logical and political: mental health professionals who see mental distress as illness misunderstand it and do a disservice to their clients, and put themselves in the position of physicians trying to cure with directive means, so taking away the **freedom** of their patients to direct their own lives. A passionate libertarian, Szasz opposes psychiatry and psychotherapy as repressive instruments. His own approach is to see psychotherapy as a philosophical enterprise that examines problems in living. Consequently he believes clients of mental health care should be free to choose for themselves, and psychotherapy should be actively chosen. Therefore, the client should pay for therapy, and the therapist should provide a clear contractual idea of what he or she will and will not provide. Furthermore, the therapist should be independent in order to safeguard the client's freedom, and should refrain from communicating with third parties. As for state-funded mental health care: as all states seek to control behaviour of which they disapprove, so state-funded psychotherapy is highly undesirable, for it will tend to control behaviour, for instance in matters of sexual behaviour and in the freedom to commit suicide.

See also **anti-psychiatry; philosophy**

technology and technological attitude

From the Greek *techne*, meaning the knowledge and method required to make something. Technology, according to **Heidegger**, discovers or reveals what can be employed, the stock (*Bestand*) of the **world**: natural resources such as trees, minerals, and fellow human beings. It reveals the **possibility** of exploiter and exploited. In some ways technology (and having a technological attitude) is a necessary phase of human development. Heidegger, however, opposes such an anthropocentric stance, seeing it as destructive and as an obscuring of **Being**. Unchecked, it threatens to engulf and overwhelm the world, to desolate the world. We ought to be detached from technology and we should reflect on it. But there is a counter to technology. Art confronts technology, and helps us think about Being.

See also **enframing; knowing and knowledge; presence; releasement**

temporality

See **time and temporality**

theology

The study of God, although it is often used more narrowly to mean the study of particular faiths or branches of faiths. Its theories and ideas address issues of God's nature and the **relationship** of humankind to God. It remains open to dispute whether theology should be regarded as a special branch of **philosophy**, i.e. of **metaphysics**, or whether, because it is grounded in faith and the revelation of sacred texts, it is quite distinct.

Existential theology is as various in style and approach as existential philosophy. And just as in existential philosophy, **existence** and **Being** are givens, so the existential theologian makes no effort to debate God's existence.

Friedrich Schleiermacher (1768–1834), a German protestant theologian, is a precursor who influenced many later existential theologians. He argued that human beings are essentially religious, and that whilst the **world** is contingent, we naturally depend utterly upon God who is necessary. This dependence on God is our human **identity**. Not to accept it is a failure, a sin. Schleiermacher also emphasises human **freedom**, and the idea that human beings discover self-knowledge only in the presence of others. He also stresses that being infinite, God transcends all human categories.

Amongst the foremost existential theorists is Karl Barth (1886–1968), a protestant Swiss theorist much influenced by **Kierkegaard**, from whom he takes the view that God, being infinite, differs from humankind so greatly that He is incomprehensible to our limited human reason. God's judgements are completely beyond human rationality. Thus, like Kierkegaard, Barth rejects reason as a way to religious conviction, arguing instead the need for faith. Kierkegaard himself, though no theologian, explored the **meaning** and significance of faith in God and he came to the conclusion that to take a **leap of faith** allows us to go beyond the narrow confines of materialistic and finite existence. For him the spiritual life is what raises us above a mere aesthetic or ethical position and is always based in an individual and personal relationship to God.

Rudolf Bultmann (1884–1976) is a German theologian influenced by **Heidegger**. He argues that a Christian believer needs no commitment to the factual claims implied in the New Testament, for the narratives in the New Testament are mythological. However, they contain an existential message, and Bultmann offers various existential accounts of their symbolism. He claims that human beings exist in a tension between **authenticity and inauthenticity** which results in an existential **anxiety**. For Bultmann, inauthenticity is the mistaken belief that we humans have any great power in the world.

Paul **Tillich** rejects the notion of a personal god. God is described by Tillich not as an object, nor even as the supreme object, but as the power of the cosmos. Tillich's work as a theologian is noteworthy in bringing theology and **psychology** together.

Dietrich Bonhoeffer (1906–45) is a Protestant theologian who, like Gabriel **Marcel**, from his Catholic perspective and Martin **Buber**, from his Jewish perspective, argues that one should treat the **Other** as a Thou, not as an It, and that we should live for Others. According to Bonhoeffer, we should resist the temptation to dominate others, to be as God rather than simply human.

See also **absurd, the; alienation; Berdyaev; contingency; I–Thou/I–You; Levinas**

therapeutic relationship
See **relationship**

thetic consciousness
See **pre-reflexive consciousness**

They, the
A term **Heidegger** uses to indicate the dominance that the anonymous They (sometimes translated, from *das Man*, as *they*) has over human beings, even though this anonymous 'one' does not actually exist. *They* don't like it. *One* doesn't do that sort of thing. *One* ought to be like them. This is the tendency to conform, to want to be the same way that we imagine others are and want us to be:

> Being-with-one-another is, unknown to itself, disquieted by the care about this distance. Existentially expressed, being-with-one-another has the characteristic of

distantiality ... Da-sein stands in *subservience* to the others. It itself *is* not; the others have
taken its being away from it. The everyday possibilities of being of Da-sein are at the
disposal of the whims of the others. (Heidegger, 1927b: 126)

According to Heidegger, we thus give up our own possibilities for **Being**, we
allow others to dominate us because we wish to be average. This is an aspect
of the Being of **Da-sein**, of *Da-sein's* essential interrelatedness. And thus our
everyday **self** is a *They-self*, a loss of the authentic self. We have become as *the
They*, we are *das Man*, the One, or the Nobody, until we are able to remove
ourselves from this fallen and inauthentic being.

When *the They* was taken up as a sociological notion, Heidegger abandoned
his use of the term.

See also **authenticity and inauthenticity; averageness; care; crowd, the;
distantiality; everydayness; herd, the; possibility**

They-self
See **call of conscience; potentiality-for-being-oneself; They, the**

thinghood
(*Dinglichkeit*). This refers mainly to **Heidegger's** description of the **existence**
of things, objects in the **world**, the *present-at-hand*, which is simply there.
Heidegger opposes this to the *ready-to-hand*, which is the object when available as a tool for human use. It is similar to **Sartre's** use of **being-in-itself**.
Heidegger distinguishes *Dinge*, things, from *Sache*, the things themselves to
which **phenomenology** incites us to return (see **phenomenological method**).
In relation to human beings, Heidegger gives various accounts of how when
we fail to be authentic, we do not allow ourselves to understand **Being**, but
we take the behaviour of the **They**, and relate **self** and being to thinghood, to
our corporeal state, our objective **presence**.

See also **authenticity and inauthenticity; being-for-itself; being-for-others;
substance; thing-in-itself**

thing-in-itself
A notion devised by **Kant**, who distinguishes between things as we perceive
them (*phenomena*) and things as they are in themselves (*noumena*). Kant
argues that we can only know phenomena, and not things-in-themselves. But
Schopenhauer thinks otherwise. Much criticised, this distinction nevertheless served as the basis for what later was systematised into **phenomenology**.
Compare also with Sartre's **being-in-itself**, or the solid object which is juxta-
posed to the **being-for-itself** of the person.

thinking
Heidegger attaches great importance to thinking (*denken*) and in his later
work he makes the connection between *denken*, i.e. thinking and *danken*, i.e.
thanking. To think deeply is to remember and to thank. Therefore Heidegger

distinguishes various forms of thought, and describes *calculative* thinking as the lowest, which has its uses, but which is limited, even blinkered. It is pragmatic thought, the thinking process of **everydayness**, of common sense and **science**. It considers beings, but only in practical terms, and it ignores the background to the practical **existence** of beings, which is **Being**.

The highest form of thought is meditative thinking, which is philosophical thinking. This is a kind of thinking that is often reflexive, that is, it considers itself. But unlike calculative thinking, which has as its end the discovery of definitive answers, meditative thinking produces answers which in turn pose further questions. Philosophical thinking poses problems and explores Being. This is because philosophical thinking, as Heidegger sees it, is a large-scale process of clearing away, of revealing, and of construction. It involves *a-letheia*, a Greek term which in his earlier writings Heidegger equates with **truth**, but which in his later writing he describes as *unconcealment*, as the preparation for truth. Good philosophical thinking for Heidegger is close in nature to poetry. He plays on the etymological connection between *denken*, thinking, and *Dichtung*, poetry.

See also **call of conscience; clearing; concealment; philosophy**

third force
See **humanistic psychology**

Thou shalt
See **Zarathustra**

Thou–Thou
See I–Thou/I–You

three worlds
See **four worlds**

thrown and thrownness
(*Geworfen* and *Geworfenheit*). Thrownness is a fundamental feature of **Dasein**, together with existence and **falling**. We are *thrown* into the there of our lives. Certain facts of our **existence** are simply thrust upon us – our gender, race, family, culture, etc., and even our very birth, our personal existence: 'The expression thrownness is meant to suggest the *facticity of its being delivered over'* (Heidegger, 1927b: 135). But where facticity refers to certain given facts of human existence, thrownness emphasises that human beings, as beings conscious of themselves, are nevertheless free only apart from the unchosen facts of their **world**.

See also *Befindlichkeit*; contingency; May; project

Tillich

Paul Tillich (1886–1965). German-born theologian and philosopher of religion. Influenced by **Plato**, Aquinas, Spinoza, Leibniz, **Kant**, **Hegel**, Schelling, **Nietzsche**, **Jung** and **Heidegger**. He influenced many Christian existentialists, especially **May**, who was his student, he thereby also influenced the American existential therapists **Bugental** and **Yalom**. Tillich's great work is *Systematic Theology* (3 vols, 1951–63), but more widely read is *The Courage To Be* (1952). Like his father, he trained and practised as a Lutheran minister, serving as an army chaplain in the Great War. He then taught **theology** and **philosophy** of religion in Berlin, Marburg, Dresden and Frankfurt. In 1933, when Hitler came to power, he went with his Jewish wife to the USA to teach, and decided to stay.

Tillich held that religious questions should be grounded in the facts of the human situation. From Heidegger, he takes the notion of Man as the being who asks **ontological** questions, and in whose very being the answers may be disclosed, since we have direct experience of Being, of the structure and elements of Being. For Tillich, the elements of human being are dimensions, e.g. freedom-destiny, individualisation-participation.

Tillich carried out a thorough investigation of **anxiety**. He distinguishes between existential and neurotic forms, and argues that the latter is a cover for the former, a psychological defence against full awareness of existential anxiety. There are, he says, three modes of existential anxiety in existence, and therefore for humankind. These are the result of encounter with **death**, **guilt** and meaninglessness. The third of these is dominant in our historical epoch, but all these anxieties are responses to the threat of non-being. They are not pure **fear**, but fear of fear. Hence, courage is required to face them. But for Tillich, God offers a practical answer to humankind's difficulties in living.

Faith is a means of organising one's life around an ultimate concern. That ultimate concern could be politics, or art, or wealth, etc. However, religious faith is a participation in God, a surrender to His authority. This allows us to trust and expect fulfilment, for God has – or *is* – infinite power to resist non-being. To participate in God is the only way to fully *be*.

Some have considered Tillich an atheist because he rejected the notion of a personal god, of God as a person. For Tillich, God is a symbol of ultimate reality that we should come to terms with in our lives.

See also **defences, psychological; meaning and meaninglessness**

time and temporality

Edmund **Husserl** argued that time is lived experience. He saw the past as made present through memory and recollection, and the future made present through anticipation, and he used a spatial metaphor, describing events as moving into the past. **Heidegger** argued that for human beings, time is neither objective nor subjective but is primordially based in human experience, that time is our *own* time. This is *temporality* (*Zeitlichkeit*), the quality and experience of being temporal, and is distinct from measured time. We use clocks to measure time objectively, and we may imagine time to be a straight line, an endless series of present moments, but this is an *inauthentic* way of dealing with time. Time is not an entity, but a human activity. Heidegger speaks of the *ek-stasies* of time in which we *ek-sist*, that is, stand outside of ourselves. These are past, present and future. The term *Augenblick* – literally the blink of an eye, or the **Moment**, or the *moment of vision*, refers to the place where we oversee past, present and future.

Sartre accounts for the past as in-itself and the present as for-itself, that is, the first is fixed and the second free. **Being-in-itself** cannot be future, for it has no possibilities, and **being-for-itself** cannot be its future:

> In short the For-itself is free, and its Freedom is to itself its own limit. To be free is to be condemned to be free. Thus the Future qua Future does not have to be. It is not *in itself*, and neither is it in the mode of being of the For-itself since it is the *meaning* of the For-itself. The future is not, it *is possibilized*. The Future is the continual possibilization of possibles. (Sartre, 1943a: 129)

Sartre, then, links future with **freedom**.

Merleau-Ponty follows from the example of Heidegger and Sartre:

> [Time] has meaning for us only because 'we are it'. We can designate something by this word only because we are at the past, present and future. (Merleau-Ponty, 1945: 430)

See also **authenticity and inauthenticity; awaiting; becoming; Bergson; change; close off; eternal return; forgetting; Minkowski; possibility**

To the things themselves!
See **Husserl; phenomenological method**

Tolstoy
(Count) Leo Nikolayevich Tolstoy (1828–1910). Russian novelist, essayist and pamphleteer. An orphan by nine and brought up by aunts. After a spell as a libertine, he joined the army and served in the Crimean War. Then he worked on his estate, developing an education system for his serfs in which classes were optional and teaching was a collaboration between pupil and teacher. At 34 he married, had 13 children, and a wife who endured his open infidelities. After a long and desperate emotional crisis, he emerged as a Christian anarchist, preaching pacifism, **love** of humankind and the blessings of the simple life. He became anti-intellectual and denounced his own fiction as insufficiently moral to be art. He opposed property-owning, gave up the copyright of his books, renounced his title, and gave his property to his wife. Like **Dostoevsky**, he saw sacrifice as beneficial.

In Tolstoy there is no systematic philosophical thought in the manner of Dostoevsky, **Camus** or **Sartre**. It is however safe to say that all Tolstoy's work focuses on intractable conflict, which can only be resolved through acceptance. Some have found in his treatment of **death** in *The Death of Ivan Ilyich* (1886) evidence of existential thinking, since he shows how the protagonist discovers a meaningful way to understand his life as he struggles with a sense of absurdity on his deathbed. In *War and Peace* (1864–69) and *Anna Karenina*

(1873–76) there are characters searching for **meaning** but failing to find it through their intellects. Those Tolstoyan characters who find contentment learn to live instinctual lives, accepting life as a flow of experience. This reflects Tolstoy's view of **history** that it is not made by individuals, but is an incomprehensible movement that sweeps human beings along with it. This may explain Tolstoy's lack of philosophical system and his recommendation not to reflect on life but to live it.

See also **absurd, the**

totalisation
In **Sartre's** philosophy, this is the individual's personal summary of their experiences, beliefs, **values** and personally defined possibilities. In fact the concept of totalisation is the existential alternative to **truth**. Totalisation is the relative, created truth, which sums up the individual's current total understanding. It is their created **world**. Moreover, the individual can become an aspect of another person's totalisation, and therefore limited within it. There are also totalisations of concepts, ideas and cultures. Totalisation is the emergent truth that is subject to a dialectical process of change. According to Sartre, the individual is responsible for their totalisation.

See also **dialectic; generosity; history; mineralisation; possibility; totality**

totality
Martin **Heidegger** claims that **metaphysics** deals with beings as beings, and always represents beings in their totality, considering their most universal traits. Thus in *Being and Time* (1927b), he searches for general statements that can be made about **Being**. He insists that human beings are more than objects objectively present. Unlike tables and chairs, hammers and nails, we possess **freedom**, and – amidst the constraints of the **world** – endless **possibility**.

When he speaks of the totality of Being or the totality of *Dasein*, Heidegger refers to something that human beings can only approximate. This is the exact opposite of **Sartre's** expression **totalisation**, which refers precisely to the best summary that a particular human being can come up with about something in a particular situation.

tragedy
According to **Aristotle**, Greek tragic drama represents the progress from happiness to misery brought upon the hero by his own error of judgement. Those who consider the human condition have their own views on how typical of human life is this representation. **Schopenhauer** views human existence as essentially miserable, for evil triumphs over innocence, and chance so often decides a person's fate. And in **absurd** drama, tragedy does not rest in the fall of an individual, but in the lot of humankind. **Nietzsche**, however, is remarkable for accepting that human life is tragic, yet believing that this tragedy can be overcome by joyful acceptance of one's **fate**. It is tragedy that often gives life its depth.

See also *amor fati*; **Bugental; Camus; Dionysian and Apollonian mentalities; laughter; Unamuno**

tragic triad
See **Frankl**

tranquillisation

An *inauthentic* way of living, referred to by **Heidegger**, who describes it as a restless state of busyness, a **falling** into a seductive delusion of the need for constant activity in which we can hide. We content ourselves with a lower level of awareness than that of which we are capable in order to soothe our fundamental **anxiety**:

> This levelling off of Dasein's possibilities to what is proximally at its everyday disposal also results in a dimming down of the possible as such. The average everydayness of concern becomes blind to its possibilities, and tranquillizes itself with that which is merely 'actual'. (Heidegger, 1927a: 194–5)

See also **alienation; authenticity and inauthenticity; entanglement**

transcendence

In **idealism** the term means that which rises above the **world**, surpasses it and is independent of it. In existential philosophy the term is used to express that which is capable of **freedom** from determinism and capable of self-determination. Human beings are described as transcendent because after everything that can be said about the physical or psychological constitution of human **Being**, there is something more. Unlike objects, and perhaps most animals, human beings have freedom. For instance, when **Sartre** explains that **existence precedes essence**, he claims that humankind defines itself; but he goes further and argues that life requires constant **choice**, constant defining of that **essence**. It is in this way that human being can be said to transcend the mundane world.

Some existential theorists describe transcendence in more mystical terms. **Jaspers**, for example, describes how transcendence is possible not only through scientific knowledge, or through **philosophy** and **psychology**, but more ultimately, through the search for God. He speaks of the encompassing, or the **comprehensive**, as that which transcends everything whilst including it all at the same time. Still other writers describe transcendence in **relationship**, as in the I–Thou described by **Buber**.

See also **ecstasy; knowing and knowledge**

transcendental ego

In his later philosophy, **Husserl**, like **Descartes**, speaks of an ego that is beyond the **body**. For Husserl, the transcendental ego is pure **consciousness**, something that remains after all phenomenological and *eidetic reduction* (see **phenomenological method**) has been made and we proceed to the transcendental reduction. The transcendental ego is something quite distinct from the psychological ego. Many who accept the value of **phenomenology** fail to see how a transcendental ego can be discovered with the phenomenological method. They argue that it leads to the risk of **solipsism**. Husserl, however, argued that the **existence** of others is included in the transcendental ego, which is conceived as a community of monads (see **other minds**).

transcendental reduction
See **phenomenological method**

transference
In **psychoanalysis** this is the displacement by the analysand of feelings for another person or object onto the analyst, the orthodox example being the patient's acting towards his therapist as if the therapist were his parent. The analyst will interpret this to the patient, so hoping to bring this displacement into **consciousness** and therefore end the psychic conflict the patient has with that person or object.

Different authors conceive of transference in different ways, and for some it refers to all projections of feeling onto the analyst. But there are a number of difficulties with the theory of transference. To the extent that a client's words or actions are interpreted as transference, the therapist can disclaim any actual influence upon the client's experience. A client may be angry with her mother, but it does not follow that she is not genuinely and distinctly angry with her therapist. Additionally, in concentrating on historical causes, present conflicts may be neglected. Thus it is that in **existential psychother-apy** the notion of transference is generally abandoned in favour of the notion of a real or genuine **relationship** or **encounter**.

Heidegger claims that talk of transference has no meaning, that nothing is transferred because the patient is simply in **attunement** to her **world**. So all experiences are aspects of the patient's *Da-sein*. And from this theoretical perspective there follows a particular psychotherapeutic practice. **Boss** argues that the patient should not be treated as if he were in error, that transference is a **phenomenon** as any other, a disclosure of the patient's Being, and needs no other kind of treatment than phenomenological investigation. Van Deurzen argues that as human **perception** is personal and distorted, the psychotherapist should take note of both her own and her client's bias, and help to clarify the constitution of that bias.

See also *Befindlichkeit*; countertransference; interpretation; phenomeno-logical method; projection

transformation
See **change**

transparency
See **sight**

transvaluation of values
See **revaluation of values**

truth

Truth is usually defined as that which is factually correct. Alternatively it can mean that which is real or genuine. The question of what truth is has taxed the minds of philosophers, scientists and artists for centuries, and no theory has general agreement. Additionally, and less obviously, the term is used in different ways. Typically it is based on a *statement*, which one can declare is true or false. Statements, if they faithfully correspond to actuality, are true: this is the so-called *correspondence theory* of truth. And classically, statements or *propositions* must obey **Aristotle's** law of excluded middle, or the *law of bivalence*, whereby a statement is either true or it is false. Nonsense and **paradox** offends this law, which subjectivists oppose.

Existential authors are more concerned with truth as a value, in the sense that life or an attitude or a **relationship** may metaphorically be said to be true. **Kierkegaard** often writes of this, and in referring to subjective truth means that **passion** and commitment and faith are necessary when objective knowledge is impossible, as it is of God. For Kierkegaard, subjectivity is the better alternative to detached and sceptical observation, and truth is defined in inwardness. **Jaspers** elaborates further kinds of truth, including pragmatic truth, truth of **existence**, truth of spirit, truth of **consciousness**, and truth of **transcendence**. He considers that all these can be brought together into a multiple truth.

It is sometimes supposed that existential philosophy is subjective with regard to **reality** and truth, but this is not so. Using the principles of **phenomenological method**, a God in His omniscience could doubtless accurately describe reality. But for mortal beings, truth cannot simply correspond with reality, for human beings are essentially a part of the **world**, beings whose outlook and judgements reflect a particular **being-in-the-world**. Human **Being** can never be detached, can never be uninvolved, can never be objective. Therefore, truth is derived from the meaning of the world for the conscious being.

In his philosophy, **Heidegger** considers the human being, *Da-sein*, to play a role in the revelation and covering up of truth. He refers to the Greek root of truth (*a-letheia*), as that which is uncovered, or literally taken out of oblivion. Thus truth lies in revealing **Being**, and what Heidegger calls *untruth* is the concealment of Being. In living without personal consideration for truth, in accepting what the **They** say, *Da-sein* is concealing truth and is thus inauthentic. But in uncovering what is in reality, *Da-sein* can achieve authenticity. For Heidegger truth and untruth, **authenticity and inauthenticity** are equiprimordially important. Heidegger gives this warning: 'The disclosure of beings as such is simultaneously and intrinsically the concealing of being as a whole' (Heidegger, 1930: 134). As soon as we pay attention to beings, we lose sight of Being as a whole and therefore any form of truth will bring an inevitable shadow of untruth. For the later **Sartre** the concept of **totalisation**, which is the best possible **interpretation** and understanding we can have of the world at any particular time, replaces the concept of truth.

Post-modernist thinking has taken Heidegger's warning even further and authors such as **Ricoeur** or **Foucault** speak of the multiplicity of truth. Deconstructionists such as **Derrida** take this view to an extreme by declaring the illusory nature of truth.

See also **pragmatism; thinking**

turbulence

Heidegger describes *Dasein*'s propensity to **falling** as an experience of turbulence (*Wirbel*). As we let ourselves be taken over by the anonymous **They**, we plunge downwards into a groundlessness that entirely takes us over:

This 'movement' of Dasein in its own Being, we call its '*downward plunge*'. Dasein plunges out of itself into itself, into the groundlessness and nullity of inauthentic every-dayness. But this plunge remains hidden from Dasein by the way things have been publicly interpreted, so much so, indeed, that it gets interpreted as a way of 'ascending' and 'living concretely'. ...

Since the understanding is thus constantly torn away from authenticity and into the 'they' (though always with a sham of authenticity), the movement of falling is characterized by *turbulence*. (Heidegger, 1927a: 178)

turn/turning

(*Kehren/Kehre*). A Heideggerian term, *turning* is an essential aspect of changing human existence. With a fondness for pictorial and spatial terminology, **Heidegger** often uses these terms to describe a switch in attitude or awareness by a human being, for instance:

Only because Da-sein is ontologically and essentially brought before itself by the dis-closedness belonging to it, *can* it flee *from* that from which it flees. Of course, in this entangled turning away, that from which it flees is *not grasped*, nor is it experienced in a turning toward it. But in turning away *from* it, it is 'there', disclosed. (Heidegger, 1927b: 184–5)

The concept of the *turn* is often used by others to describe Heidegger's change in attitude and style after *Being and Time*, when he adopts a less technical style, turning to a more poetical and mystical approach in which he speaks less of *Dasein* and more of human beings and **Being**. Some see this as a radical shift, a U-turn, and distinguish between *early Heidegger* and *later Heidegger*, while others argue that this turn is not an overthrowing of his earlier thought, but a development of it. In this way there are many such turns in Heidegger's writing as he adjusts the emphasis of his favourite words or concepts.

See also **disclosedness; entanglement; ontological**

Übermensch
See **superman**

Überwelt
See **four worlds**

Uexkull, von
See **lived world**; *Merkwelt*

ultimate meaning
See **will to meaning**

Umwelt
See **four worlds**

Unamuno
Miguel de Unamuno y Jugo (1864–1936). Spanish philologist, philosopher, poet and novelist. His most important work is *The Tragic Sense of Life in Men and Nations* (1913). His other publications include *Peace in War* (1897), often considered the first existential novel, and *The Life of Don Quixote and Sancho* (1905). He was influenced most of all by Pascal and **Kierkegaard**, but also by **Schopenhauer** and **Nietzsche**. A religious and political thinker, his **philosophy** springs from the tension he felt between his intuitive faith in eternal life and his rational doubt of it. This conflict between faith and reason is reflected in the tensions between life and thought and culture and civilization.

Unamuno's philosophy is individualistic, for he regards man as an end in himself, and society and humanity as mere abstractions. In the midst of our lives there lies an awareness of **time** and of **death**, and so every human being yearns for immortality. For if there is no God and no afterlife, we will return to **nothingness**, yet if we derive from and will return to God, then our earthly human lives are doomed. Unamuno has faith that **consciousness** cannot die, but he knows reason cannot prove it, and this is the **tragedy** of human **existence**, that there is anguish and sorrow without resolution, and the only redemption lies in commitment to a rationally unjustifiable ideal. In Christ and in Don Quixote Unamuno sees an awareness of this tragedy as well as a **passion** to commit to what is beyond reason. The authentic life is a committed life. Like Kierkegaard, Unamuno urges a commitment to faith. Only the heart can confirm faith, and if faith cannot overcome reason then one must have faith in faith.

uncanniness

Unheimlichkeit, literally not-at-homeness. In the **metaphysics** of **Heidegger**, an account is given of basic moods, one of which is angst (see **anxiety**), a troubled state in which we feel *homeless*, and everything seems unfamiliar. While angst makes us feel ill at ease, this feeling of uncanniness or homelessness is nevertheless a fundamental state of **Being**, which corresponds to the intrinsic temporary nature of human existence. This feeling of uncanniness may lead *Dasein* to engage in metaphysical questioning, for it calls on us to consider our actual state of Being rather than hide in the **They**.

uncertainty principle

See **freedom and free will**

unconscious

See **consciousness and unconsciousness; pre-reflexive consciousness**

uncover, uncovering

See **truth**

understanding

Heidegger insists that understanding (*Verstehen*) is not an intellectual process. He opposes *Verstehen* to *Verstand*, our intellectual understanding, whereas *Verstehen* is the total grasp of something in a phenomenological fashion. There is no need of an expedition to collect data from which to construct theories, for every human being (that is, *Dasein*) has an intrinsic understanding of **Being**, and we possess **ontological** knowledge of how to do things, of how to be in the **world**. Understanding in this sense is simply the way we are **thrown** into the world and the way we are projected towards the world. Although we may not always comprehend the world, we always understand it in a particular way. Distortion and **covering up** make the world unintelligible through inauthenticity, an attitude to living which alienates us from **truth**. State of mind, **disposition**, understanding and **discourse** are the fundamental existentialia that underpin human being.

See also **authenticity and inauthenticity; knowing and knowledge**

undifferentiation

A Heideggerian concept. Though *Dasein* is mostly torn between **authenticity and inauthenticity**, previous to this struggle it starts out as being undifferentiated. *Dasein* sets out to be indifferent in its average form of **Being**, from which emerge the possibilities of being authentic and inauthentic:

> This undifferentiated character of Dasein's everydayness is *not nothing*, but a positive phenomenal characteristic of this entity. Out of this kind of Being – and back in to it again – is all exiting, such as it is. We call this everyday undifferentiated character of Dasein 'averageness'. (Heidegger, 1927a: 43)

See also **averageness; everydayness; Heidegger; possibility**

Unheimlichkeit
See **uncanniness**

unity
Heidegger uses *Einheit* in a number of circumstances, but especially to emphasise the unity of **self** and **world**, which he terms **being-in-the-world**. It is hyphenated, he explains, to show it is a primary fact, a unified **phenomenon**, and indivisible. Nevertheless, being-in-the-world has structural features that can be separately examined, including being, in-the-world, and being-in. Heidegger's emphasis on the unity between *Dasein* and world stems from **Husserl's** phenomenological approach, which seeks to describe the world and **consciousness** in a united fashion, demonstrating them to be intrinsically interrelated. The notion of the unity of the human being is an important element in **Nietzsche's** philosophy, which proclaims the unity of **body** and soul.

See also **phenomenology**

utilitarianism
See **pragmatism**

values

Values play a central role in existential *praxis*. **Nietzsche** speaks of the re-evaluation of all values:

> Let us therefore *limit* ourselves to the purification of our opinions and evaluations and to the *creation of our own new tables of values* ... (Nietzsche, 1882: 335)

Similarly, **Heidegger** is opposed to value ethics, for the reason that values are not essential givens but rather existential evaluations of specific conditions. **Sartre** and de **Beauvoir** write about ethics as *praxis*. We are obliged to determine for ourselves how to evaluate our existence and this is done, for de Beauvoir (1948) in a context of **ambiguity** and for Sartre (1983) in a context of scarcity.

The practice of psychotherapy cannot be neutral, cannot be amoral, cannot be free of values. Enabling a client to examine his or her own values is therefore of central importance, not in order to impose values on them but in order to clearly establish what values they live by and wish to live by. At the same time the therapist will be aware that the physical environment of the consulting room, the psychotherapist's clothes and manners all suggest certain values. And the new client will soon realise that certain things are of interest to the therapist, and are selected for particular attention. The therapist will challenge the client to reconsider some matters, and not others, for the therapist brings his or her cultural and moral values to the consulting room, and cannot help but judge the success or failure of the therapy according to those values.

Practitioners of **existential psychotherapy** believe in the values of **choice** and of **freedom**, and therefore encourage their clients towards self-examination and purposeful action.

See also **revaluation of values**

verification

Term used by **Husserl** to describe an essential phase of the phenomenological, eidetic and transcendental reductions (see **phenomenological method**). It is the process of checking whether our observations and findings after the process of reduction are coherent with the natural experiences we have of the **world**, and thus an essential way of validating the conclusions we derive in the process of **phenomenology**. After intuitions have been reduced and cleared, they are verified against personal experience and the experience of others. This intersubjective validation is considered to be an act of reflection. This was also an important concept for **Marcel**.

See also **intuition**

Verstehen
See **understanding**

vision
See **sight**

vital reason
See **Ortega**

voice of conscience
See **call of conscience**

Vorhandenheit
See **world**

Vorspringen
See **leaping ahead**

Vorstellung
See **representation**

Weltanschauung
See **Dilthey**; **Jaspers**

Wesenschau
See **intuition**

West, Ellen
One of the most discussed patients in the history of existential psychotherapy. Her case study by **Binswanger** was published in *Existence* (May et al., 1958). A patient of several psychiatrists, Ellen was a 33 year old woman who had been brought up by controlling parents, and who had been forced by them to break off an engagement to marry. When she felt that her **identity** and her **freedom** were under threat, she began to eat a great deal, but ridiculed by peers, resorted to dieting. Controlling her life through this anorexia nervosa, she became severely underweight. She began **psychoanalysis**, but ended it and made a suicide attempt.

It was at this point that she went to the Kreuzlingen Sanatorium, where Binswanger diagnosed her as schizophrenic, although other physicians suggested melancholia and obsessive-compulsive neurosis. Ellen kept a diary, which Binswanger's case description is based upon, showing her struggle with the contradictory aspects of her experience of the **world**. It was known she was suicidal, nevertheless she was discharged and three days later took a fatal dose of poison. Binswanger argued that she had finally claimed her independence and asserted herself, a judgement that has been the subject of much professional debate (see, for instance, Rogers, 1961b).

will to live
Schopenhauer's concept of the will to live – or simply, the *will* – is an endless striving, a restlessness which entails human beings can never be fulfilled, and which indicates (to Schopenhauer's bleak satisfaction) an unconscious rapaciousness in humankind. Schopenhauer extends this will beyond human motivation to all nature (to gravity, for instance).

For most existentialists, the main interest in this idea lies in its genesis of the notion of **will to power**, which unlike Schopenhauer's metaphysical doctrine, is a claim of empirical fact. Not an existentialist, Schopenhauer believed in a reality behind phenomena – the **thing-in-itself**, which he identified with will:

> The concept of *will* is of all possible concepts the only one that has its origin not in the phenomenon, not in the mere representation of perception, but which comes from within. (Schopenhauer, 1818: 112)

For Schopenhauer, the will to live is derived from a metaphysical will of which it is the physical manifestation, as the physical **body** is an embodied will and action is objectified will. But by *will*, Schopenhauer does not mean rational volition; indeed, he sees the intellect as merely the servant of the greater will, and in its necessity he sees a depressing entrapment in a deterministic **world**, an entrapment from which there is little escape except that aesthetic contemplation offers passing relief, since it is disinterested. The only lasting escape from the unhappiness of determinism (see **freedom and free will**) is to abandon personal concern for **existence**. Thus, the self-denial of saints, but an idea that **Nietzsche** derides, seeing the exercise of will to power in such denial.

will to meaning

In logotherapy (see **Frankl**) it is assumed that the search for **meaning** is an overriding motivation in human life. Frankl distinguishes two kinds of meaning: *meaning of the moment* and *ultimate meaning*. The first is the understanding of everyday life, the second is of greater principles, of God and nature, principles which can only be glimpsed. Logotherapists hold that the stifling of the will to meaning leads to neurosis. Psychotherapy directly addresses this neglect, focusing on the search for meaning.

Baumeister, in *Meanings of Life* (1991), argues that meaning can be judged according to four existential criteria: purpose, value, efficacy and self-worth.

will to power

Nietzsche's concept of the basic tendency of a human being or other life-form to assert itself. Unlike **Schopenhauer**'s notion of the **will to live**, this is a fully existential idea, making no claim to an ultimate **reality** behind the phenomenon of the **world**. It is both an empirical claim and an explanatory hypothesis, and in its generality equally incapable of proof or falsification.

With this idea Nietzsche prefigures **Freud** in going beyond merely accusing human beings of egoism, as philosophers such as Hobbes had already done, but in offering an explanation of human motivation. In the notebooks that were posthumously published as *The Will to Power*, Nietzsche writes: '*The most fearful and fundamental desire in man, his drive for power – this is called freedom*' (Nietzsche, 1901: 720). Nietzsche does not mean will as conscious volition, and the will to power is more than a psychological hypothesis, it is a foundational theory of what it is to be human. Like Freud, Nietzsche shows a discrepancy between how we are and how we perceive ourselves or like to see ourselves. And with his observation of this incongruity, and his insistence of our human hypocrisy, Nietzsche demands that we look afresh at our moral judgements:

> By doing good and doing ill, one exercises one's power upon others – more one does not want! ... Certainly, the condition in which we do ill is seldom as pleasant, as unmixedly pleasant, as that in which we do good – it is a sign that we still lack power. (Nietzsche, 1882: 13)

Here, Nietzsche predates Kurt Goldstein's concept of self-actualisation, and shows his influence on **humanistic psychology**.

According to Nietzsche, the will to power may manifest itself in paradoxical ways:

> Whether we make a sacrifice in doing good or ill does not alter the ultimate value of our actions; even if we stake our life, as the martyr does for the sake of his Church – it is a sacrifice to our desire for power. (Ibid.: 13)

Yet although it is a general theory, again and again Nietzsche's examples are of the direct experience of power. For instance, he writes:

> [W]herever I found living creatures, there too I heard the language of obedience. All living creatures are obeying creatures ... Where I found a living creature, there I found will to power; and even in the will of the servant I found the will to be master. The will of the weaker persuades it to serve the stronger; its will wants to be master over the weaker still: this delight alone it is unwilling to forego ... And where sacrifice and service and loving glances are, there too is will to be master. There the weaker steals by secret paths into the castle and even into the hearts of the powerful – and steals the power. And life itself told me this secret: 'Behold,' it said, 'I am that which must overcome itself again and again ... Only where life is, there is also will: not will to life, but – so I teach you – will to power!' (Nietzsche, 1883: 137–8)

For the therapist who uses Nietzschean ideas, the will to power may provide a conceptual underpinning with which to make psychological assessments. More broadly, depression, cruelty, anger, and so on – all these may be hypothesised as frustrated will to power. Furthermore, the pain of being thwarted may be seen as stimulating the will to power. And the pursuit of control, or the seeking of knowledge may be viewed as expansive instances of the will to power. Such a therapist will probably agree with Nietzsche when he writes, *'What is the strongest remedy? – Victory'* (Nietzsche, 1881: 200).

See also **master–slave dialectic; sublimation; superman**

witnessing
See **anti-psychiatry**

Wittgenstein
Ludwig Josef Johann Wittgenstein (1889–1951) changed twentieth-century **philosophy** with the one small book published in his lifetime, *Tractatus Logico-Philosophicus* (1921), and the posthumous *Philosophical Investigations* (1953), much of the later work being an attack on the earlier.

Born into a wealthy Viennese family, Wittgenstein came to England in 1908, where he then remained but for active service in the Austrian Army during the Great War, and a later spell in Austria as a schoolteacher. A troubled and unhappy man, he had few friends, was seldom light-hearted and lived an ascetic life.

In the *Tractatus* Wittgenstein argues that language can be measured against **reality**, but in the *Investigations* he overturns this, claiming that there is no correlation between language utterances and logic or **truth**. So to examine

intentionality, one should not look at the **world** but at the grammatical relations of the language used.

Wittgenstein thought deeply about **psychology** and **psychoanalysis**, and he saw philosophy as therapeutic insofar as it removes confusion.

Wittgenstein is not an existentialist. Indeed, although he is usually described as analytical, it is hard to classify his philosophy. But his sparse, questing approach to life and philosophy, and the closely descriptive quality of his writing, show a relationship to the phenomenological tradition. He argues that many people, including psychotherapists, confuse reason and cause. In *Philosophical Investigations* he insists there is no need to penetrate phenomena to seek ultimate causes, that nothing is really hidden, it is all open to view. He is always at pains to clarify, to remove conceptual conceptions: 'What is your aim in philosophy? To show the fly the way out of the fly-bottle' (Wittgenstein, 1953: 309).

Wittgenstein is adamant that philosophy has no content, no body of **knowledge**. It is purely a process of examination. This is a warning for those who seek ready-made answers in philosophy. According to Wittgenstein, all they will find is the means to analyse and clarify human thought. As he wrote: 'I should not like my writing to spare other people the trouble of thinking' (ibid.: viii).

work
See **practico-inert**

world
According to **Heidegger**, we are **thrown** into the **world**. This means that we find ourselves in a world that is already there before us and will be there after we are gone and in which we have to take certain givens into account. This is often referred to as our **facticity**. In our given world there are other *Daseins*, and there are physical objects. The things in the world first of all come to our attention when we use them and find them ready-to-hand, like tools. *Zuhandenheit*, readiness-to-hand (also translated as readiness-*at*-hand), refers to objects as they are of use to us: equipment, tools, gear. Heidegger claims that readiness-to-hand is ontologically prior to presence-at-hand, in that we look first of all for usefulness or significance in things. We notice that a hammer is a hammer, we do not first see that it is a shank of wood attached to a metal block. In this way, whilst *Dasein* is itself thrown, it creates a great deal of thrownness, of things with fixed **Being**.

It is only when things break down and fail us in some way that we become aware that they exist in their own right. This is when we discover presence-at-hand, *Vorhandenheit*. We now realise that things are simply there, and have no useful function for us. They simply exist in the world. Presence-at-hand is objective **presence**, and the world is the sum of all that is present-at-hand. But what is present-at-hand does not stand in meaningful relationship to us. Yet the quality of presence-at-hand can only be understood by *Dasein* in relationship to itself.

However, the idea of world is much more complex than just in relation to physical objects. Heidegger uses **Husserl's** notion of worldliness, **being-in-the-world,** to sketch out *Dasein's* complex relationship to its environment, showing that our attitude towards the world colours our *world relations* and our *worldview.*

See also **four worlds; sight**

world relations
See **Binswanger**

worldview
See **Jaspers**

Yalom

Irvin Yalom (b. 1931). American psychiatrist and psychotherapist. After his original contributions to the literature on group therapy, his most notable publications include *Existential Psychotherapy* (1980), *Love's Executioner and Other Tales from Psychotherapy* (1989) – a set of case studies, *When Nietzsche Wept* (1992) – a fictional account of a psychotherapy conducted by Breuer for Nietzsche, and then by Nietzsche for Breuer, *Lying on the Couch* (1996) and *The Gift of Therapy* (2001). Yalom's approach to therapy is primarily based on a psychoanalytical and medical foundation, and he maintains a belief in the unconscious and in the usefulness of ascribing psychopathological diagnoses. However, in place of a Freudian theory that states that unconscious drives create **anxiety** to which the psychological response is to create defence mechanisms, Yalom sees anxiety as induced by four ultimate existential concerns: **death, freedom**, isolation, and **meaninglessness**. This notion can be traced back to his mentor Rollo **May**, and to May's teacher Paul **Tillich**. Yalom's case studies are a lively illustration of the human issues that emerge in therapy, and his books have done much to popularise the existential approach in the United States.

yes-saying

This is the act of affirming life, according to **Nietzsche**. It is a positive acceptance of life as it is. Sometimes he refers to it as *amor fati*, the love of one's fate.

For Nietzsche, the person who aspires to transcend his or her limitations must go through three metamorphoses of the spirit (see **Zarathustra**): the camel, the lion, and the child, so that they first choose to bear the burdens of life, then, they will find the courage to make a new start, then lastly they forget all and find innocence. Then it is possible to affirm life as it is:

> Yes, a sacred Yes is needed, my brothers, for the sport of creation: the spirit now wills *its own* will, the spirit sundered from the world now wins *its own* world. (Nietzsche, 1883: 55)

Nietzsche contends that much of life is hardship, hence his idea of **eternal return** is a test of our ability to be positive, to say yes in the face of adversity, to cry *encore* to life when we know we will experience pain again and again. Therefore, to genuinely affirm life one must allow for this test of strength. Not to do this, to want only the pleasant parts of life, this is not an embracing of life, it is a **no-saying** to the **world**.

Zarathustra

A Persian prophet of approximately 1,000 years BC, whose teachings form the basis of Zoroastrianism (Zoroaster, the Greek form of his name, is often used). His approach and some of his ideas were conducive enough to **Nietzsche** for the latter to use Zarathustra as a mouthpiece for his own ideas in *Thus Spoke Zarathustra*. Zarathustra teaches that one should pursue the path of **truth**. But it takes courage to do this when one's discoveries run against the cultural grain. Zarathustra was obliged to flee when his teachings (that the gods his people followed were evil) aroused active hostility. Nietzsche had sympathy with this prophet, even though Zarathustra's beliefs were that there exists objective good and evil in the world (more-or-less balanced, until the end of the world, when good triumphs). Zarathustra's courage in the face of adversity impressed Nietzsche. But in *Thus Spoke Zarathustra*, Nietzsche's portrays the prophet courageously rescinding his views, teaching instead that there is no objective good and evil.

A psychotherapy employing ideas from *Thus Spoke Zarathustra* would probably stress the necessity of self-overcoming: '[H]e who cannot obey himself will be commanded' (Nietzsche, 1883: 137). Thus, we should discover our own volition and pursue truth for ourselves, not meekly accept what is given us. Such a therapy would emphasise the need of courage to pursue truth:

> [T]here is something in me that I call courage: it has always destroyed every discouragement in me ... Courage also destroys giddiness at abysses: and where does man not stand at an abyss? Is seeing itself not – seeing abysses? (Ibid.: 177)

Nietzsche's Zarathustra also speaks of the *three metamorphoses of the spirit*, which in his metaphorical style, he calls the *camel*, the *lion* and the *child*. The camel-like spirit is reverential, and seeks to endure heavy burdens, to be heroic and to rejoice in its strength. For instance, to refuse comfort when troubled, or to display its folly so as to mock its own wisdom. The lion-like spirit seeks to oppose the *great dragon* of subjugation: 'The great dragon is called "Thou shalt". But the spirit of the lion says "I will!"' (ibid.: 55). And the need for the spirit to metamorphose from a camel into a lion is developed further:

> Once it loved this 'Thou shalt' as its holiest thing: now it has to find illusion and caprice even in the holiest, that it may steal freedom from its love: the lion is needed for this theft. (Ibid.: 55)

But the lion-like spirit needs to become a child if it is to realise its full potential. Just as the iconoclastic lion is able to say No, so the innocent child is able to utter a sacred Yes, to make a new beginning (see **yes-saying**).

Above all, Nietzsche's Zarathustra urges a questioning attitude to life, and argues that individuals must decide for themselves what is good and what is evil.

See also **superman; values; will to power**

Zeitlichkeit
See **time and temporality**

Zollikon Seminars
In 1947 the Swiss psychiatrist and psychotherapist **Boss**, having put much effort in trying to understand the significance of *Being and Time*, wrote to **Heidegger**, asking for help. To his great surprise, the author replied by return of post. Unknown to Boss, Heidegger had for some while wished to apply the psychological insights of his work. At first they corresponded, but eventually Heidegger visited Switzerland to hold seminars for Boss. Judging that it would be selfish to have the great man's attention just for himself, Boss invited dozens of psychiatrists and students to these meetings, held at his home each semester from 1959 until 1969, when the philosopher became too frail to travel.

Boss quickly realised the significance of these meetings – that an important philosopher was personally engaging with and offering tuition to mental health practitioners, and he began to keep notes of both the seminars and his own conversations with Heidegger on **phenomenology** and psychotherapy. In the seminars, Heidegger outlined the basis of his phenomenology, and compared it with the established scientific manner of thinking – a manner with which he was clearly exasperated, for as he explained to his students, scientific thought deals only with simple **causality**, and applies to things, not to human beings: more exactly, **science** deals with beings and not with **Being**. Science sets aside the possibility of **freedom**, and **consciousness**, and confuses motivation with causality.

From Boss's commentary it is evident that Heidegger had only 'contempt' (Heidegger, 1987: xvii) for the prevalent psychological and psychopathological theories, and that when he read **Freud**'s metapsychological theories 'he never ceased shaking his head' (ibid.: 309), and reported that he felt physically ill. But we also learn that his view of Freud's *practice* was more approving, and that he felt it to be in accord with his own **philosophy**. These reactions show not only the degree of **passion** in Heidegger's philosophy, but more specifically, that he saw a contradiction between Freud's philosophical assumptions and his therapeutic practice. Heidegger believed Freud was blind to the discrepancy between the Galilean-Newtonian physics that was the basis of his **ontology**, and the everyday belief he had in human freedom and individual **choice**, and which was present in his analytic method.

Heidegger insisted to his listeners that it is a mistake to imagine human Being as fixed, and that:

> Psychological theories arise under the pressure of tradition because tradition does not know anything else than the character of being as substantiality, objectification and reification ... *Psyche* and psychology are attempts to objectify the human being. (Ibid.: 216)

This hints at something surprising: that notwithstanding the difficulty of Heidegger's philosophy, there is a core idea to it, which is elaborated and explored, but from which there is seldom any deviation. As he remarked to his Zollikon audience, quoting **Socrates**: 'To say the same thing is what's difficult. To say the same thing about the same thing is the most difficult' (ibid.: 24). In natural science, laws of causality are taken for granted, and so the investigation of an individual **phenomenon** requires only data collection from which a more specific law can be formulated or an outcome calculated. Heidegger's 'same thing' is to speak of the fallacy of applying such a science to human beings – indeed, to *Being*, and that natural science cannot represent *Da-sein*. Heidegger was instead at pains throughout his teaching to demonstrate the phenomenological task of accessing phenomena through **intuition**, and reflecting on **space**, and **time**, the human being and causality.

See also **technology and technological attitude**

Zuhandenheit
See **world**

References

Anderson, R. and Cissna, K. (1997) *The Martin Buber–Carl Rogers Dialogue: A New Transcript with Commentary*. New York: State University of New York Press.

Arendt, H. (1951) *Origins of Totalitarianism*. London: Secker & Warburg.

Arendt, H. (1958) *The Human Condition*. Cambridge: Cambridge University Press.

Arendt, H. (1963) *Eichmann in Jerusalem: A Report on the Banality of Evil*. London: Faber.

Barthes, B. (1957) *Mythologies*, trans. A. Lavers, 1972. London: Cape.

Barthes, B. (1966) *Criticism and Truth*, trans. K.P. Keuneman, 1987. London: Athlone.

Baumeister, R.F. (1991) *Meanings of Life*. London: Guilford Press.

Beauvoir, S. de (1948) *The Ethics of Ambiguity*, trans. B. Frechtman, 1970. New York: Citadel Press.

Beauvoir, S. de (1949) *The Second Sex*, trans. H.M. Parshley, 1953. Harmondsworth: Penguin.

Berdyaev, N.A. (1916) *The Meaning of the Creative Act*, trans. D.A. Lowrie, 1955. London: Gollancz.

Berdyaev, N.A. (1923) *The Meaning of History*, trans. G. Reavey, 1936. London: Geoffrey Bles.

Berdyaev, N.A. (1939) *Slavery and Freedom*, trans. R.M. French, 1939. London: Geoffrey Bles.

Berdyaev, N.A. (1947) *The Beginning and the End*, trans. R.M. French, 1952. London: Geoffrey Bles.

Bergson, H.-L. (1889) *Time and Free Will*, trans. F.L. Pogson, 1910. New York: Swan Sonnenschein.

Bergson, H.-L. (1896) *Matter and Memory*, trans. N.M. Paul and W.S. Palmer, 1911. New York: Swan Sonnenschein.

Bergson, H.-L. (1901) *Laughter*, trans. C.S.H. Brereton and F. Rothwell, 1911. London: Macmillan.

Binswanger, L. (1942) *Grundformen und Erkenntnis menschlichen Daseins*. Zurich: R. Asanger Verlag.

Boss, M. (1957a) *The Analysis of Dreams*, trans. A.J. Pomerans, 1958. New York: Philosophical Library.

Boss, M. (1957b) *Psychoanalysis and Daseinsanalysis*, trans. L.B. Lefebre, 1982. New York: Dacapo Press.

Boss, M. (1979) *Existential Foundations of Medicine and Psychology*, trans. S. Conway and A. Cleaves, 1994. New York: Aronson.

Brentano, F. (1874) *Psychology from an Empirical Standpoint*, trans. A.C. Rancurello, D.B. Terrell and L.L. McAlister, 1973. London: Routledge & Kegan Paul.

Buber, M. (1923/1957) *I And Thou*, trans. W. Kaufmann, 1970. Edinburgh: T. & T. Clark.

Buber, M. (1929) *Between Man and Man*, trans. R.G. Smith, 1947. London: Kegan Paul.

Buber, M. (1965) *The Knowledge of Man: Selected Essays*, trans. M. Friedman and R.G. Smith. New York: Harper & Row.

Bugental, J. (1965) *The Search for Authenticity*. New York: Holt, Rinehart & Winston.

Bugental, J. (1978) *Psychotherapy and Process*. London: Addison-Wesley.

Camus, A. (1942a) *The Myth of Sisyphus*, trans. J. O'Brien, 1955. London: Hamish Hamilton. Reprinted in 1975, Harmondsworth: Penguin.

Camus, A. (1942b) *The Outsider*, trans. J. Laredo, 2000. Harmondsworth: Penguin.

Camus, A. (1944) *Caligula*, trans. D. Grieg, 2003. London: Faber.

Camus, A. (1947) *The Plague*, trans. S. Gilbert, 1948. New York: Knopf.

Camus, A. (1951) *The Rebel: An Essay on Man in Revolt*, trans. A. Bower, 1954. New York: Vintage.

Camus, A. (1956) *The Fall*, trans. J. O'Brien, 2000. Harmondsworth: Penguin.

Camus, A. (1960) 'Reflections on the Guillotine: An Essay on Capital Punishment'. In *Resistance, Rebellion and Death*, trans. J. O'Brien, 1961. London: Hamish Hamilton.

Cooper, D. (1967) *Psychiatry and Anti-Psychiatry*. New York: Barnes & Noble.

Cooper, D. (1971) *The Death of the Family*. London: Allen Lane.

Cooper, D. (1974) *The Grammar of Living: An Examination of Political Acts*. London: Allen Lane.

Derrida, J. (1967) *Of Grammatology*, trans. G.C. Spivak, 1976. Baltimore, MD: Johns Hopkins University Press.

Derrida, J. (1967) *Speech and Phenomena*, trans. D.B. Alison, 1973. Evanston, IL: Northwestern University Press.

Derrida, J. (1967) *Writing and Differance*, trans. A. Bass, 1978. London: Routledge & Kegan Paul.

Descartes, R. (1637) 'Discourse on the Method'. In R.M. Eaton (trans.) (1927), *Descartes: Selections*. New York: Scribners.

Descartes, R. (1641) 'Meditations on First Philosophy'. In R.M. Eaton (trans.) (1927), *Descartes: Selections*. New York: Scribners.

Deurzen, E. van (1998) *Paradox and Passion in Psychotherapy*. Chichester: Wiley.

Deurzen, E. van (2002) *Existential Psychotherapy and Counselling in Practice*, 2nd edn. London: Sage.

Dilthey, W. (1985) *Selected Works* (6 vols), ed. R.A. Makkreel & F. Rodi. Princeton, NJ: Princeton University Press.

Dostoevsky, F. (1864) *Notes from the Underground*, trans. J. Coulson, 1973. Harmondsworth: Penguin.

Dostoevsky, F. (1866) *Crime and Punishment*, trans. D. McDuff, 2003. Harmondsworth: Penguin.

Dostoevsky, F. (1868) *The Idiot*, trans. D. Magarshack, 1973. Harmondsworth: Penguin.

Dostoevsky, F. (1871–72) *The Possessed*, trans. D. Magarshack, 1973. Harmondsworth: Penguin.

Dostoevsky, F. (1879–80) *The Brothers Karamazov*, trans. D. McDuff, 2003. Harmondsworth: Penguin.

Dostoevsky, F. (1886) *The Gambler*, trans. J. Coulson, 1973. Harmondsworth: Penguin.

Foucault, M. (1961) *Madness and Civilization*, trans. R. Howard, 1967. London: Tavistock.

Foucault, M. (1966) *The Order of Things: An Archaeology of the Human Sciences*, trans. A. Sheridan, 1970. London: Tavistock.

Foucault, M. (1969) *The Archaeology of Knowledge*, trans. A. Sheridan, 1972. London: Tavistock.

Foucault, M. (1976–84) *The History of Sexuality*, trans. R. Hurley, 1979–91. Harmondsworth: Penguin.

Frankl, V.E. (1946) *Man's Search for Meaning*, trans. I. Lasch, 1962. London: Hodder & Stoughton.

Frankl, V.E. (1955) *The Doctor and the Soul: From Psychotherapy to Logotherapy*, trans. R. Winston and C. Winston, 1973. Harmondsworth: Pelican.

Frankl, V.E. (1967) *Psychotherapy and Existentialism*. New York: Washington Square Press.

Freud, S. (1900) *The Interpretation of Dreams*, trans. J. Crick, 1999. Oxford: Oxford University Press.

Gadamer, H.-G. (1960) *Truth and Method*, trans. G. Barden and J. Cumming, 1975. London: Sheed & Ward.

Gadamer, H.-G. (1965) *Truth and Method*, trans. G. Barden and J. Cumming, 1975. London: Sheed & Ward.

Heidegger, M. (1924) *The Concept of Time*, trans. W. McNeill, 1992. Oxford: Blackwell.

Heidegger, M. (1927a) *Being and Time*, trans. J. Macquarrie and E. Robinson, 1962. Oxford: Blackwell.

Heidegger, M. (1927b) *Being and Time*, trans. J. Stambaugh, 1996. Albany, NY: State University of New York Press.

Heidegger, M. (1927c) *The Basic Problems of Phenomenology*, trans. A. Hofstadter, 1982. Bloomington, IN: Indiana University Press.

Heidegger, M. (1929) *What Is Metaphysics?*, trans. D.F. Krell. In M. Heidegger, *Basic Writings*, ed. D.F. Krell (rev. edn), 1993. London: Routledge.

Heidegger, M. (1930) *On the Essence of Truth*, trans. J. Sallis. In M. Heidegger, *Basic Writings*, ed. D.F. Krell (rev. edn), 1993. London: Routledge.

Heidegger, M. (1935) *An Introduction to Metaphysics*, trans. R. Manheim, 1959. Garden City, KS: Doubleday Anchor.

Heidegger, M. (1947) *Letter on Humanism*, trans. F.A. Capuzzi. In M. Heidegger, *Basic Writings*, ed. D.F. Krell (rev. edn), 1993. London: Routledge.

Heidegger, M. (1954a) *The Question Concerning Technology*, trans. W. Lovitt. In M. Heidegger, *Basic Writings*, ed. D.F. Krell (rev. edn), 1993. London: Routledge.

Heidegger, M. (1954b) *What Is Called Thinking?*, trans. F.D. Wieck and J.G. Gray. In M. Heidegger, *Basic Writings*, ed. D.F. Krell (rev. edn), 1993. London: Routledge.

Heidegger, M. (1954c) 'Building Dwelling Thinking', trans. A. Hofstadter. In M. Heidegger, *Basic Writings*, ed. D.F. Krell (rev. edn), 1993. London: Routledge.

Heidegger, M. (1959) 'The Way to Language', trans. D.F. Krell. In M. Heidegger, *Basic Writings*, ed. D.F. Krell (rev. edn), 1993. London: Routledge.

Heidegger, M. (1983) *The Fundamental Concepts of Metaphysics: World, Finitude, Solitude*, trans. W. McNeill and N. Walker, 1995. Bloomington, IN: Indiana University Press.

Heidegger, M. (1987) *Zollikon Seminars*, ed. M. Boss, trans. F. Mayr and R. Askay, 2001. Evanston, IL: Northwestern University Press.

Hölderlin, F. (2004) *Poems and Fragments*, trans. M. Hamburger (4th edn). London: Anvil Press Poetry.

Husserl, E. (1891) *Philosophy of Arithmetic*, trans. D. Willard, 2003. London: Kluwer Academic.

Husserl, E. (1900) *Logical Investigations*, trans. J.N. Findlay, 1970. London: Routledge.

Husserl, E. (1913) *Ideas*, trans. W.R. Boyce Gibson, 1931. New York: MacMillan.

Husserl, E. (1928) *Cartesian Meditations*, trans. D. Cairns, 1960. The Hague: Martinus Nijhoff.

Husserl, E. (1929) *Formal and Transcendental Logic*, trans. D. Cairns, 1969. The Hague: Martinus Nijhoff.

Husserl, E. (1938) *The Crisis of European Sciences and Transcendental Phenomenology*, trans. Q. Lauer, 1965. New York: Harper & Row.

Irigaray, L. (1974) *Speculum of the Other Woman*, trans. G.C. Gill, 1985. Ithaca, NY: Cornell University Press.

Irigaray, L. (1984) *An Ethics of Sexual Difference*, trans. C. Burke and G.C. Gill, 1993. Ithaca, NY: Cornell University Press.

Jaspers, K. (1913) *General Psychopathology*, trans. J. Hoenig and M.W. Hamilton, 1963. Baltimore, MD: Johns Hopkins University Press.

Jaspers, K. (1932) *Philosophy* (3 vols), trans. E.B. Ashton, 1969–71. Chicago, IL: University of Chicago Press.

Jaspers, K. (1938) *Philosophy of Existence*, trans. R.F. Grabau, 1971. Oxford: Blackwell.

Jaspers, K. (1950) *The Way to Wisdom*, trans. R. Manheim, 1951. London: Gollancz.

Kierkegaard, S. (1841) *The Concept of Irony*, trans. H.V. Hong and G.H. Hong, 1989. Princeton, NJ: Princeton University Press.

Kierkegaard, S. (1843a) *Either/Or: A Fragment of Life*, trans. A. Hannay, 1992. Harmondsworth: Penguin.

Kierkegaard, S. (1843b) *Fear and Trembling*, trans. W. Lowrie, 1941. Princeton, NJ: Princeton University Press.

Kierkegaard, S. (1843c) *Repetition*, trans. W. Lowrie. In *A Kierkegaard Anthology*, ed. R. Bretall, 1946. Princeton, NJ: Princeton University Press.

Kierkegaard, S. (1844a) *Philosophical Fragments*, trans. H.V. Hong and E.H. Hong, 1962. Princeton, NJ: Princeton University Press.

Kierkegaard, S. (1844b) *The Concept of Anxiety*, trans. R. Thomte and A.B. Anderson, 1980. Princeton, NJ: Princeton University Press.

Kierkegaard, S. (1846a) *Concluding Unscientific Postscript to 'Philosophical Fragments'*, trans. H.V. Hong and E.H. Hong, 1992. Princeton, NJ: Princeton University Press.

Kierkegaard, S. (1846b) *The Present Age: A Literary Review*, trans. A. Dru. In *A Kierkegaard Anthology*, ed. R. Bretall, 1946. Princeton, NJ: Princeton University Press.

Kierkegaard, S. (1847a) *Purity of Heart Is to Will One Thing*, trans. D. Steere, 1938. New York: Harper and Row.

Kierkegaard, S. (1847b) *Works of Love*, trans. W. Lowrie. In *A Kierkegaard Anthology*, ed. R. Bretall, 1946. Princeton, NJ: Princeton University Press.

Kierkegaard, S. (1848) *The Point of View*, trans. W. Lowrie. In *A Kierkegaard Anthology*, ed. R. Bretall, 1946. Princeton, NJ: Princeton University Press.

Kierkegaard, S. (1849) *The Sickness Unto Death*, trans. W. Hannay, 1989. Harmondsworth: Penguin.

Lacan, J. (1966) *Écrits: A Selection*, trans. A. Sheridan, 1977. London: Tavistock.

Lacan, J. (1973) *The Four Fundamental Concepts of Psychoanalysis*, trans. A. Sheridan, 1977. London: Hogarth Press.

Laing, R.D. (1959) *The Divided Self*. London: Tavistock.

Laing, R.D. (1961) *Self and Others*. Harmondsworth: Penguin.

Laing, R.D. (1967) *The Politics of Experience*. Harmondsworth: Penguin.

Leibniz, G. (1697) 'On the Ultimate Origin of Things'. In P.P. Wiener (trans.) (1951), *Leibniz: Selections*. New York: Scribners.

Levinas, E. (1935) *On Escape*, trans. B. Bergo, 2003. Stanford, CA: Stanford University Press.

Levinas, E. (1961) *Totality and Infinity*, trans. A. Lingis, 1960. The Hague: Martinus Nijhoff.

Levinas, E. (1974) *Otherwise than Being*, trans. A. Lingis, 1981. The Hague: Martinus Nijhoff.

Lewin, K. (1935) *A Dynamic Theory of Personality*, trans. D.K. Adams and K.E. Zener. New York: McGraw-Hill.

Marcel, G. (1935) *Being and Having: an Existentialist Diary*, trans. 1965. New York: Harper & Row.

Marcel, G. (1948) *The Philosophy of Existence*, trans. M. Harari, 1948. London: Harvill Press.

Marcel, G. (1950–51) *The Mystery of Being*, Vols 1 and 2, trans. G.S. Fraser, 2001. South Bend, IN: St. Augustine's Press.

May, R. (1950) *The Meaning of Anxiety*. New York: Norton.

May, R. (1953) *Man's Search for Himself*. New York: Norton.

May, R. (1967) *Psychology and the Human Dilemma*. New York: Norton.

May, R. (1969a) *Existential Psychology*. New York: Random House.

May, R. (1969b) *Love and Will*. New York: Norton.

May, R., Angel, E. and Ellenberger, H.F. (1958) *Existence: A New Dimension in Psychiatry and Psychology*. New York: Basic Books.

Merleau-Ponty, M. (1942) *The Structure of Behaviour*, trans. A.L. Fisher, 1965. London: Methuen.

Merleau-Ponty, M. (1945) *Phenomenology of Perception*, trans. C. Smith, 1962. London: Routledge.

Merleau-Ponty, M. (1948) *Sense and Non-Sense*, trans. H. Dreyfus and P. Dreyfus, 1964. Evanston, IL: Northwestern University Press.

Merleau-Ponty, M. (1961) *The Primacy of Perception*, trans. and ed. J.M. Edie, 1964. Evanston, IL: Northwestern University Press.

Merleau-Ponty, M. (1964a) *Consciousness and the Acquisition of Language*, trans. H.J. Silverman, 1973. Evanston, IL: Northwestern University Press.

Merleau-Ponty, M. (1964b) *The Visible and the Invisible*, trans. A. Lingis, 1968. Evanston, IL: Northwestern University Press.

Merleau-Ponty, M. (1992) *Texts and Dialogues*, ed. H.J. Silverman and J. Barry. London: Humanities Press.

Minkowski, E. (1927) *Schizophrénie: Psychopathologie des schizoides et des schizophrenes.* Paris: Payot Bibliothèque Scientifique.

Minkowski, E. (1933) *Lived Time*, trans. N. Metzel, 1970. Evanston, IL: Northwestern University Press.

Minkowski, E. (1966) *Traité de Psychopathologie.* Paris: Presses Universitaires de France.

Nietzsche, F. (1872) *The Birth of Tragedy*, trans. C.P. Fadiman, 1927. New York: Modern Library.

Nietzsche, F. (1878–9) *Human, All Too Human*, trans. R.J. Hollingdale, 1986. Cambridge: Cambridge University Press.

Nietzsche, F. (1879) *Assorted Opinions and Maxims*, trans. R.J. Hollingdale. In *A Nietzsche Reader*, ed. R.J. Hollingdale, 1977. Harmondsworth: Penguin.

Nietzsche, F. (1881) *Daybreak*, trans. R.J. Hollingdale. In *A Nietzsche Reader*, ed. R.J. Hollingdale, 1977. Harmondsworth: Penguin.

Nietzsche, F. (1882) *The Gay Science*, trans. W. Kaufmann, 1974. New York: Random House.

Nietzsche, F. (1883) *Thus Spoke Zarathustra*, trans. R.J. Hollingdale, 1961. Harmondsworth: Penguin.

Nietzsche, F. (1886) *Beyond Good and Evil*, trans. R.J. Hollingdale. In *A Nietzsche Reader*, ed. R.J. Hollingdale, 1977. Harmondsworth: Penguin.

Nietzsche, F. (1887) *On the Geneology of Morals*, trans. W. Kaufman and R.J. Hollingdale, 1969. New York: Vintage Books.

Nietzsche, F. (1889) *Twilight of the Idols*, trans. R.J. Hollingdale. In *A Nietzsche Reader*, ed. R.J. Hollingdale, 1977. Harmondsworth: Penguin.

Nietzsche, F. (1901) *The Will To Power*, ed. W. Kaufmann, trans. W. Kaufmann and R.J. Hollingdale, 1968. New York: Vintage Books.

Ortega y Gasset, J. (1914) *Meditations on Quixote*, trans. E. Rugg and D. Marin, 1961. New York: Norton.

Ortega y Gasset, J. (1931) *The Revolt of the Masses*, trans. A. Kerrigan, 1985. Notre Dame: Notre Dame University Press.

Ortega y Gasset, J. (1933) *Man and Crisis*, trans. M. Adams, 1959. London: Allen & Unwin.

Ricoeur, P. (1950) *Freedom and Nature*, trans.   E.V. Kohák, 1966. Evanston, IL: Northwestern University Press.

Ricoeur, P. (1965) *Freud and Philosophy*, trans. D. Savage, 1970. New Haven, CT: Yale University Press.

Ricoeur, P. (1969) *Conflict of Interpretations*, trans. D. Ihde, 1974. Evanston, IL: Northwestern University Press.

Ricoeur, P. (1983–85) *Time and Narrative*, trans. K. McLaughlin and D. Pellauer, 1984–88. Chicago, IL: University of Chicago Press.

Rogers, C.R. (1940) 'Newer Concepts in Psychotherapy'. A paper delivered to the University of Minnesota, later revised and published as Chapter 2 of Rogers's *Counseling and Psychotherapy* (1942). Boston, MA: Houghton Mifflin.

Rogers, C.R. (1951) *Client-Centered Therapy.* Boston, MA: Houghton Mifflin.

Rogers, C.R. (1957) 'The Necessary and Sufficient Conditions of Therapeutic Personality Change'. Originally in *Journal of Consulting Psychology*, 21 (2): 95–103. Reprinted in H. Kirschenbaum and V.L. Henderson (eds) (1990) *The Carl Rogers Reader.* London: Constable.

Rogers, C.R. (1961a) *On Becoming a Person: A Therapist's View of Psychotherapy.* Boston, MA: Houghton Mifflin.

Rogers, C.R. (1961b) 'Ellen West – and Loneliness', *Review of Existential Psychology and Psychiatry*, 1 (2): 94–101.

Rogers, C.R. (1964) 'Towards a Science of the Person'. In T.W. Wann (ed.), *Behaviourism and Phenomenology*. Chicago, IL: University of Chicago Press.

Rogers, C.R. (1974) 'Remarks on the Future of Client-centered Therapy'. In D.A. Wexler and L.N. Rice (eds), *Innovations in Client-Centered Therapy*. New York: John Wiley.

Rogers, C.R. (1980) *A Way of Being*. Boston, MA: Houghton Mifflin.

Russell, B. (1959) *Wisdom of the West*. London: Macdonald.

Sartre, J.-P. (1936a) *The Imagination*, trans. B. Frechtman as *The Psychology of Imagination*, 1948. London and New York: Routledge.

Sartre, J.-P. (1936b) *Imagination: A Psychological Critique*, trans. F. Williams, 1962. Ann Arbor, MI: University of Michigan Press.

Sartre, J.-P. (1938) *Nausea*, trans. R. Baldick, 1965. Harmondsworth: Penguin.

Sartre, J.-P. (1939) *Sketch for a Theory of the Emotions*, trans. P. Mairet, 1971. London: Routledge.

Sartre, J.-P. (1943a) *Being and Nothingness: An Essay on Phenomenological Ontology*, trans. H.E. Barnes, 1958. London: Methuen.

Sartre, J.-P. (1943b) *Two Plays*, trans. S. Gilbert, 1947. New York: Knopf.

Sartre, J.-P. (1945a) *The Age of Reason*, trans. E. Sutton, 1947. London: Hamish Hamilton.

Sartre, J.-P. (1945b) *The Reprieve*, trans. E. Sutton, 1947. London: Hamish Hamilton.

Sartre, J.-P. (1946) *Existentialism and Humanism*, trans. P. Mairet, 1948. London: Methuen.

Sartre, J.-P. (1948) *What Is Literature?*, trans. B. Frechtman, 1949. New York: Philosophical Library.

Sartre, J.-P. (1949) *Iron in the Soul*, trans. E. Sutton, 1950. London: Hamish Hamilton.

Sartre, J.-P. (1952) *Saint Genet: Actor and Martyr*, trans. B. Frechtman, 1964. London: W.H. Allen.

Sartre, J.P. (1960) *Critique of Dialectical Reason*, trans. A. Sheridan-Smith, 1976. London: Methuen.

Sartre, J.-P. (1964) *The Words*, trans. I. Clephane, 2000. Harmondsworth: Penguin.

Sartre, J.-P. (1971) *The Family Idiot*, trans. C. Cosman, 1981–91. Chicago, IL: University of Chicago Press.

Sartre, J.-P. (1983) *Notebooks for an Ethics*, trans. D. Pellauer, 1992. Chicago, IL: University of Chicago Press.

Saussure, F. de (1916) *Course in General Linguistics*, ed. C. Bally and A. Sechehaye with A. Reidlinger, trans. R. Harris, 1983. London: Duckworth.

Scheler, M. (1931) *Nature of Sympathy*, trans. P. Heath, 1954. London: Routledge & Kegan Paul.

Schopenhauer, A. (1818) *The World as Will and Representation*, trans. E.F.J. Payne, 1958. Indian Hills, CO: Falcon's Wing Press.

Spinoza, B. (1677) *Ethics*, trans. G.H.R. Parkinson, 2000. Oxford: Oxford University Press.

Szasz, T.S. (1961) *The Myth of Mental Illness*. New York: Hoeber-Harper.

Szasz, T.S. (1965) *The Ethics of Psychoanalysis*. Syracuse, NY: Syracuse University Press.

Szasz, T.S. (1978) *The Myth of Psychotherapy*. Garden City, KS: Anchor Press.

Szasz, T.S. (1999) *Fatal Freedom*. Westport, CT: Praeger.

Tillich, P. (1951–63) *Systematic Theology*. Chicago, IL: University of Chicago Press.

Tillich, P. (1952) *The Courage to Be*. Newhaven, CT: Yale University Press.

Tolstoy, L. (1864–69) *War and Peace*, trans. L. Maude and A. Maude, 1992. London: Everyman.

Tolstoy, L. (1873–76) *Anna Karenina*, trans. L. Maude and A. Maude, 1992. London: Everyman.

Tolstoy, L. (1886) *The Death of Ivan Ilyich*, trans. R. Edmonds, 1960. Harmondsworth: Penguin.

Turgenev, I.S. (1862) *Fathers and Sons*, trans. R. Freeborn, 1999. Oxford: Oxford University Press.

Unamuno y Jugo, M. de (1897) *Peace in War*, trans. A. Lacy, M. Nozick with A. Kerrigan, 1983. Princeton, NJ: Princeton University Press.

Unamuno y Jugo, M. de (1905) *The Life of Don Quixote and Sancho*, trans. H.P. Earle, 1927. New York: Knopff.

Unamuno y Jugo, M. de (1913) *The Tragic Sense of Life in Men and Nations*, trans. J.E.C. Flitch, 1921. London: Macmillan.

Wittgenstein, L.J.J. (1921) *Tractatus Logico-Philosophicus*, trans. D.F. Pears and B.F. McGuiness. London: Routledge & Kegan Paul.

Wittgenstein, L. (1953) *Philosophical Investigations*, trans. G.E.M. Anscombe, 1953. Oxford: Blackwell.

Yalom, I.D. (1980) *Existential Psychotherapy*. New York: Basic Books.

Yalom, I.D. (1989) *Love's Executioner*. New York: Basic Books.

Yalom, I.D. (1992) *When Nietzsche Wept*. New York: Harper-Collins.

Yalom, I.D. (1996) *Lying on the Couch*. New York: Basic Books.

Yalom, I.D. (2001) *The Gift of Therapy*. New York Harper-Collins.